MONEY ADVISER
1998

▶ STEVE GELMAN
AND THE EDITORS OF MONEY

MONEY BOOKS
Time Inc. Home Entertainment
1271 Avenue of the Americas
New York, NY 10020

MONEY STAFF

managing editor Robert Safian

TIME INC. HOME ENTERTAINMENT

managing director David Gitow

CONSUMER MARKETING DIVISION

MONEY BOOK SERIES

▶ CONTENTS

CHAPTER 1

WHERE YOU SHOULD PUT MONEY NOW

Last year we urged you to follow a conservative investing strategy. The wisest choices among stocks, we advised, would be reasonably priced shares of large companies likely to post solid earnings gains even if the economy slowed. We favored mutual funds with a proven record of posting solid gains in choppy markets, and we also said there would be nothing wrong with raising your cash reserves to more than 25% of your portfolio as a defense against a stock market pullback. We were correct when we told you that long-term interest rates would fall. But we were far off the mark predicting that economic growth would drop to 2% in 1997; instead, the economy expanded around 3.7%. And instead of the feeble 7% return we saw for blue chips, top-quality stocks gained around 24% in 1997.

Even so, it is clear that investors are getting increasingly edgy. The Dow Jones industrial average climbed for seven years without a 10% pullback, but that magic time ended last October when turmoil in Asia knocked down the Dow more than 13% from its Aug. 6, 1997 peak. Your foremost objective for 1998 is to ensure that you'll be in a position to ride out expected high volatility. To do that, you'll need to make sure your portfolio is as well diversified as possible. For starters, take a look at how much money you have in stock or equity funds. Because of soaring share prices over the past three years, you may be far more heavily weighted in stocks than you realize. If you had 65% of your money in stocks in 1994, for instance, that stake may have swelled to more than 75% of your portfolio today.

You should take advantage of market upswings to unload some of your winners—particularly any stocks with price/earnings ratios above 25. Don't feel you need to reinvest that money in stocks right away. Instead, you should begin writing down a buy list of at least two or three dozen stocks you would like to own for the next 10 years and the prices at which you would be willing to buy each of them if the stock market were to break tomorrow.

A well-diversified portfolio should always include high-quality long-term bonds, such as Treasury issues maturing in 10 years or more, as well as cash reserves. In 1998, those income investments will be even more important than usual. Since bond prices rise when the economy slows and interest rates fall, keeping as much as 20% of your money in Treasury bonds or high-grade bond funds will help offset any stock market decline resulting from an economic slowdown that crimps corporate profits.

We appreciate the long-term strength of the U.S. economy—but still think it's smart to be wary in this high-flying market. We believe that stocks remain the best choice for investors who want to accumulate wealth for retirement and other long-term goals, such as buying a home or paying for children's college tuition. Yet, there are ample reasons that investors should be cautious—in particular, stocks are overpriced and the economy looks poised for a moderate slowdown. Therefore, your strategy this year should be to try to cash in on long-term growth while minimizing your chances of short-term losses that actually might scare you into leaving the market rather than riding out the ups and downs. Here's a detailed outline of what we expect in 1998:

▶ **The economy.** Growth will slow to an annualized rate of 2.5% by late 1998, down from around 3.7% last year.

▶ **Inflation.** Consumer prices will rise a tad faster than they did in '97, but inflation will remain well below 3%.

▶ **Short-term interest rates.** The slower economy will persuade Federal Reserve chairman Alan Greenspan that it's safe to lower short-term interest rates, and the 90-day Treasury bill yield will fall below 5%.

▶ **Bond yields.** Long-term Treasury bond yields will hover at around 5.75% or less.

▶ **Corporate profits.** Average earnings growth will slow to 7% next year, down from 12% in late 1997.

▶ **Stock prices.** With the Dow likely to remain locked in a trading range, swinging sharply between 7000 and 8500, we see blue chips ending the year with a 7% price gain, and small stocks up about 12%.

MONEY'S FINANCIAL FORECAST FOR 1998

The long-term outlook for the U.S. economy is little short of brilliant: Inflation is low, workers' productivity is soaring, and U.S. companies are more competitive than they have been since the 1960s. But there are also reasons for investors to be on guard: Stocks are overpriced right now and the economy is poised for a temporary slowdown. As a result, shareholders are edgy and every scrap of bad news seems to trigger at least a brief selloff. So over the next 12 months, you can expect to feel like you're on a seesaw with a bear. But if you take advantage of temporary downswings to buy first-rate stocks and mutual funds, you can come out on top when stocks resume their long climb.

The economy will weaken. The late October collapse in the Hong Kong stock market helped drive the Dow down 554 points in a single day, largely because investors know the U.S. market is overpriced and worry that any bad news could spark a decline. But the striking fact is that collapsing stock markets and falling real estate prices in a handful of Southeast Asian countries won't have much impact in our hemisphere. The U.S. economy was likely to weaken in 1998 even before the Asian troubles began; they will simply be an additional drag. There's an important domestic reason for a slower economy: Increasingly nervous lenders are forcing overindebted consumers to slow their borrowing.

Interest rates will fall. The brightest spot in our economic outlook for 1998 is that interest rates are likely to fall. In 1994, Fed chairman Greenspan raised short-term interest rates nearly three percentage points. Although short rates have come down about half a point from their early 1995 high of 6%, they remain above normal levels, based on the current rate of inflation. The reason: Greenspan has hesitated to lower rates significantly because he fears that rising labor costs will re-ignite inflation. However, once economic growth slows to an annual rate of about 2.5%—as we believe it will in 1998—Greenspan could permit short-term rates to come down.

Rapid economic expansion also kept long-term yields above their normal range. We expect to see long-term yields, which decreased signifcantly in January, remain low.

THE DOW WILL SWING WILDLY IN '98

Stocks started rising faster than corporate profits in 1995. From today's market levels, share prices will be extremely volatile in 1998, with the Dow dipping as low as 7000.

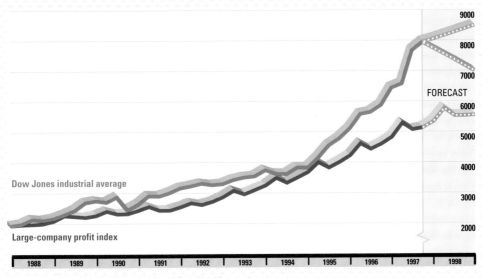

Sources: Bloomberg Financial Markets, Prudential Securities, MONEY estimates

We used Prudential's data on large companies' profits to create an index that was set to equal the Dow at the start of 1988. As you can see, stocks have outrun the earnings that support them over the past three years.

Profit margins will shrink. Consumer price increases have been low primarily because corporations lack pricing power. That's economist-speak for a company's ability to charge more for its products without losing sales. In addition to the corporate downsizing of the past 15 years, which has made workers more restrained in their wage demands, global competition has kept a lid on the cost of consumer goods.

This is what puts corporations in a profit vise. But even if little inflation shows up at the consumer level, companies will be faced with rising production costs. Growth in workers' average hourly earnings has been accelerating since 1992. Much of that increase has been offset by some stunning—if sporadic—gains in productivity. In the third quarter of 1997, for instance, productivity rocketed up 4.5%, the strongest advance in five years. But if

Inflation

(change in consumer prices vs. a year earlier)

FORECAST

7% · 6 · 5 · 4 · 3 · 2

| 1991 | 1992 | 1993 | 1994 | 1995 | 1996 | 1997 | 1998 |

...THOUGH LABOR COSTS WILL RISE

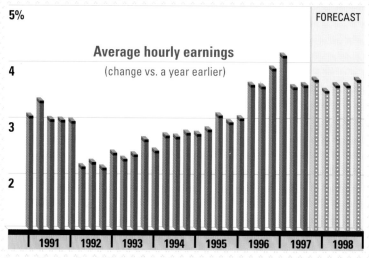

Average hourly earnings

(change vs. a year earlier)

FORECAST

5% · 4 · 3 · 2

| 1991 | 1992 | 1993 | 1994 | 1995 | 1996 | 1997 | 1998 |

Sources: Bloomberg Financial Markets, Bureau of Labor Statistics, Merrill Lynch, MONEY estimates

Inflation in consumer prices will remain negligible, even though workers' average hourly earnings will continue rising, as they have been for the past five years. Reason: Sharp gains in productivity keep offsetting higher labor costs. However, if companies avoid raising prices in today's highly competitive market and workers' earnings continue to climb—as we predict—look for profit margins to shrink, slowing corporate earnings growth next year.

THE FED HAS KEPT RATES HIGH...

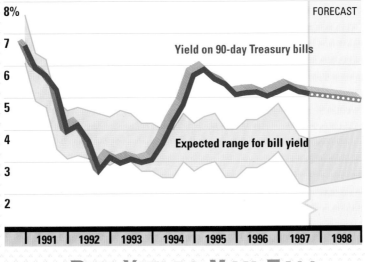

FORECAST

8%

7

Yield on 90-day Treasury bills

6

5

4

Expected range for bill yield

3

2

| 1991 | 1992 | 1993 | 1994 | 1995 | 1996 | 1997 | 1998 |

...BUT YIELDS MAY FALL

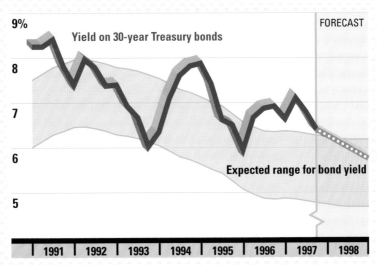

FORECAST

9%

Yield on 30-year Treasury bonds

8

7

6

Expected range for bond yield

5

| 1991 | 1992 | 1993 | 1994 | 1995 | 1996 | 1997 | 1998 |

Sources: Bloomberg Financial Markets, Bureau of Labor Statistics, Merrill Lynch, MONEY estimates

Interest rates have been high since 1994, when Federal Reserve chairman Alan Greenspan hiked short-term rates to restrain the booming economy. Over the past three years, rates have hovered as much as a percentage point above the range economists consider normal given the rate of inflation. We expect the economy to slow, encouraging Greenspan to lower short-term rates below 5% and allowing bond yields to hover at 5.75% or less.

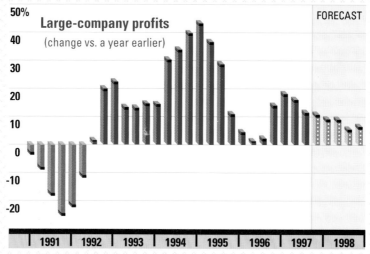

Large-company profits

(change vs. a year earlier)

FORECAST

Sources: Prudential Securities, MONEY estimates

The stock market stalled in 1994, anticipating the drop-off in corporate profit growth that began in '95. Since late '96, profits have rebounded, fueling the stock boom. This year, however, the earnings of large companies are likely to slow again to an average of 7%, down from 12% in late '97. The result: Share prices could move sideways and will be vulnerable to temporary sell-offs.

corporations can't raise prices, and wages continue to rise—as we expect they will—sooner or later businesses will see profit margins shrink.

Stock gains will slow. The effect of a slowing economy in the U.S. and overseas could hold blue chips' earnings gains to 7% in 1998, compared with recent annual increases of 12% or more. Since at their recent average of 20, price/earnings ratios for blue chips were already near record highs, it seems unlikely that the average stock's P/E will increase, particularly in the face of a likely earnings slowdown.

Without P/E expansion, stocks can move up only as much as profits rise—a projected 7% as we see it. Add in current dividend yields of about 2%, and investors in blue chips would be likely to earn a total return (capital gains plus dividends) of only about 9%, just below the historical average for top-quality stocks. It appears unlikely, therefore, that the Dow would top 8500

We know we can't have all the answers about the 1998 economy and markets. Some of the top experts on Wall Street disagree with us and with one another.

Here's what four top forecasters are predicting. Although we don't agree with these opinions, we do think there are underlying insights that most of us seem to share: The stock market will be riskier and more volatile than ever. There's a growing danger of a big market drop before 2000. Inflation will be negligible for the foreseeable future. Bonds will not only diversify your portfolio but could boost your returns.

▶ **Edward Yardeni**, chief economist at Deutsche Morgan Grenfell in New York City, has been one of the most optimistic forecasters over the past seven years. Although still bullish on balance, he's started to sound a few cautionary notes on stocks—and he's turned more positive on bonds. "The Asian meltdown could trigger a global recession in 1998. There's a 25% chance of a recession in the U.S. in 1998, rising to a 40% chance of a worldwide recession by the year 2000. U.S. government bond yields could fall to 5.5% by mid-1998."

▶ **Richard Rippe**, chief economist at Prudential Securities, also sees ripples from Asia that could hurt stocks and help bonds. His analysis: Weaker economies overseas will crimp the earnings of U.S. multinationals slightly but reduce inflation in the U.S. "The prices of imports from Asian countries will be lower because of the declines in Asian currencies. With core consumer price inflation already running low, cheaper imports could restrain U.S. inflation a bit more."

▶ **Abby Joseph Cohen**, portfolio strategist at Goldman Sachs, issued an unequivocal call to buy when the Dow dropped 554 points in a single day in late October. And she is a prominent proponent of the view that stocks are cheap at today's prices. "The U.S. is an oasis of growth in a sluggish global economy. Moreover, the S&P 500 market currently looks undervalued. We calculate that from late 1997 prices the S&P 500 could return 13% to 15% over 12 months. And we recommend boosting equity holdings to above normal levels."

▶ **Rao V. Chalasani**, chief investment strategist at Everen Securities in Chicago, expects the Dow to trade in a range from 7200 to 8000 over the next few months. But he sees at least a possibility that the U.S. stock market will undergo a boom-and-bust cycle over the next four years. "Similarities are developing between the current U.S. stock market and the Japanese stock market in the late '80s. More conditions are developing that could lead to a speculative bubble in the U.S."

or so in 1998. Moreover, any bad news—from a spike in inflation or interest rates to an unexpected shortfall in quarterly profits—could send stocks into a tailspin, knocking down the Dow as low as 7000 before prices rebound.

Blue chips will be outpaced. Many strategists believe that small stocks—particularly those in industries such as technology and health care—will do better than blue chips over the next couple of years. In the third quarter of 1997, small and mid-size stock mutual funds returned an average of at least 14.5%, compared with only 7.3% for S&P 500 index funds, according to Lipper Analytical Services in Summit, N.J. Smaller stocks could continue to turn in market-beating numbers for two reasons. Many are relatively cheaper when you compare their P/Es to their growth rates than the highest-flying blue chips. Also they tend to be less exposed to economic problems overseas because a greater proportion of their profits are earned in the U.S.

Bonds can boom. Lower interest rates will be bullish for stocks but will boost bonds even more. If the Dow returns 9% in '98—as we are forecasting—bonds and other top-quality income investments could earn 10% or more. Most important, in the unlikely event of a serious economic slump that depresses stock prices by more than 15%, interest rates would fall even more sharply than we project. That, in turn, would boost bond prices and could produce returns of more than 15% on many income investments, which would offset losses on stocks in your portfolio.

OUR ALL STAR BROKERS' TOP PICKS

How did your portfolio perform since MONEY published its 1997 list of 10 All Star brokers and their choices of top stocks? Did you match the S&P 500's incredible 36% rise over the 11 months of our contest? Four of our superstar brokers did, indeed an impressive feat when you consider that only 26% of U.S. stock fund managers matched or outpaced the S&P 500 during that period. Those four 1997 All Stars return on our 1998 team, the eighth we've chosen since 1988. We asked them and the six newcomers to name the stocks they're most confident can score superior returns in today's high-anxiety market. The resulting recommendations, in the opinion of our stars, have the potential to earn market-beating returns by the end of '98.

Leading the four returning All Stars is Smith Barney's Jeff Auxier, a 14-year veteran broker from Portland, Ore. Auxier, who is making his second appearance as an All Star, scored an average 54% gain in '97. Merrill Lynch's Charles Dare, a third-year man and 37-year vet from suburban Detroit, finished No. 2 with a 53% profit. Rauscher Pierce's Frank Sloan, a second-year All Star and 25-year pro from Dallas, came in third with 49%. No. 4 with 40% was Paine Webber's Cynthia Bassett, another second-year All Star and a 29-year veteran from Cleveland.

To identify our exemplars, we asked money managers and prominent brokers to nominate brokers at firms other than their own. Candidates had to be willing to take new accounts of $150,000 or less and to have spotless records of professional conduct according to the National Association of Securities Dealers, the best source of disciplinary actions taken against brokers. Then we focused on attributes such as accountability and independent thinking that set All Stars apart from journeymen. Our 10 All Stars customarily base their recommendations on their own research as well as that of analysts. They personally own the stocks that are on their buy lists, avoid selling most brokerage products whose gold-plated fees can weigh down clients' returns, and give regular customers commission discounts of 20% to 25% in many cases.

The following profiles begin with the four returning All Stars in order of their average gain. Their six new teammates are then listed alphabetically. The profiles feature each broker's top three picks (or pans) and market outlook over the next 12 months. Three are bullish; six are anxious; one is bearish. The brokers see their 30 recommendations appreciating 41% as a group in '98 in step with earnings growth averaging a bustling 29%. That's four times the 7% profit growth forecast for companies in the S&P 500. Yet the picks are priced 14% below the market's earnings multiple, recently 20 based on analysts' consensus estimates for '98.

JEFF AUXIER   + 54%

FIRM: Smith Barney in Portland, Ore.; 800-835-9556. AGE: 38. ROOKIE YEAR: 1983. CLIENT HOUSEHOLDS: 150. ACCOUNT MINIMUM: $100,000. AVERAGE ACCOUNT: $500,000. OUTLOOK: Bullish

RÉSUMÉ: Native of Portland; graduate of University of Oregon; career broker

CLIENTELE: Local business executives and wealthy families including that of paper and textile magnate Robert Pamplin, who *Forbes* estimates is worth $550 million. Says Auxier: "Bob Pamplin has been a mentor and customer since my first job mowing neighborhood lawns 27 years ago at age 11."

COMMENT: "My demanding clients expect me to match or beat the S&P 500's return without taking a lot of risk," says Auxier. None of his three picks a year ago disappointed our readers. One of them, $16 billion financial supermarket American Express, quickly soared past his 12-month target price, prompting Auxier to recommend its sale at $68, a 46% profit, in our All Star midyear update. He held his two other choices, $2.2 billion (assets) Selective Insurance (up 57%) and $71 billion tobacco titan Philip Morris (up 37%). What about his replacement pick at midyear? Auxier recommended $6.6 billion property insurer TIG Holdings, which rose 24%, beating the market's corresponding 14% gain.

PICKS FOR '98: Again buy **Philip Morris** (New York Stock Exchange, recommended at $42). The New York City firm derives 65% of its profits from cigarette brands dominated by No. 1 Marlboro. By the end of 1998, Auxier sees the stock at $51, a 21% gain, as investors favorably anticipate a much-debated Congressional settlement of smoking-related lawsuits. What if a deal is struck earlier, say, in the first half of '98? "Then the stock could hit $56, or 33% more, by year-end," predicts Auxier. Buy $1.5 billion (assets) **PMI Group** (NYSE, recommended at $65). This San Francisco firm has a 15% share of the fast-consolidating $33 billion mortgage insurance market. Auxier expects California's resurgent housing sector (22% of PMI's premiums) to help boost earnings 16% in '98, elevating the stock 26% to $82 within the year. And buy $280 million **Binks Sames** (American Stock Exchange, recommended at $44). A year from now, says Auxier, this obscure Franklin Park, Ill. maker of industrial-strength paint spray guns will be wrapping up a two-year restructuring and earning about $3.50 a share. His 1998 target for the stock is $53, a 20% profit.

CHARLES DARE	+53%

FIRM: Merrill Lynch in Farmington Hills, Mich.; 800-937-0446. AGE: 63. ROOKIE YEAR: 1960. CLIENTS: about 500. MINIMUM: None. AVERAGE: $1 million. OUTLOOK: Bullish

RÉSUMÉ: Native of nearby Bloomfield Village; graduate of Michigan State, where he lettered in tennis; career broker who heads a five-adviser group that includes son Charles Jr., 32

CLIENTELE: Senior executives and professionals in the U.S. and abroad

COMMENT: Dare, a growth stock investor, last year recommended three companies whose price/earnings ratios averaged 19, representing a risk-reducing 27% discount to their projected 26% profit growth as a group. Pacing the trio was $1 billion Genesis Health, a nursing-home chain whose stock rose 72%. Credit-card whiz First USA, with $23 billion in card receivables, promptly charged ahead 68% and was sold at midyear. But its replacement, $5 billion credit-card processor First Data, slid 5% when earnings didn't live up to analysts' forecasts. (For the latest on First Data, see All Star John Jaeger.) Dare's other choice, $6 billion software house Oracle, gained 23%.

PICKS FOR 1998: Buy $4 billion **Corning** (NYSE, $43) in Corning, N.Y. "The world's dominant producer of optical fiber is a terrific but often overlooked way to bet on today's rapidly expanding telecom, computer and cable-TV networks," says Dare. He sees the stock propelling to $65 in '98. Buy $423 million **Paychex** (Nasdaq, $39). More and more small businesses, notes Dare, are hiring this superefficient Rochester, N.Y. data processor to streamline accounting chores such as payroll, withholding taxes and corporate tax filings. Over the past five years, earnings have grown an amazing 33% annually while net profit margins have doubled to almost 19%. He sees profits rising 31% next year and the stock hitting $50, a 28% gain. Also buy $2.5 billion (assets) **MGIC Investment** (NYSE, $63), a leading mortgage insurer based in Milwaukee. Dare's 1998 forecast for this low-risk stock is at least $72, a 14% profit.

FRANK SLOAN   +49%

FIRM: Rauscher Pierce Refsnes in Dallas; 800-677-2154. AGE: 53. ROOKIE YEAR: 1972. CLIENTS: 225. MINIMUM: $100,000. AVERAGE: $350,000. OUTLOOK: Anxious.

RÉSUMÉ: Native of Odessa, Texas; graduate of the University of Texas; career broker

CLIENTELE: Business owners and executives who appreciate Sloan's focus on companies based in Texas or the Southwest

COMMENT: "I read lots of Wall Street research on firms in my area," says Sloan. "But I won't buy until I've completed my own grass-roots assessment." That can include interviews with a company's customers, competitors and mid-level management as well as top brass. Last year Sloan recommended three seemingly undervalued Dallas companies led by $8.5 billion computer chipmaker Texas Instruments. The stock shot up a Texasesque 173%, amply offsetting two losing small-cap picks—$140 million driller Triton Energy (down 2%) and $126 million computer repairer PC Service Source (down 23%). Two of Sloan's three choices this year also have headquarters in his backyard.

PICKS FOR 1998: Again buy **Triton Energy** (NYSE, $39) before a major oil company swallows the exploration firm to gain control of its stakes in promising wells in Colombia and the Gulf of Thailand. Unexpected production headaches plagued Triton in '97, says Sloan. For 1998 he sees cash flow more than doubling and the stock approaching $60, a 54% rise from here. Buy $370 million art auctioneer **Sotheby's** (NYSE, $19) based in New York City and controlled by Detroit real estate magnate Alfred Taubman, who owns 63% of voting shares. Sloan notes that an investment group representing the billionaire Bass family of Texas scooped up 8.5% of the stock this past summer. What's up? Sloan expects Sotheby's to rise to $27. And buy Dallas' $13 billion **Kimberly–Clark** (NYSE, $51), maker of Huggies diapers, Kleenex tissues and other paper products. Glitches in integrating Scott Paper, acquired in late 1995, slowed profit growth in '97, says Sloan. For 1998, however, he sees earnings jumping 19% and the stock cracking $70, a 37% gain.

CYNTHIA BASSETT   +40%

FIRM: Paine Webber in Cleveland; 800-533-6386. AGE: 58. ROOKIE YEAR: 1969. CLIENTS: 250. MINIMUM: None. AVERAGE: $900,000. OUTLOOK: Anxious

RÉSUMÉ: Native of Cleveland; graduate of the University of Wisconsin; began career in 1962 as assistant to two veteran brokers

CLIENTELE: Monied Cleveland clans whose accounts often extend through three generations

COMMENT: Last year Bassett recommended three blue chips that, she predicted, "could quickly recover from earnings stumbles that had hobbled the stocks." All three delivered. Bankers Trust, with $130 billion in assets, rose 47%, while $29 billion Pepsico gained 34%. By midyear, third pick $29 billion Motorola had rebounded 42% to $64, two bucks above her target price, and was sold. But her streak was broken by Motorola's replacement, $400 million boating emporium West Marine. Its stock dropped 3% after the company reported earnings below analysts' estimates.

PICKS FOR 1998: Buy brash $7 billion telecom consolidator **Worldcom** (Nasdaq, $30) in Jackson, Miss. for Bassett's end-of-year target price of $50, a 67% profit. Worldcom's proposed $37 billion stock swap to buy $19 billion long-distance rival MCI appears to have vanquished MCI suitor GTE, a $22 billion local phone carrier. The record-setting MCI bidding war, says Bassett, "is revealing the enormous hidden value of leading phone and data networks, particularly Worldcom's." Buy $4.8 billion **Staples** (Nasdaq, $28), a Westborough, Mass. chain of office-supply superstores, for a 1998 target of $35, a 25% rise. And buy Minneapolis-based **Norwest** (NYSE, $32), the nation's 11th largest commercial bank with $85 billion in assets and one of the nation's largest mortgage lenders. She figures earnings increases of 13% will boost the stock 25% to $40 by the end of the year.

FIRM: Donaldson Lufkin & Jenrette in Los Angeles; 800-237-5022. AGE: 56. ROOKIE YEAR: 1972. CLIENTS: 250. MINIMUM: $50,000. AVERAGE: $500,000. OUTLOOK: Bearish

RÉSUMÉ: Native of Los Angeles; graduate of California State Polytechnic; former aerospace engineer at McDonnell Douglas

CLIENTELE: Conservative investors, often in the entertainment business, who have placed their personal and retirement accounts under his control

COMMENT: "Clients expect me to maintain a sturdy balance between growth and income," notes Frankel. "They're more comfortable earning consistent 12% to 15% annual returns than trying to beat a runaway bull market." Besides, Frankel predicts that 1998 will mark the start of a bear market sparked by a slowdown in corporate profits or a spike in long-term interest rates to the neighborhood of 7.5% to 8%. The bogeyman? Frankel sees one in Asia's mounting currency and credit crunches, which figure to force many banks and companies there to liquidate their stashes of U.S. Treasury bonds, depressing prices.

PICKS FOR 1998: Sell short **Standard & Poor's Depositary Receipts**, nicknamed "spiders" (ASE, $92), which mirror moves in the S&P 500 index. This year, Frankel sees S&P 500 companies' earnings rising about 6%, roughly 50% below brokerage DLJ's estimate of 13%, and spiders falling 20% to $74. Sell short $10 billion PC powerhouse **Dell Computers** (Nasdaq, $76) in Round Rock, Texas. Frankel's only knock on the stock is its gold-plated price, which toward the end of '97 was 22 times estimates of '98 earnings. His end-of-1998 target is $58, a 24% drop. And buy $68 million **Interneuron Pharmaceuticals** (Nasdaq, $12) in Lexington, Mass. In September, the firm pulled its Redux weight-loss drug off the market, citing safety concerns. Fears about potential liability lawsuits dragged the stock down 64% from its '97 peak of almost $33. But Frankel says Interneuron has limited liability, ample insurance, $140 million in cash and several other major drugs now undergoing clinical trials that support his end-of-year target price of $22.

FIRM: Merrill Lynch in New York City; 800-624-6122. AGE: 54. ROOKIE YEAR: 1965. CLIENTS: 250. MINIMUM: $150,000. AVERAGE: $1 million. OUTLOOK: Anxious

RÉSUMÉ: Native of Manhattan; graduate of Fairleigh Dickinson University; career broker who heads a four-adviser group that includes sons Gregory, 30, and Andrew, 28

CLIENTELE: Top executives at Merrill Lynch and in the media, one of the market sectors his group follows closely

COMMENT: While Merrill Lynch analysts cover more than 1,000 companies around the world, says Heilbronn, "we focus on only 30 to 40 undervalued stocks in industries like media that our clients know intimately." Among his largest media holdings are $13 billion Time Warner, parent of MONEY, and $10 billion Westinghouse. But Heilbronn isn't recommending either pet stock because, he says, "we've got three other ideas, including a Japanese turnaround, that promise more upside in '98."

PICKS FOR 1998: Buy $4 billion **Corning** (NYSE, $43) for the same reason cited earlier by All Star Charles Dare. Heilbronn adds that many investors fail to recognize how Corning has refocused itself as a technology company by selling its consumer-products unit (Corning, Pyrex and Revere cookware) and spinning off health-care businesses (mainly testing labs). Heilbronn's 1998 target, like Dare's, is $65, a 51% profit. Buy Japan's $39 billion **NEC Corp.** (Nasdaq, $53), which has commanding 50% shares of that stalled economy's computer and telecom equipment markets. The stock fell 28% from its '97 peak of $74 in expectation of an 18% earnings decline in the fiscal year ending March 31, 1998. Heilbronn sees both corporate cost-cutting and a modest economic upturn in Japan fueling a 48% profit rebound in fiscal '99 that will lift the stock 51% to $80. And buy $818 million **Callaway Golf** (NYSE, $32) to cash in on golfers', including Heilbronn's two sons', insatiable appetite for this Carlsbad, Calif. firm's larger, longer-hitting and premium-priced titanium woods and irons. His end-of-year target for it is $45, a 41% rise, aided by a 17% earnings hike in 1998.

JOHN JAEGER   NEW ALL STAR

FIRM: BT Alex. Brown in Baltimore; 800-638-2596. AGE: 56. ROOKIE YEAR: 1968. CLIENTS: 200. MINIMUM: $50,000. AVERAGE: $1 million. OUTLOOK: Anxious

RÉSUMÉ: Native of Aberdeen, Md.; graduate of Brown University; career broker

CLIENTELE: Wealthy people, about half of whom pay Jaeger's annual fee (averaging 1% of assets) to manage their money

COMMENT: "Working at Alex. Brown's Baltimore headquarters gives me a competitive edge," says Jaeger. Why? Software whizzes Microsoft, Oracle and Sun Microsystems are among the famous growth stocks brought public by the well-connected investment bank. So scores of wannabe Bill Gates flock to Brown's headquarters each month to make presentations that, quips

Jaeger, "I faithfully attend to gain insights and determine, once the slide show begins, whether the top brass, you know, glows in the dark."

PICKS FOR 1998: Buy $5 billion **First Data (**NYSE, $29), down 37% from its '97 peak of $46 after posting disappointing third-quarter profits. For 1998, Jaeger sees earnings at the Hackensack, N.J. credit-card processer rising 19% and the stock bouncing 66% to $48, aided by innovations such as FDC's joint venture with Microsoft to allow consumers and businesses to pay bills via the Internet. Buy $2.4 billion **Amgen** (Nasdaq, $52), down 25% from 1997's $69 high on news of slower sales of Epogen, the Thousand Oaks, Calif. biotech firm's best-selling drug for combating anemia. Jaeger believes Amgen's $52 stock is a short-lived bargain in light of the firm's lineup of promising new drugs under development and $1 billion cash horde, much of it earmarked for buying back shares. His end-of-year target is $65, a 25% profit. Also buy $594 million (assets) **IPC Holdings** (Nasdaq, $32), an unrecognized gem among specialty insurers operating from tax haven Bermuda. IPC's forte is excess property/catastrophe coverage, providing an average of $15 million in protection that kicks in only after the first $2 billion in damages. What could the stock fetch by the end of the year? "I'm aiming for $39, or 22% more, not counting the fat 7% dividend yield," says Jaeger.

ALEX LIEBLONG   NEW ALL STAR

FIRM: Lieblong & Associates in Little Rock; 888-805-4705. AGE: 47. ROOKIE YEAR: 1977. CLIENTS: 350. MINIMUM: none. AVERAGE: $500,000. OUTLOOK: Anxious

RÉSUMÉ: Native of Conway, Ark., where Lieblong sits on the board of the local bank; never finished college; ran Paine Webber's 20-broker Little Rock office for 10 years; launched his own three-broker boutique in June

CLIENTELE: Entrepreneurs and bankers whom he first encountered while checking out their firms as prospective investments

COMMENT: "The banking crisis of the early '90s was a bonanza for asset players like me," says Lieblong. In 1992, Lieblong told MONEY he and his clients were loading up on the $12 to $13 shares of crippled megabank Citicorp. He still owns those shares, which have been trading at $123. And Lieblong was the main source for our recommendation of Los Angeles' Coast Savings at $16 in the May 1995 Buy Sell Hold column. Coast was recently commanding $60, a 275% profit over 2 1/2 years, pending its acquisition by rival California thrift H.F. Ahmanson.

PICKS FOR 1998: Buy $460 million (assets) **Servico** (NYSE, $17), a West Palm Beach, Fla. firm that owns or operates 44 mostly full-service hotels affiliated with major chains, including Holiday Inn. "Servico is a master at acquiring mundane properties and transforming them into cash cows within three years," says Lieblong. He sees the stock escalating 47% to $25 in '98. Buy $587 million **Grand Casinos** (NYSE, $13). This low-profile Minnetonka, Minn. concern, initially a manager of gambling parlors on Indian reservations, owns three thriving Mississippi riverboat casinos led by GND's 18-month-old casino/convention center at Tunica, 30 miles south of Memphis. "Grand's stock trades at only half the cash flow multiple of its competitors," says Lieblong. He's betting that surging receipts at Tunica will pump earnings up 33% in 1998, boosting the stock 54% to $20. And buy $250 million **Virco** (ASE, $27) for a projected 30% rise to $35 powered by a 67% surge in earnings this year. The impetus? As a leading maker of sturdy school furniture, the Torrance, Calif. firm is Lieblong's favorite way to profit from the baby-boom echo-kids born in a bulge of nest-building in the late '80s, who are now swamping many school systems.

ROBERT McLEAN　　　NEW ALL STAR

FIRM: Paine Webber in Philadelphia; 800-345-7941. AGE: 44. ROOKIE YEAR: 1979. CLIENTS: 300. MINIMUM: $100,000. AVERAGE: $500,000. OUTLOOK: Anxious

RÉSUMÉ: Native of Philadelphia; graduate of Brown University; scion of the *Philadelphia Bulletin* media empire founded by his great-grandfather and sold in 1982; career broker

CLIENTELE: Wealthy families and institutional investors

COMMENT: "My customers are on the lookout for smaller growth stock ideas that are thoroughly researched but not shopworn," says McLean. To spot timely buys, he taps into his Bloomberg database to discover stock purchases by corporate insiders that are not related to the exercise of options. "Such insider buying has popped up at two of my current picks, Triton Energy and Diacrin," he explains. "That's bullish in my book even if the purchases are fairly modest."

PICKS FOR 1998: Buy $140 million exploration outfit **Triton Energy** (NYSE, $39) for the same reasons mentioned earlier by All Star Frank Sloan. Delays in ramping up oil production in Colombia have turned off impatient investors, says McLean. He sees Triton's daily output more than doubling to 500,000 barrels by midyear, turning heads on Wall Street and pushing up the stock 54% to $60. Buy Charlestown, Mass. biotech startup **Diacrin** (Nasdaq, $10) for McLean's 1998 target of $18, a projected 80% rise. The trigger? This summer, he predicts, Diacrin will disclose the promising results of clinical trials of transplanting living pig cells into humans suffering from neurological diseases including Parkinson's. (It's the first such study permitted by federal regulators.) Sell short Newark, Del.'s **MBNA Corp.** (NYSE, $27), the nation's No. 2 credit-card issuer with $45 billion in account receivables. Rivals, including $18 billion Advanta and $14 billion Capital One, already have fessed up that mounting charge-offs of uncollectable receivables are depressing profits. So will MBNA, predicts McLean. He figures '98 earnings will come in about 10% below expectations, knocking the stock down at least 26% to $20.

JIM STROUD   NEW ALL STAR

FIRM: McDonald & Co. in Hudson, Ohio; 800-216-4638. AGE: 43. ROOKIE YEAR: 1985. CLIENTS: 200. MINIMUM: $50,000. AVERAGE: $200,000. OUTLOOK: Bullish

RÉSUMÉ: Native of Cleveland; graduate of the State University of New York at Fredonia (B.A.) and Akron University (M.A.); manager of seven-broker McDonald office in Hudson, a Cleveland suburb

CLIENTELE: Owners and executives of Ohio-based companies

COMMENT: Stroud and partner Craig Pickering, 48, have complementary roles. Jim concentrates on researching stocks, while Craig is the customers' man. "We favor prosperous, low-profile companies whose stocks are priced at a risk-reducing discount to their growth rates," says Stroud. For example, his three picks as a group are projected to increase their earnings an average of 21% next year. Yet the trio trades for an affordable average of 12 times earnings—a 43% discount to that 21% growth rate.

PICKS FOR 1998: Buy $4.2 billion personal computer disk-drive maker **Western Digital** (NYSE, $21). The stock of this Irvine, Calif. firm fell 62% from its '97 high of $55 after WDC disclosed that escalating price wars would result in 1997 earnings coming in significantly below analysts' forecasts. This year, however, Stroud sees WDC's push into brawnier, high-priced drives pumping up profit margins and propelling earnings 15%. His 1998 target is $37, a 76% rebound. Buy $241 million **Encore Wire** (Nasdaq, $30), a highly efficient maker of low-margin copper wiring used mainly in houses and buildings. Thanks in part to a 10% drop in copper prices over the past year or so, Stroud says earnings at the McKinney, Texas firm figure to soar, elevating the stock 40% to $42. And buy $293 million **In Focus Systems** (Nasdaq, $33) in Wilsonville, Ore., a Portland suburb. In Focus is the leading maker of PC-powered, graphics-rich overhead projectors that are becoming standard equipment in corporate conference rooms. In 1998, Stroud sees earnings rising 28% and the stock hitting $44—a projected 33% profit for shareholders.

In the six months ending November 1, shares of companies with a market capitalization of around $1 billion or less returned 27%, more than double the S&P 500's 13% and 14 points higher than the 13% returns that small stocks have averaged historically. Why are the wee ones doing so well? The short answer is: It's their turn. "Many of the multinationals have become so overvalued that investors are shifting to small caps to find cheap stocks," explains Hugh Johnson, chief investment strategist at First Albany in Albany, N.Y. Moreover, since small companies do most of their business domestically, their profits are largely insulated from the international turmoil that threatens the earnings growth of many multinationals. For both these reasons, we expect that this year small stocks will match their historical results and return 12%, the best outlook for any asset class in 1998.

You can increase that return significantly through solid stock-picking rather than relying on a small-stock index fund. Says Claudia Mott, the small cap guru at Prudential Securities: "The best move for next year is to own a diversified collection of high-growth small caps that have limited risk."

Since high growth with limited risk sounds like an oxymoron, we asked Mott to screen Prudential's database of 6,000 equities to isolate the companies with market capitalizations of $200 million to $1 billion. Then, to ensure solid growth, we requested a projected long-term earnings growth rate of at least 20% a year. To limit risk, we asked for stocks with price/earnings ratios (based on estimated 1998 earnings) lower than their long-term earnings growth rates. Finally, we vetted the 120 stocks that cleared those hurdles with roughly two dozen fund managers, investment advisers and security analysts who make a specialty of small stocks. They added suggestions of their own and then helped us narrow the recommendations. None pays a dividend, but all are expected to gain at least 25% through 1998.

▶ **Americredit** (NYSE, recently traded at around $22). The leading purveyor of so-called subprime automobile loans, $210 million Americredit is growing 300% a year in both revenues and profits. It maintains plump 25% net profit margins by making loans averaging $12,000 to consumers with less than perfect credit histories and charging them an average 20% interest. By contrast, the interest on a prime bank auto loan averages 9%. This year Americredit will open 50 new lending offices across the country, bringing the total to 150. Prudential analyst Mary Rhei thinks the added real estate along with fewer competitors will help boost earnings a full 33% through 1998.

Nearly 75% of Americredit's competitors have gone out of business in the last three years because many of their customers defaulted on loans. "The key to subprime lending is choosing borrowers a bank would overlook, but who won't default," says Michael Durante, an analyst at Salomon Brothers. "Americredit is the best in the business at finding those borrowers," he adds. As a result it is able to hold loan losses to around 5.5% a year, well below the industry average of 7%. Nonetheless, the stock trades at only 16 times earnings, despite a projected earnings growth rate of 25% a year through 2002. Durante thinks that this year Americredit will rise to $40.

▶ **Volt Information Sciences** (NYSE; around $49). This $1.7 billion temporary employment and telecommunications services company is the Rodney Dangerfield of the NYSE. Despite a torrid eightfold increase in the stock price since 1994, a red hot 40% earnings growth rate and a moderate 20 P/E, no Wall Street analyst actively follows it. But, says fund manager Catherine Lawson of the Highland Growth Fund in Fairfield, Conn.: "Wall Street won't ignore Volt for long."

The New York City company has two main lines of business, both in areas of the economy growing 20% a year or more. One is supplying professional temporary staffing mostly to large tech companies like Lucent Technologies. The other is bulding and installing telecommunications equipment for companies like Bell Atlantic and Sprint. "Volt benefits from the outsourcing trend," says Andy Knuth, of Westport Asset Management in Westport, Conn., "and also from the deregulation of telecommunications, which is spurring installation of equipment." Lawson thinks earnings will grow 30% during 1998, pushing the stock to $95.

▶ **Curative Health Services** (Nasdaq; around $31). Headquartered in East Setauket, N.Y., this $114 million company operates 141 chronic wound care units in hospitals and freestanding clinics around the country, where it treats victims of recurring ailments on an out-patient basis. "Curative uses proprietary computer modeling, therapies and drugs to find the best treatment for poor blood circulation, diabetic ulcers and bed sores," says Andrew Gitkin, an analyst at Smith Barney. And Curative is able to handle its patients at two-thirds the cost of conventional hospitals.

Although Curative has no publicly traded competitor serving the $2 billion wound market, the stock trades at a 26 P/E. "It would be incredibly difficult for a private physician group to gain the size needed to challenge Curative nationwide," says Gitkin. Equity strategist Phil Dow at Dain Bosworth in Minneapolis looks for the company to keep its earnings growing 30% annually for the next five years, while Gitkin expects the stock to reach $38 for a 25% gain in 1998.

▶ **Showbiz Pizza Time** (Nasdaq; around $21). All six analysts who follow this $390 million food and entertainment company, known for its Chuck E. Cheese pizzas, rate the stock a buy. That's quite a change from a few years ago when the stock dropped from $24 in 1993 to $5 in 1995 as a result of turf wars with Discovery Zone, a glitzy upstart bankrolled by uber-financier Wayne Huizenga. Two years ago, Showbiz parried Huizenga's attack by initiating an aggressive, $78 million campaign to improve the food, decor, service and entertainment with the result that sales at existing stores increased 18% a year. That move established Chuck E. Cheese's superiority and reduced the threat of punishing price wars by helping to drive Discovery Zone into bankruptcy in 1996. "After the renovations, Chuck E. Cheese became by far the best entertainment for families, and it still is," says Robert Derrington at Equitable Securities in Nashville.

The Irving, Texas company isn't slowing down. But its P/E of only 14 reflects its rocky past and reduces the risk in its buoyant future. Over the next two years, it plans to add 30 new stores to its existing 312 nationwide. The company recently spent $150,000 to $170,000 per store to install newer and better video games and entertainment. That facelift helped boost same-store sales 10% during 1997, while helping raise net profit margins from 5% in 1996 to 13%. Dennis Telzrow, an analyst at Principal Financial in Dallas, expects Showbiz to boost earnings at an average annual rate of 20% for the next five years. Derrington expects 21% earnings growth in 1998, pushing the stock to $28, a deep-dish 33% return.

BLUE CHIPS TO BANK ON

With their impeccable pedigrees, blue-chip companies are the royalty of the investing world. But recently, many seem to be in danger of losing their crowns. Toward the end of 1997, when the market as a whole was down only 8% from its all-time peak, Coca-Cola had tumbled 23% from its 1997 high, Merck had fallen 18%, and Gillette had lost 14%.

The outlook for 1998 doesn't appear much brighter. Given the economic troubles in Asia and other international markets, multinational corporations won't be able to count on big earnings boosts from overseas. In addition, with the U.S. economy likely to slow from 3.7% in 1997 to about 2.5% in

1998, growth in domestic profits will be limited. And to top it all off, blue chips are far from cheap. The 30 stocks in the Dow have been trading at an average of 18 times projected 1998 earnings. That's roughly a 13% premium over the Dow's historical 16 price/earnings ratio. As a result, lots of investors are asking: Who needs 'em?

The fact is, blue chips should still be the cornerstone of your portfolio. "They have the characteristics that, over time, make stocks winners," says Charles Smith, managing director of J. & W. Seligman, an investment advisory firm in New York City. "These companies are No. 1 or No. 2 in their industry, have control over pricing and generate all the capital they need to keep growing." In short, they are stocks you can buy and hold for five years or longer.

Of course, you want to identify those blue chips that stand the best chance of outpacing corporate America's slowing profit growth. To find such stocks, we canvassed more than two dozen security analysts and money managers for recommendations. Then we winnowed their favorite blue chips to a group expected to post at least 14% growth in earnings per share this year, or twice the amount that MONEY projects for the average company. The pros' top picks are listed below in descending order of their projected 1998 total return (capital gains plus dividends).

▶ **Xerox** (NYSE; recently traded at around $75). Xerox is redoubling its efforts to hold on to its core corporate clientele, particularly its production publishing unit, which is growing at a rate of 27% a year. At the same time, this $19 billion Stamford, Conn. company is busily creating a new image for itself as the dominant supplier of copiers and printers for the rapidly growing home-office market. In September, sporting its new look, the company announced that CompUSA will sell Xerox's new Document HomeCentre, which delivers professional-level color printing, copying and scanning, and Document WorkCentre, which integrates color printing with faxing, PC faxing, copying and scanning. The CompUSA deal doubles to 3,000 the retail outlets carrying Xerox products in the U.S. and Canada. That increased retail reach will help Xerox tap into the booming home-office market, which the industry forecasts will grow nearly 30% a year from $26 billion in 1997 to $54 billion by the year 2000. Oppenheimer analyst Rudolf Hokanson says Xerox could boost its revenues from this line of business to $4 billion annually by 2000, up from only $1 billion today. That works out to a compound annual growth rate of nearly 60% over three years.

In addition, for corporate clients, Xerox's new line of laser printers comes with a free, one-year service contract. "That's something that most of its rivals aren't matching right now," says Tim Ghriskey, head of value stock research at Dreyfus. And then there's Xerox's new DocuColor 40, a digital copier launched in March 1996, that churns out 40 color reproductions a minute, making it five times faster than any other copier/printer while carrying a base price of $130,000—about half as much as a digital color press. This model helped digital product sales spurt 26% in the third quarter of 1997. For all these reasons, Prudential analyst Alexander Henderson looks for the company to post earnings growth of 15% in 1998 and a share price of $100, for a total return of 35%.

▶ **Compaq Computer** (NYSE, around $29). Already the world's largest manufacturer of personal computers, the $29 billion Houston company shipped 19% of the 8.4 billion domestic PCs ordered in the third quarter of 1997, compared with 13.5% the year before. At the same time, the firm boosted its share of global PC sales to 14.3%, up 3.5 percentage points from the year earlier. What makes Compaq so popular? "The PC business is a tough one, but because Compaq is the No. 1 PC company, it has leverage when it comes to purchasing and brand-name recognition when it comes to sales," says Goldman Sachs analyst Richard Schutte. "That's a winning combination."

Compaq now has a two-pronged approach in place to capitalize on the 15% rise in PC demand that the Semiconductor Industry Association expects in 1998. First, last July the company launched a build-to-order manufacturing process to challenge rivals like Dell and Gateway 2000, which have long been successful with this approach. The build-to-order process allows corporate customers and retailers to mix and match features from an array of models to get a machine tailored to their specific needs. The computer is not actually built until the order is placed, which enables the company to keep product inventories low. Savings are passed on to consumers. For example, Compaq's new build-to-order Deskpro 2000 models are up to 28% cheaper than similar Hewlett-Packard machines. At the same time, through acquisitions such as the purchases of Tandem Computer and Digital Equipment Corporation, Compaq is expanding its position in the corporate market for complex computer networks. The combination of new products and a boarding house reach for market share have David Wu, an analyst at ABN Amro Chicago, calling for significant earnings growth in 1998.

▶ **Kroger** (NYSE; around $34). Like a homemaker clipping coupons from the Sunday paper, the $27 billion Cincinnati grocer is always scouting for ways to cut costs. Kroger is the nation's largest supermarket chain, holding the No. 1 or No. 2 position in 26 of its 28 largest markets. Since 1995, it has invested $70 million in projects to reduce spending on distribution, transportation and storage. It has consolidated many of its warehouses and begun to coordinate grocery purchases across entire regions rather than allowing individual stores to buy from local wholesalers. "Buying in bulk should result in better pricing deals, which will boost Kroger's profit margins," says Phil Schettewi, manager of Loomis Sayles' Strategic Value fund.

From 1998 through 1999, Kroger also expects to invest up to $800 million annually to build, expand or acquire stores and increase its square footage by nearly 6% a year. As a result, even though low inflation has kept food prices stagnant, Kroger's total sales during the third quarter of 1997 were up 4.7% from a year earlier, to $7.7 billion. That kind of performance has Smith Barney analyst Gary M. Giblen predicting a 19% earnings increase in 1998, and a $42 share price, for a total return of 25%.

▶ **Home Depot** (NYSE; around $57). Houses built before 1980 account for 86% of the U.S. housing stock, which means that some 75 million older homes need new roofs, siding, plumbing, wiring, painting, papering—you name it. That's why the Home Improvement Research Institute projects that industry sales will hit $167 billion by 2001, up from $135 billion in 1996. And benefiting from that favorable trend is the $30 billion do-it-yourself retailer Home Depot. Its roughly 559 stores across the nation stock over 50,000 different kinds of building materials, home-improvement supplies, interior-design items and lawn products and have 14% of the market nailed down.

Not that the Atlanta company plans to stop there: Its goal is to have 1,100 stores by 2000. "They're taking business away from the mom-and-pop outfits by going into underserved areas and providing customers with top-notch service," says Gary Dennis, an analyst at J.C. Bradford in Nashville. Moreover, the company is expanding into every corner of the home-improvement market. Its five EXPO Design Centers, ranging from 80,000 to 145,000 square feet, sell upscale interior-design products like hand-painted Italian marble tile and also offer professional design consulting services to customers undergoing major home renovations. Thus, Gary Balter, an analyst at Donaldson Lufkin & Jenrette, anticipates earnings growth of 25% in 1998, driving the company's share price to $70, for a total return of 24%.

▶ **AirTouch Communications** (NYSE; around $39). Taking its cue from a more conventional kind of phone company, the San Francisco provider of worldwide wireless communications services is reaching out to touch someone—the citizens of Europe. Only about 10% of that continent's population uses cellular phones, compared with 20% of the U.S. population. So AirTouch is boosting the number of customized phone plans it offers to European customers, like the pre-paid service plan it began offering last year in Italy and Spain. As a result, the $4 billion company added 366,000 customers to an international pool that now tallies 2.6 million—vs. 3.9 million in the U.S—and its third quarter 1997 was the best ever for international sales.

Analysts expect the company to maintain this kind of momentum because, says Jack Reagan of Legg Mason Wood Walker in Baltimore, "It is in very stable countries where government regulation of the industry keeps competition low and, therefore, the cost of cellular service high." Meanwhile, Bear Stearns analyst David Freedman notes that AirTouch will lose no time entering local European cellular businesses that are about to be deregulated and will allow private cellular companies to offer subscribers additional services. In fact, Reagan says, "AirTouch's international portfolio is the growth engine that will keep the company expanding at double-digit rates through 2005." For the next 12 months, Reagan is calling for 45% earnings growth and a target price of $45, for a total return of 15%.

▶ **Carnival Corp.** (NYSE, around $56). Cruise lines start targeting their customers when they are as young as 25 and have a household income of $20,000 or more. That market is almost half the U.S. population. But even so, only about 7% of the general population has actually set sail. To boost that paltry number, this $2.6 billion cruise ship and tour operator is "continually enhancing its fleet, adding innovations that attract travelers," says Smith Barney analyst Jill Krutick. For example, the Miami company offers a spa menu with healthy food selections low in calories, fat and sodium, and in December 1998 it will christen the world's first smoke-free cruise ship. In addition, Carnival—which has 34 ships plying routes to Alaska, Asia, the Bahamas, the Caribbean, Europe, Hawaii, the Mexican Riviera and the Panama Canal—is offering the following guarantee on some of those routes through 1998: If you're dissatisfied with your cruise, you can disembark in the first non-U.S. port of call and receive a refund for the unused portion of your cruise fare, as well as a free flight back to the ship's home port.

Such moves increased advance bookings for the first half of 1998 from the same period in 1997. And analysts like Krutick think Carnival can see exciting growth overseas, now that the company owns a 50% stake in Costa Crociere S.p.A., the largest cruise operator in Europe. A scant 2% of Europeans take cruises. In addition, Carnival owns a portion of Airtours, one of the

United Kingdom's leading travel and tour operations. "Carnival has proved it knows how to expand its customer base in the U.S., and the same approach should work in Europe," says David Anders, an analyst at Credit Suisse First Boston in New York City. That's why he believes Carnival's earnings will rise 14% in 1998.

FOREIGN STOCKS ON A FAST TRACK

When it comes to investing these days, you may think there's no place like home. After all, once you step off U.S. shores, you risk being swept up in a global market tornado like the one last October that began in Southeast Asia. The crisis that sprang from Thailand's currency devaluation drove Hong Kong's Hang Seng stock index down 30% and Japan's already depressed Nikkei average down 5.7%. Then it hit Latin America, where Brazil plunged 32.7%.

But over the long haul, stashing all your investment dollars in the U.S. would be a big mistake. Here are three reasons:

Basic philosophy. The recent storms in Southeast Asia haven't altered the fundamental case for international diversification. Even though small overseas markets have an alarming tendency to crash, putting foreign equities in a well-balanced portfolio can actually reduce your overall volatility. That's because markets here and abroad often move in different cycles, even in these days of increasing global economic links. "During major drops, it may seem as if all markets go down together," says Princeton University economics professor Burton Malkiel. "But generally, international stock market returns have been moving in step less often during the last five years than during the preceding fifteen years. So by investing abroad, you lower the risk of your portfolio."

Growth potential. Many foreign markets are poised to outperform Wall Street. "The U.S. bull market is slowing and likely to suffer more shake-outs," says Nicholas Bratt, head of the global equity group at investment firm Scudder, Stevens & Clark in New York City. "But many international markets are likely to deliver 15% to 20% gains over the next year." Indeed, with U.S. stocks posting extraordinary gains over the past three years, it's been easy to forget just how rewarding foreign investing can be. But since 1970, according to research by senior international strategist Douglas Johnson at Merrill Lynch in New York City, foreign equities have outpaced U.S. stocks by an average of one-half to one percentage point annually.

Company quality. Some of the world's best companies are based overseas. According to investing experts, there are many fast-growing overseas companies, with the best prospects today to be found in Europe and Latin America. "Right now many European companies resemble American firms just after the wave of restructuring in the '80s," says Mark Holowesko, manager of the Templeton Foreign fund. "As those companies cut costs and improve productivity, their share prices will climb."

Thus, it's still smart for long-term investors to keep 20% of their stock portfolio in foreign equities. If you have $20,000 or more to invest, and you enjoy picking stocks, your best move is to buy American Depositary Receipts (ADRs), which are the U.S.-traded equivalent of foreign stocks. But investors with only a small amount to put away—as well as those who don't know a baht from a bat—should choose a diversified foreign stock fund. Either way, you should plan to hang on for at least three to five years so you can ride out the inevitable downdrafts.

To help you make the most of global opportunities, we asked more than two dozen investment strategists, money managers and stock and fund analysts for their recommendations. Here are stocks they are high on:

▶ **Pan American Beverages** (NYSE, recently traded at around $30). For a foreign stock with an all-American flavor, try $2.5 billion (1997 sales) Pan American Beverages. The Mexican-based company is the largest Coca-Cola bottler outside the U.S., accounting for 28% of Coke's sales in one of its fastest-growing regions. With a dominant 60% market share, Panamco has been the biggest beneficiary of Coca-Cola's drive to consolidate its foreign operations in the hands of key bottlers. Last year, for instance, Panamco acquired Venezuela's chief Coke bottler, which had earlier defected from Pepsi. The deal, which raised Coke's stake in Panamco to 24%, is expected to lift the company's revenues by $600 million in 1998. "As more mom-and-pop bottlers sell out, Panamco will be in a good position to acquire them, which will further increase its market share," says Dan Jaworski, chief investment officer for BPI Global Management, an investment firm in Orlando.

Meanwhile, with operations in six Latin American countries—including Brazil, its largest market, Colombia, and Costa Rica—Panamco is well-positioned to ride out any isolated downturns. "In 1995 Mexico was in economic trouble, but Brazil was booming," says Smith Barney analyst Francisco Chevez. "Now Mexico is doing well, and Brazil is sluggish, but Panamco has maintained 27% earnings growth over the past two years. " Chevez expects the company's profits to climb 28% this year. Panamco shares are currently trading at a discount to other Latin American bottlers because its shares can be bought only in the U.S. and not in local markets. But as Wall Street catches on to the stock's potential, Chevez thinks Panamco's shares could hit $50 in 1998 for a bubbly 66% gain.

▶ **Philips Electronics N.V.** (NYSE, around $62). Based in the Netherlands, this $40 billion semiconductor and consumer electronics behemoth makes everything from televisions to telephones to compact disc players. For years Philips' stock price lagged its peers', in part because the company was seen as poorly managed. But chairman Cor Boonstra, who took the reins in 1996, has launched a restructuring program that analysts believe will streamline the company and boost profits. "Boonstra is moving decisively to expand earnings by 15% annually over the next five years," says Mike Gerding, manager of the Founders Worldwide Growth Fund.

For starters, Boonstra is shedding dozens of Philips' less profitable divisions. Just last October, the company announced plans to sell its car systems group, which makes radios and navigation devices, to Mannesmann VDO—a move that analysts say will save the company $100 million a year. And to further trim costs, Boonstra is planning more joint ventures—toward the end of '97, he announced a $2.5 billion deal with U.S. firm Lucent Technologies to develop telephones and other communications products. The restructuring program should help lift Philips' earnings from $3.80 a share last year to $5.70 in 1998, according to Richard Foulkes, manager of the Vanguard International Growth fund. Foulkes, who has 2.7% of the fund's $7 billion stashed in Philips, expects the stock to hit $100 a share in 1998.

▶ **Sedgwick Group** (NYSE, around $11). With $1.7 billion in revenues, Sedgwick is the world's third largest insurance broker, selling property and casualty coverage to large corporations worldwide. And at its recent price/earnings ratio of just 9.5, Sedgwick trades far more cheaply than market leader Chicago-based $5.5 billion Aon, which carried a 16 P/E. Add to that the company's lofty 5.3% yield, and "you have an extraordinary value," declares David Herro, manager of the Oakmark International fund, who has roughly 4% of his $1.6 billion fund invested in the company.

Sedgwick's stock price has been hurt by a long-term slump in insurance rates, which has pulled down the share prices of most U.K. insurers. Even so, Sedgwick has kept its insurance sales climbing a steady 4% annually. Moreover, the company operates a booming employee benefits consulting unit that now accounts for 26% of revenues, up from just 11% in 1992. And with consulting fees poised to surge 17% in 1998, Merrill Lynch analyst Roman Cizdyn figures Sedgwick's share price will shoot up to $14 over the next 12 months. Combined with Sedgwick's dividend, that would provide investors with a total return of 39%.

▶ **Novartis** (Nasdaq, around $77). The world's largest drug company, $22 billion Novartis was formed in 1996 by the merger of Swiss pharmaceutical giants Ciba-Geigy and Sandoz. Aided by that combination, prescription drug sales, which account for a third of revenues, were up a hefty 14% in 1997's third quarter, according to Bear Stearns analyst David Molowa. The firm's big money makers include top-seller cyclosporin, which fights transplant rejections, ($1.2 billion in annual sales) and antifungal medication Lamisil ($600 million). Novartis is also the leading producer of agricultural chemicals.

Over the next five years, analysts expect Novartis' sales growth to accelerate as the company launches several promising new drugs. For example, Exelon, a treatment for Alzheimer's disease, will deliver revenues of $350 million by 2002, according to Molowa. Even so, Novartis stock has been trading at a P/E of 24, which is 15% less than the average for its drug company peers, mainly because 40% of its sales come from its less profitable agricultural business. But that sluggishness is more than offset by Novartis' fast-growing pharmaceutical revenues. Mark Yockey, manager of the Artisan International fund, who keeps 3.2% of his portfolio in Novartis, figures the company's profits will grow 20% to 25% annually through 2002. And in 1998, Molowa says, the stock will reach $92 a share, giving shareholders a healthy 24% return.

▶ **Total** (NYSE, around $54). If you want a relatively safe way to tiptoe into emerging markets consider France's $34 billion (sales) Total. This fully integrated oil giant, which operates everything from oil production to gas stations, excels at finding new petroleum reserves, particularly in developing nations, according to Donaldson Lufkin & Jenrette analyst John Hervey. Moreover, Total manages to pump out that oil and gas with Gallic thriftiness: At just 86 cents a barrel, the company's exploration costs are the second-lowest in the industry.

Currently Total has two-thirds of its oil and gas reserves scattered throughout Africa, Latin America and Southeast Asia. This wide distribution reduces the risk that a regional political crisis will disrupt its supplies. (Potential investors should know, however, that Total disregards U.S. efforts to impose trade sanctions on certain nations. For example, the company recently agreed to invest $800 million to develop a gas field in Iran, which is off limits to U.S. oil giants.) Over the next five years, Total's oil production will grow a slick 7%

to 8% annually, according to Hervey. But at its recent price of $54, Total stock trades at a slight discount to oil majors that have slower growth prospects. Hervey figures the share price will hit $65 next year for a total return of 22%.

WHY BONDS ARE BETTER THAN EVER

In 1998, you can rely on bonds to perform their traditional role as your portfolio's calming influence. Consider the evidence: During Halloween week last October, when stock prices were zig-zagging like a bunch of panicky teens fleeing a monster on Elm Street, the price of the benchmark 30-year U.S. Treasury bond barely moved and finished the week about where it started. In contrast, stocks tanked more than 7% on their worst trading day of the week.

Better yet, any swing that bond investors feel in 1998 is likely to be in their favor. That's because, with inflation subdued, the Federal Reserve is expected to leave interest rates alone, or even to lower them. That's why we think 30-year Treasury yields could hover in the neighborhood of 5.75%, and some forecasters see a drop to around 5.5%. Such yields could produce total returns—interest or dividends plus price appreciation—on bonds and other income investments that will beat the 9% you are likely to earn on the average blue-chip stock.

Whether you're adding to a well-established portfolio or just beginning to invest, the 10-year Treasury is this year's best bond to own. It recently yielded 5.85%, which means bondholders stand to earn a 9.6% total return for the year, assuming rates drop by half a point. In comparison, bonds with longer maturities pay higher yields—but not enough to justify the additional risk of losing principal if rates rise.

Your worst bond buy in '98 is a high-yield issue, better known as a junk bond. Junk recently yielded an average of 8.5%—just 2.5 percentage points more than Treasuries. "With this spread, you are not being paid enough for the extra default risk," says analyst James Floyd of Leuthold Weeden Research in Minneapolis.

BUILD UP YOUR FUND PORTFOLIO

As always, certain basic investment wisdom remains unchanged. Last year, in the midst of unprecedented prosperity, we reminded you that stock prices do fall as well as rise. We said that basic fact of life has been easy to forget during a record-breaking bull market that began way back in 1982. And we offered advice that you should continue to heed today.

Specifically, we urged you to understand that a solid fund portfolio requires three basic building blocks, including U.S. stocks, foreign stocks and bonds. By spreading your money among a variety of investments that don't move in lockstep with one another, the current winners in your portfolio help offset the losers, allowing you to earn the highest possible gains for the level of risk you can live with.

In the long run it's the behavior of the broad market that does most of the work for even the most brilliant investment pro. Money manager Gary Brinson of Brinson Partners in Chicago has painstakingly analyzed the roles that various factors play in determining investment returns. Brinson and a team of researchers found that 92% of investment results can be explained purely by your asset mix. That's the proportion of a portfolio you dedicate to broad investment categories like stocks and bonds. In the long run, an investor with 80% in stocks and 20% in bonds will fare differently from one with 60% in stocks and 40% in bonds.

Your choice of mutual funds does matter, of course. But before you dedicate any energy to selecting individual funds, you should step back and look at your overall portfolio. Ask yourself, "Am I forgetting to use all three building blocks?" And follow these fundamental rules:

Cushion your ride. Stocks traditionally produce the biggest rewards but also carry the greatest risk, so you also want to own some bond funds. Mix in some international stock funds, too, so that the fortunes of your portfolio aren't pegged solely to U.S. stocks.

Pay attention to style. Be sure to own funds whose managers practice a broad variety of investing styles. For example, you should diversify within asset categories, so that the stock section of your portfolio is not limited to funds that specialize in large companies, but includes those that buy midcap and small-fry firms as well. Similarly, you want to diversify by holding funds that look for growth companies (those with rapidly accelerating revenues and earnings) and funds that look for value stocks (those that are undervalued relative to their earnings or assets) or funds that offer a blend of both.

Keep expenses down. The higher a fund's annual fees, the harder it is for the manager to outperform similar funds and market benchmarks. So scrutinize the expenses of funds you own or are thinking of buying, and whenever possible aim for U.S. stock funds with expense ratios below 1.5% and domestic bond funds that charge 0.75% or less.

HOW TO TUNE UP YOUR FUNDS TODAY

We believe the market is in for a period of volatility that will reward savvy stock selection more than riding market trends. That means the big mutual fund winners in recent years—portfolios that move in sync with a broad index such as the S&P 500—may be in for some lean times. For 1998, there-fore, here's one good move: Add to your holdings of index and other diver-sified funds one or more portfolios managed by seasoned stock pickers who put their money into just a few dozen issues they truly love. "We're moving into a difficult investing environment that should give active management an advantage over passive indexing," says Edward Goldfarb, research director at Wellesley, Mass. money management firm Kobren Insight Funds. "Portfolios concentrated in a few dozen issues run by proven managers have the best chance of taking advantage of the opportunities volatility offers."

Making sizable bets on a handful of companies is nothing new, of course. But recently, concentrated portfolios have become all the rage in the fund world. Fortunately for investors, the less-is-more strategy can generate outsize gains. A recent study by Chicago fund tracker Morningstar conclud-ed that, on average, focused funds don't outpace the typical diversified fund. But the study also found that concentrated portfolios run by managers who have successful long-term records do in fact outperform their peers, as well as the market. One reason: Even in the hands of a talented stock picker, a fund cluttered with hundreds of stocks is likely to perform a lot like an index fund (but with higher expenses). When a stock savant loads his fund with just a handful of issues, however, a couple of big winners can truly boost returns. "Our goal is to outperform the S&P 500 by three or four per-centage points a year over the long term," says James Oelschlager, co-man-ager of the 25-stock $361 million White Oak Growth Stock fund. "We can't do that if we are widely diversified."

To find the best of the picky portfolios, we examined nearly 165 domes-tic and foreign equity funds in the Morningstar database that currently own fewer than 40 stocks. We looked specifically for ones that have beaten the S&P 500 or other relevant indexes over the past three or more years, although we also considered new portfolios whose managers boast sterling long-term records. Our six choices span a broad range of investing styles.

Two—**White Oak Growth Stock** (launched in 1992) and **Strong Growth 20** (1997)—invest in growth stocks, while **Oakmark Select** (1996) and **Clipper** (1984) seek undervalued shares. **Papp America–Abroad** (1991) buys shares of U.S. companies that derive at least half their revenues overseas, and **Harbor International Growth** (1993) focuses on fast-growing foreign stocks.

To be sure, focused funds can plummet if just a couple of their stocks run into trouble. Still, we managed to find two—Clipper and Papp America-Abroad—whose managers have generated market-beating returns without stomach-wrenching dives. White Oak Growth Stock and Harbor International Growth are more volatile than the average equity fund but have compensated shareholders with outsize returns. As for the two young funds on our list, we anticipate that value-oriented Oakmark Select will deliver superior gains with relatively low volatility, while Strong Growth 20 shareholders should expect a profitable but bumpy ride.

▶ **Oakmark Select.** Bill Nygren, manager of Oakmark Select, sure knows how to make a dramatic entrance. Select's 63.1% gain in its first 12 months through October 1997 made the 32.1% rise in the S&P 500 look practically shabby. Nygren, who has been research director at Harris Associates—the adviser to five Oakmark funds—since 1989, is careful to warn current and prospective shareholders not to expect an encore of Select's astounding debut. His long-term goal is to outperform the index by an average of two to three percentage points annually, not 20 or 30. And despite its stellar start, investors need to know that Select could be a big dipper if any single issue implodes. That's because Nygren has 71% of assets jammed into the fund's top 10 holdings.

To select the fund's 20 or so stocks, Nygren searches for companies with market value of $1 billion or more that sell for at least 33% less than he figures they are worth. The value-seeking manager is especially fond of companies whose executives own plenty of the stock. His two biggest holdings—$2.5 billion conglomerate US Industries and $325 million cable operator Tele-Communications/Liberty Media (up 44% and 92% in the 12 months since Nygren bought them at the fund's launch in November 1996)—each account for 15% of fund assets. Despite their sizzling gains, Nygren figures the two stocks are still trading at least 20% below their intrinsic value. Considering that these two companies are industry leaders, have savvy management teams and aren't shy about buying back their own shares, Nygren is confident that there's plenty more upside in both stocks.

▶ **Papp America–Abroad.** L. Roy Papp and his daughter-in-law Rose, who head up Papp America–Abroad, are armchair travelers. Rather than invest directly in foreign firms, they stick to U.S. companies that are global leaders and that derive at least a third of their revenues from international sales. "We get all the benefits of international exposure without many of the disadvantages of investing abroad, such as poor liquidity, poor accounting standards and no SEC oversight," says Roy, who dealt with plenty of such problems first-hand during his two-year stint as U.S. director of the Asian Development bank.

Their don't-leave-home approach led to stately 17.3% annualized gains during the large-cap fund's first six years. Given the recent upheaval in international markets, it's understandable if you think that you should be avoiding U.S. multinational firms. In the case of this fund, at least, you would be wrong. By concentrating on 30 global firms "that are the industry leaders now and the innovators that will dominate in the future," says Roy, "we know we have the premier firms that will continue to prosper both here and abroad." The fund certainly held on well in 1997, posting a gain that matched the S&P 500.

Indeed, the father-and-daughter-in-law team seeks companies that are the paragons of consistency. "We want to see earnings growth of at least 12% in eight of the past 10 years, and we pray for 15%," says Roy. One big holding that exemplifies the Papps' ideals is General Electric, which represents 4% of assets. GE generates 36% of its $87 billion in revenue in foreign markets and has racked up annual earnings growth of 12% over the past decade.

▶ **Harbor International Growth.** Unlike the Papps, Howard Moss and Blair Boyer of Harbor International Growth are happy to spread their assets around the globe. And they pride themselves on the intensity of their research. "Given the size of our bets, we need to have a deep degree of conviction about our stocks," says Boyer. Most of their 31 issues are large companies with growth rates that exceed their P/E ratios—and that the managers believe can deliver a 50% return within three years. (Asia-phobes have no need to panic; the $1 billion fund has less than 10% of assets invested in the Pacific.) They struggled to eke out a 1997 gain. But overall in the four years following Clipper's 1993 inception, the managers parlayed their focused foreign strategy into a powerful 13.9% annualized gain. By comparison, the typical foreign fund and the Morgan Stanley index of Europe, Australia and Far East stocks both climbed only 7.5%.

▶ **White Oak Growth Stock.** By plowing big chunks of their portfolio's money into shares of large companies that sell at bargain prices relative to their earnings, Jim Oelschlager and Douglas MacKay have generated index-whipping returns. In the five years following its 1992 launch, the $361 million portfolio boasted a 23.2% annualized gain compared with the 18.7% climb of the S&P 500.

Oelschlager and MacKay are careful not to overpay for rapidly increasing earnings. While the average annualized earnings growth for their 25-stock portfolio is forecast at 23% over the next five years—nearly twice the 13% projected for the S&P 500—the fund's average P/E ratio of 22 barely exceeds that of the benchmark index.

Of course, any concentrated portfolio with a high-growth tilt is going to be vulnerable to severe downdrafts. According to Morningstar's proprietary risk score, which measures by how much and how often a fund's performance lags the return of risk-free Treasury bills, White Oak was 44% more volatile than the average equity fund over the past five years. But investors have been well compensated for the periodic wild swings, as this fund outgained its peers by more than eight percentage points a year during that stretch.

The extra volatility stems partly from the huge stakes the managers have placed on a few market sectors. Oelschlager and MacKay have plowed 58% of the fund's assets into fast-growing technology issues, with $4 billion computer network Cisco Systems accounting for the largest piece (6%) of the portfolio. Financial firms, including $315 billion (assets) global banking and securities powerhouse Citicorp, represent the next largest holding.

▶ **Clipper.** Just about everything the 18-issue Clipper fund does sails against the winds of conventional wisdom. At the end of 1997 co-managers James Gipson, Michael Sandler and Bruce Veaco had only 63% of their portfolio invested in stocks, with the remaining 37% stashed in cash and Treasury bonds. By comparison, the average equity fund has more than 90% of assets invested in stocks. The shares the Clipper iconoclasts prefer also set them apart: ugly beaten-up issues scorned by Wall Street that the co-managers calculate are trading at least one-third below their true value.

Daring to be different has paid off. Clipper's 17% annualized gains during the past 10 years outpaced the 14.5% gains for similar funds that feed on large undervalued issues. Over that stretch the fund also experienced 7% less volatility than the average equity fund, according to Morningstar. In addition to the usual number crunching, Clipper's managers spend a lot of time getting to know a company's management, suppliers and competitors.

"When we buy, we plan on owning for at least three years," says Veaco. "We need that level of patience given our value approach. So we want to have a high degree of confidence in our investment." They currently have plenty of faith and money in $425 billion (assets) Federal National Mortgage Association (Fannie Mae) and $200 billion Federal Home Mortgage (Freddie Mac); each represents 10% of assets. All told financial services companies account for 45% of the funds' stock assets, followed by a 26% bet on retailers such as $117 billion Wal-Mart and $11.5 billion Toys R Us.

▶ **Strong Growth 20.** Fund investors probably know Strong Growth 20 manager Ron Ognar best for his record at Strong Growth fund, whose 25.3% annualized gain during its first four years easily outdistanced the S&P 500's 22% rise. But that fund has $1.7 billion invested in 118 stocks. In contrast, his spanking-new 1997 baby, Strong Growth 20, has just $54 million in assets in 25 stocks and will never own more than 30 issues. "The real advantage with Growth 20 is that it is much smaller and I have a lot of flexibility," says Ognar. "It will take five years to measure our success, but I would expect it to outperform the bigger fund, though with more volatility." In its first three months—a period so short we hesitate to mention it at all—the fund gained 20% compared to 7.5% for the market.

Ognar is a cautious growth investor, preferring to stick with stocks whose P/E ratios do not tower above their projected earnings growth rates. When it comes to market caps, he'll snap up stocks of any size, as long as they can deliver huge profit increases. At the end of 1997 more than 80% of the fund's assets were invested in firms with capitalizations of at least $1 billion (the biggest stake: a 5.4% bet on $1.8 billion McKesson and a 5.2% position in Cisco Systems), but Ognar was eyeing "a rotation into small-caps once we see an extended market correction."

A FEW REIT BARGAINS REMAIN

The stocks of Real Estate Investment Trust companies, which invest in apartment complexes, office buildings and other properties, have boomed for two years as bargain hunters bid up the prices. But REITs have begun to cool as their shares have become more expensive. Thus in '98, the average REIT will likely track the S&P 500's forecast 9% return. But you can still find REITs that yield more than the industry's 5.8% average and also offer potential capital gains. Two examples:

▶ **Associated Estates Realty** (NYSE, recently traded at around $22; recent yield, 8.3%). Because its properties are in relatively slow-growth areas, cash-flow gains will slow at this $94.4 million Cleveland REIT, which owns apartment buildings in Indiana, Kentucky, Michigan, Ohio and Pennsylvania. But Baltimore-based analysts Catherine Creswell of brokerage BT Alex. Brown and Rod Petrick of Legg Mason still favor the REIT. That's because lack of competition will allow it to hold rents steady. In the meantime, as interest rates fall, Petrick sees AEC'S stock rising to $25 in 1998 for a 21% total return.

▶ **Health and Retirement Properties** (NYSE, around $19; 7.8% yield). This $208 million REIT is the owner of 110 nursing homes and 26 assisted-living facilities, which serve elderly clients who can mostly take care of themselves but need help with some activities, such as housework. The REIT recently bought 29 office buildings in 15 states that are rented by various U.S. government agencies. Analysts Robert Thornburg of brokerage D.A. Davidson in Great Falls, Mont. and Helen O'Donnell of PaineWebber in New York City have confidence in the staying power of the REIT's yield. In addition, O'Donnell believes falling interest rates could help the stock top $20 in 1998 for at least a 15% total return.

CHAPTER 2

SLASH YOUR TAXES WITH THE NEW LAW

T here are some great current and future savings in store for you if you follow the advice in this chapter. First, we will help you make the most of the confusing package of federal income tax breaks passed by Congress last year. Then we'll pass along strategies for taking maximum advantage of the new Individual Retirement Accounts, timely tips on cutting the tax on your mutual fund gains and the lowdown on how new rules can make it easier for you to deal with the IRS. We'll also show you how to put together an estate plan that will provide your heirs with the biggest possible bonanza.

LATEST WAYS TO PAY LESS FEDERAL TAX

You know the line about how you should never watch legislation or sausages being made? Well, add last summer's messy Taxpayer Relief Act to the list. With Capitol Hill lawyers pulling all nighters to help write it, the 800–odd–page law included baffling provisions compounded by a dearth of information about how to put the changes into practice. What's more, the clarifications that have been trickling out from Congress and the IRS have revealed surprising ways to cut your taxes that had been obscured by the '97 law's dense legalese. For example, it turns out that if you paid tax on the sale of your home within the past three years, you may have a refund coming—of the entire amount you paid. Or if you have college-bound kids and want to take some courses your-self, you may be able to claim new writeoffs for everyone's expenses.

Meantime, the President and lawmakers in Washington have turned their focus to the next round of tax cuts. The two likeliest goodies this year: some relief from the marriage penalty (the quirk that can cause working couples to pay more tax than they'd owe if each were still single) and reform of the alternative minimum tax—a provision originally designed to hit the super-rich but that has increasingly punished middle-class taxpayers.

Right now, however, you need to focus on getting the most out of the latest tax law. For starters, we'll tell you about a slew of ways to benefit, grouped in four broad categories: capital gains, home sales, tuition tax credits and other college savings plans. Each section begins with an overview of the rules followed by our advice on how to grab the new breaks and avoid the inevitable tax traps.

Cash in on changes for capital gains.
Under the new law, starting July 29, 1997, the top tax rate on capital gains has dropped to 20% for investments you've owned for more than 18 months before selling, or 10% if you're in the 15% bracket (joint filers with taxable income under $42,351; singles with taxable income under $25,351). The old top rate of 28% (or 15% if you're in the 15% bracket) still applies if you hold your asset for more than a year but not more than 18 months. And if you unload a winner that you've owned for a year or less, look out! You'll pay capital-gains tax at your top income tax rate—as high as 39.6% if your taxable income tops $278,449 in 1998.

There are two major exceptions. For real estate investors, the top long-term rate is 25% on the portion of a gain attributable to any depreciation you claimed. And the maximum capital-gains rate on the sale of collectibles remains at 28% and applies to assets you hold for more than a year.

Here's how to get the biggest savings from the new capital-gains rules:

▶ **Budget your losses.** Take your investment losses in years when you report short-term gains, which are otherwise taxed at your top income tax rate of up to 39.6%. The new law requires you to group your gains and losses according to the tax rates that apply to their holding periods. For example, the gain on a stock you held for more than 18 months—which would be taxed at a top rate of 20%—gets offset first by losses on assets you held for more than 18 months. Similarly, the gain on the sale of a stock you held for, say, 13 months—which would be taxed at 28%—is offset first by losses on assets that you have held for more than a year and not more than 18 months. But here's the boon: If your losses in any group exceed your gains in that group, the excess can be used to offset your other gains, starting with the gains that are subject to the highest rate of tax.

Consider the differing tax savings from a $10,000 loss you take on a stock held for more than 18 months: If you sell the loser in a year when you also have a $10,000 gain on stock you owned for more than 18 months, you must deduct the loss against that gain, which would otherwise be taxable at 20%. Thus, your savings come to $2,000 ($10,000 times 20%). But if you dump the $10,000 loser in a year when you have gains only from assets owned for less than a year—taxable at your highest income tax rate, say, 31%—your tax savings from your loss jumps to $3,100 ($10,000 times 31%).

▶ **Use losses to cut ordinary income.** If your losses exceed all your gains, write off the excess against $3,000 in ordinary income. Even if you don't anticipate selling any investments for a gain in 1998, you ought to comb through your portfolio later in the year to turn up dogs you could unload for a loss of up to $3,000. By using a capital loss to shelter $3,000 in ordinary income, you'll save $840, assuming you're in the 28% bracket.

▶ **Go for long-term gains.** Try to hold your investments for more than five years, especially if your taxable income is around $40,000 if you're married or $25,000 if you're single. In an important, but little noted, section of the new law, truly long-term investors reap an even bigger tax boon: Starting in 2001, if you're in the 15% income tax bracket and sell an asset you've owned for more than five years, you'll pay tax on your capital gain at a superlow 8%. That could amount to a tax savings of as much as $1,200 on a $10,000 gain, assuming that you were in a 28% bracket or higher when you bought the asset but had dropped into a 15% bracket by the time you sold the asset at least five years later. Such a bracket drop is not uncommon if, for example, you retire or your spouse leaves the work force. Any stock you bought before 1996 will qualify for the 8% rate, as long as you put off selling until 2001; similarly, stock you buy now will qualify for the 8% rate in 2003.

Your best move is to identify the investments you plan to hold for at least five years and, unless a company falls apart in a fundamental way, stick with them.

Push up your home profits. For home sales on or after last May 7, married joint filers can now exclude from tax up to $500,000 in profits; single filers can shield $250,000. Moreover, you can use the exclusion as often as every two years. To qualify, you must have owned and lived in the home as your principal residence for at least two out of the five years before the sale.

When you compute the gain on your current home, you must include any profits you previously deferred by trading up. So if you've been pyramiding your profits over many years and the accumulated deferrals plus the gain on your current home exceed the new exclusion, you'll owe tax on the amount above the limit when you sell. Here are other tips.

▶ **Look for a refund.** You may have an income tax refund coming if you traded down within the past three years when you were age 55 or older. The new law repeals the once-in-a-lifetime exclusion of up to $125,000 of profit on the sale of your home if you were 55 or older at the time of the sale. So if you qualified for the $125,000 exclusion in the past but didn't use it—say, because you had a smallish gain on your sale and expected a larger profit on a future home sale—you unwittingly forfeited a huge tax saving opportunity. Thankfully, you may have recourse: If you traded down and paid the tax within the past three years, you can file an amended return using Form 1040X (available by calling the IRS at 800-829-3676 or off the Web at irs.ustreas.gov) to retroactively claim the $125,000 exclusion and get a refund.

The savings could be substantial. Assume you were 55 in 1995 when you sold your home, exposing a $40,000 capital gain to tax. Also assume that you expected your new home to appreciate by more than $40,000 and so chose not to use the one-time exclusion. Rather, you paid the $11,200 tax due on your gain. By filing an amended return, you can get a full refund.

Unfortunately, this ploy won't work if you filed the tax return for the sale more than three years ago, since you get only three years from the return's due date—or, if you filed late, the date you actually filed—to ask for a refund. One exception: If you paid your tax late, you have two years from the time you paid the tax to file an amended return.

▶ **Check out partial tax exclusions.** What if you're selling but haven't lived in your home for two of the last five years? The new law lets you claim a pro rata share of the exclusion if you must sell your home because of a job transfer, ill health or another significant unexpected event.

▶ **Make a marriage split less taxing.** Under the old law, if you separated or divorced and moved out of the family home but retained sole or joint ownership, you could not defer the tax on your share of the gain when the house was sold, because at the time of the sale, the home was no longer your principal residence. But for home sales on or after May 7, 1997, a separated or divorced taxpayer can now exclude from tax his or her share of the gain—as long as the ex-spouse has been living there under a separation or divorce agreement for at least two of the five years before the sale.

The law is unclear, however, on whether the spouse who moved out will be held to an exclusion limit of $250,000 (the max for single filers) or can exclude as much as $500,000, provided he or she has remarried and is filing jointly.

▶ **Hang onto records.** Because the majority of home sellers will no longer owe tax, you might think you don't have to retain documents proving your home's purchase price and the cost of improvements anymore. Wrong. If you claim the home sale exclusion on your return and are subsequently audited by the IRS, you'll be asked for records to prove the amount of your gain. You will also need records of your home's purchase price and improvements (such as invoices and cancelled checks) to compute any casualty loss deduction if fire, flood or other calamity damages your home.

Take these tuition tax breaks.

If you, your spouse or your dependents are in college—or soon will be—and your Adjusted Gross Income (AGI) is less than $80,000 for joint filers ($40,000 for singles), you can cut your tax bill with the new law's Hope tuition credit and Lifetime Learning credit. (The credit phases out as AGI rises above the $80,000 and $40,000 thresholds and disappears once AGI exceeds $100,000 for couples, $50,000 for singles.)

Starting this year, the Hope credit lets you slash your tax by up to $1,500 a year per student for tuition you pay during the first two years of college. (The full credit is 100% of the first $1,000 of tuition you pay; 50% of the next $1,000.) So if you pay at least $2,000 apiece in tuition for your college freshman and sophomore this year and your income is below the phaseout range, you can claim the maximum Hope credit for each of them—for a 1998 tax cut of $3,000.

In contrast, the full Lifetime Learning credit is $1,000 a year—20% of up to $5,000 in tuition payments—but can be claimed for any year in which you don't also take the Hope credit for the same student's tuition. Say that your AGI is $70,000 in 1998 and you pay $4,000 in tuition for your college senior plus $2,000 for your spouse's graduate school tuition. Up to $5,000 of the payments qualify for the 20% credit.

Here's how to make the most of these credits:

▶ **Know what expenses qualify.** Only payments for tuition and required fees, such as lab costs, qualify for the credits—not other wallet busters such as room, board, books and athletic fees. Moreover, the law allows only your out-of-pocket outlays. So, for example, if your child has a merit scholarship that fully covers tuition or your employer provides tax-free reimbursement for your tuition, you can't claim these credits.

▶ **Pay tuition at the right time.** To qualify for either credit, the education must occur within the tax year in which the payment is made or within the first three months of the following year. This requirement is trickier than it seems: For most taxpayers, the tax year is the same as the calendar year, but a calendar year rarely tracks an academic year. To ensure your eligibility, bear in mind that you can claim the Hope credit for tuition you pay starting this year as long as the classes start or continue through March 1999. The Lifetime credit is available for tuition paid after June 30, 1998 and for instruction that takes place through March 1999.

▶ **Claim your child as a dependent.** In order for you to take either tuition tax credit, your child must be listed as a dependent on your tax return. Conversely, if your child wants to claim either of the credits on his or her own return, he or she can't be claimed as a dependent on anyone else's return.

This rule means that your son or daughter cannot claim the credit, even if he or she pays the tuition, as long as you're eligible to claim the child as a dependent. Under the law, you're eligible to take the dependency exclusion if you provide more than half the support of your child who is under age 24 and attends college at least half time.

Tuition paid by your dependent child is treated as if you paid it for purposes of taking the credits. Assume that your college senior will pay $1,000 of her tuition this year. As long as she is your dependent, you can claim a Lifetime Learning credit against her payment for a $200 tax savings.

▶ **Use loan proceeds.** Feel free to use proceeds from a home-equity loan or credit line to pay the tuition and take these tax credits. You can use the credits against tuition payments made with loan proceeds as long as you claim the credit in the year you pay the tuition, not the year in which you repay the loan.

would receive if you had saved the money in your own name. Reason: The formula for computing aid assumes that students ante up 35% of their assets each year to pay for college, while parents are expected to contribute only 5.65% of assets. So skip funding an Education IRA unless you already know you won't qualify for aid or your children are so young that you prefer the certainty of building up your own savings to speculation about future financial aid.

Consider a state prepaid tuition plan only if you are confident that your child will attend a participating school. That's because if your kid doesn't go to one of the schools in the program, most plans will only return your principal plus a paltry 3% to 5%. One more point: Chances are you can accumulate more money by investing in stocks on your own—which historically return about 10% a year—than you can by saving through a prepaid plan, which currently grows by about 5% a year.

And get this: If you contribute to a state prepaid plan for your child, you can't also contribute to an Education IRA for him or her. If you fund both types of plans in the same year, you will be slapped with a 6% excise tax on the Education IRA contribution. That would be tantamount to flunking out of Tax Savings 101.

HOW TO PICK THE BEST IRA

There are now three types of Individual Retirement Accounts: Traditional deductible IRAs, which are generally best for older or less affluent investors; new Roth IRAs, which are named after William Roth (R-Del.), chairman of the Senate Finance Committee, and best for the young and wealthy; and nondeductible IRAs, which are suitable for anyone not eligible for the other two options. Also, you may be able to convert old IRAs into Roths. Salivating over potential commissions and fees on the $1.3 trillion that is currently invested in IRAs, the nation's banks, brokerages and mutual fund companies are now jockeying to help you figure out exactly which flavor is best for you. While these companies are generally hyping the Roth IRA as the best thing since the self-cleaning oven, you can get burned if you don't consider all your options carefully.

It's true that the Roth IRA plus new rules that make it easier for millions of people to qualify for deductible IRAs will save Americans a total of $20 billion in taxes over the next 10 years, according to the Congressional Joint Committee on Taxation. But how to get your share of that windfall is hardly straightforward. "A lot of professionals, never mind investors, haven't figured out the IRA changes," says Ben Norquist, a consultant at Universal Pensions, a financial services advisory firm in Brainerd, Minn.

To get an accurate picture of which IRA moves are wisest, you have to make some assumptions about your age, current tax rate and your anticipated retirement age and tax rate once you start taking the money out. Then—there's no getting around it—you have to do the math. For that, either consult a financial planner or use mutual fund company T. Rowe Price's IRA Analyzer on CD-ROM and diskette (800-333-0740) or fund behemoth Vanguard's free Web calculator (www.vanguard.com).

To make your task easier, we've interviewed three dozen of the nation's top tax lawyers, policymakers and financial planners. Armed with their advice, we'll first help you decide which kind of IRA to invest in (probably a Roth). Then we'll address whether you should convert your existing IRA or IRAs to a Roth (think twice). And finally, we'll suggest the best investments for any IRAs you open in 1998.

Size up the three types of IRAs.

Let's begin with a brief refresher course on the new IRA rules laid out by the 1997 tax law, distinguishing the three places you can invest your $2,000 a year:

▶ **Traditional deductible IRAs.** As you probably know, universally deductible IRAs, introduced by Congress in 1981, give you a tax benefit right away. You deduct contributions from your taxable income in the tax year that you make them. The earnings grow tax deferred until you withdraw the money, when you pay taxes on the balance. Perhaps you contributed to these IRAs in the '80s, but stopped after 1986 when Congress limited the amount of income you could earn and still get the up-front write-off. If so, it may be time to take a fresh look.

That's because Congress just raised the Adjusted Gross Income threshold for deducting an IRA, even if you have an employer-sponsored retirement plan. The new thresholds: $50,000 this year (rising to $80,000 in 2007) for married couples; $30,000 for singles ($50,000 in 2005). That's up from $40,000 and $25,000, respectively. What's more, if your spouse is covered by a pension plan at work but you're not, you can now deduct a full $2,000 contribution, so long as your combined AGI is under $150,000. Another important change: If neither of you has a retirement plan but one of you has earned income, you can each deduct up to $2,000. Consequently, this year, over 90% of American adults will qualify to contribute to deductible IRAs.

▶ **Roth IRAs.** As of January 1, 1998, each spouse of a married couple with a total AGI of up to $150,000 ($95,000 for singles) can make a $2,000 annual contribution to a Roth, whether he or she has a retirement plan at work or not. While you'll have paid income taxes on the money you put into a Roth, the IRS never gets a bite of the earnings you build up—even when you take the money out—as long as you meet certain withdrawal requirements. (Exception: If you withdraw your money before your account is five years old, the earnings are taxed and you may face a 10% penalty to boot.)

▶ **Nondeductible IRAs.** This third type of IRA gives you tax-deferred earnings but taxable withdrawals and no up-front writeoff. It is still available for people who fail to meet the income cutoffs for the other two IRAs.

With all three IRAs you can withdraw cash without owing the 10% early-withdrawal tax penalty if you are buying your first home (subject to a $10,000 limit), funding a college education for you, your spouse, your children or your grandchildren (no income limit) or paying for medical expenses that total 7.5% or more of your AGI. And all three offer penalty-free withdrawals for any reason starting at age 59 1/2.

But the Roth has two key withdrawal advantages. Deductible and nondeductible IRAs require you to start pulling out your money at age 70 1/2. With Roths, you may leave your money untouched as long as you like. Also, since you contribute after-tax money to a Roth, you can withdraw your contributions (but not your earnings) without penalty or further taxes at any time, no matter what your age.

What kind of IRA is best for you? So what's better for your new IRA dollars: a nondeductible IRA, a deductible or a Roth? That depends on your situation, of course. But here are four helpful rules of thumb:

1. A Roth IRA always beats a nondeductible IRA. If you're married and your AGI is between $50,000 and $150,000 ($30,000 to $95,000 for singles), the decision is a no-brainer. Since you aren't eligible for a deductible IRA, a Roth is your best deal. With a nondeductible IRA, you defer paying taxes on the earnings of your after-tax contributions, but a Roth means never having to pay taxes on the earnings.

2. A Roth beats a deductible IRA if your tax bracket will stay the same or rise after you retire. Because the decision between a Roth IRA and a deductible IRA boils down to taxes now vs. taxes later, one big factor in choosing between the two is how your tax bracket will change over time. Most people find their tax bracket declines in retirement because their pension, Social Security savings, and portfolio income fall short of their former paychecks. If you expect your tax bracket will fall—say, from 36% to 28%—a deductible IRA will most likely put you ahead.

But if you think you have a good chance of maintaining or even boosting your income in retirement, then the Roth wins hands down. For example, a 40-year-old investor who stays in the 28% federal tax bracket (5% state) from now until retirement and contributes $2,000 a year to a Roth IRA earning 8% annually will have $158,000 when he turns 65. That's 9% more than the $145,000 after taxes he'd get with a deductible IRA.

3. The longer you can wait to tap your IRA after you retire, the more attractive a Roth becomes. Since you needn't begin taking distributions from a Roth IRA at 70 1/2, you can get a huge financial lift by keeping your retirement stash tucked away in a Roth into your 70s and beyond. If you're age 70 and earn a modest 7% a year in a Roth IRA, you can literally double your money by age 80 by leaving it there instead of withdrawing it and spending it.

What if you're over 70 1/2 and want to keep saving? A Roth IRA is your only option. With a deductible or nondeductible IRA, once you hit 70 1/2, you have to start taking money out of your account and you must stop contributing. But just as you can keep your money in a Roth for as long as you like, you can keep adding to it each year, too, so long as you have earned income. Those attributes make the Roth IRA a powerful estate planning tool for people who will continue to work part time in retirement. When you die, the Roth IRA will go to your beneficiary and no one will ever have to pay income tax on the money. (However, your estate might owe taxes on your IRA—at a rate of 37% or higher—just as it might on any other asset you own.)

4. Roths make great sense for kids with part-time jobs. Because you can make penalty-free withdrawals from a Roth IRA to pay your child's college bills, opening one in your own name is a great way to save for tuition. But you might also consider opening Roths in your kids' names. As long as they have earned income, they can contribute up to $2,000 a year or their entire income, whichever is lower. And retirement savings are currently not factored into the federal financial aid formula, so unless the government changes the rules, their IRAs shouldn't reduce the amount of federal aid your kids can qualify for. Even if your kids don't use the money for college, they'll get 50 or more years of tax-free compounding for their retirement with this IRA.

Should you convert to a Roth?

If you're like the one in three American households that already has at least one IRA, you'll need to determine whether a Roth conversion will make sense. No, that's not a new kind of religious experience. It's a way to move your existing IRA into a Roth and avoid owing taxes on the withdrawals in retirement. You're eligible if your individual 1998 AGI is $100,000 or less, whether you're married or not.

Converting will sting at first: You'll owe immediate taxes on any deductible contributions you've made and on all the earnings in your account. The 1997 tax law softens the blow a bit by requiring you to pay just one-fourth of the tax bill annually for the next four years. (The amount you convert is not included in the $100,000 AGI conversion ceiling or the $160,000/$110,000 AGI ceiling for contributions.) For example, if you have a deductible IRA balance of $100,000 from a former pension rollover and stay in the 28% bracket, you'll owe the IRS $28,000 for the privilege of converting, or $7,000 a year for four years.

"Converting to a Roth IRA is a huge and complicated decision," warns Michael Chasnoff, a certified financial planner in Cincinnati. "You need to run the numbers to see if it makes sense for you." A quick way to figure out whether converting to a Roth may be a good move is to see what kind of people shouldn't convert. If you clear the following four hurdles, give converting a serious look. But don't convert if:

1. You believe your tax rate will fall in retirement.

One of the most important factors when assessing whether it pays to convert is your tax rate when you withdraw the money. Suppose you are 40 years old, have $50,000 in a deductible IRA that earns 8% a year and figure your tax bracket will drop from 28% now (5% state) to 15% (5% state) when you start withdrawing at age 65. You'd be smart to sit tight with your deductible IRA. That's because in 25 years you would have an after-tax balance of just $237,000, or 2% more than the $233,000 you'd be sitting on if you converted to a Roth now after paying the taxes to convert. However, if you expect your tax rate will rise to 31% in retirement, you'd be better off converting now. Then your deductible IRA would be worth $200,000, or 14% less than the Roth amount.

2. You'll start withdrawing the money within five years.

Biting the tax bullet now with a Roth conversion pays off only if you can keep the retirement account for at least five years. If you take converted money out of a Roth IRA sooner, by law you'll probably be hit with a 10% withdrawal penalty. In addition, because you'd be paying taxes on the conversion over the next four years, your tax rate might go up immediately—which means that you'd not only be paying taxes on the IRA now, you'd be paying higher taxes on all your income in the coming four years. "In general, the more years until you'll withdraw the money, the more sense it makes to convert to a Roth IRA," says Judith McMichael, a vice president of marketing at Fidelity.

3. You would have to raid the IRA to pay the conversion taxes.

"If you use your IRA account to pay the taxes for converting to a Roth in 1998 and you are under age 59 1/2, you may suffer a special 20% early-withdrawal penalty," points out Martin Nissenbaum, director of retirement planning at Ernst & Young in New York City. That rule is in a technical corrections bill pending in Congress that is anticipated to become law in 1998.

4. Converting means you'll forfeit valuable tax breaks.

The extra income you'll have to report on your tax returns from 1998 to 2001 by converting might not only raise your bracket, it could push your AGI over the limit for some valuable tax credits, deductions and exemptions. "Ask your tax preparer to estimate how converting will affect your total tax picture, including eligibility for child or education credits," says Nissenbaum.

One more thing: If you think your AGI might exceed $100,000 in 1998, wait awhile. If you convert now and discover later this year that your AGI exceeds the cutoff, you'll have to roll back the money to the original IRA at tax time—a real hassle. It's smarter to make the conversion decision at the end of the year, when you can better gauge what your AGI will be. Then get ready to make some bread instead of getting burned.

Where should you invest for your IRA? The advent of the Roth IRA requires a serious shift in your thinking about which investments to put in your IRAs. The traditional advice has been to keep income-producing investments in your tax-deferred IRA and equity holdings in your taxable accounts. That way you'd defer paying the higher ordinary income tax rate on income-producing securities (top rate: 39.6%) while your equities would be taxed at the capital-gains rate, now capped at 20%, down from 28% last year.

Enter Roth IRAs. Vanguard analyst Joel Dickson says that if you will now own taxable accounts, a tax-deferred traditional IRA or 401(k) and a new Roth IRA, you should keep your stocks in both the Roth IRA and taxable accounts and put fixed-income investments in the standard IRA. This way, you'll still defer income taxes on your fixed-income investments and you'll accrue tax-free earnings on the asset that's likely to appreciate the most over the long-term: stocks.

BEAT BACK MUTUAL FUND TAX BITES

Ignoring the effect taxes have on your mutual funds' returns can cost you real money. A 1993 study estimated that fund shareholders paid an extra $1 billion in taxes because portfolio managers do little to minimize the tax bite on shareholders' returns. And since the new tax law effectively rewards funds that deliver long-term capital gains taxed at a maximum 20% rate—and punishes those that generate income and short-term profits that face a top rate of 39.6%—it's more important than ever to evaluate funds based on how well they fend the IRS.

Don't look to the fund companies for much help. The majority of managers don't give taxes much thought. "Taxes are important, but I'm paid to produce the largest gains possible, not to participate in an intellectual exercise," says John Wallace, manager of $303 million Robertson Stephens Growth & Income. He's right. Fund managers' annual bonuses—which can exceed $1 million—are based on their performance *before* taxes, not after.

To assure that more of your funds' gains end up in your pocket rather than the IRS', follow our four tax-smart investing strategies below.

Home in on after-tax returns. Fund investors need to invoke the mantra you hear on basketball courts all over the country: *Nothing But Net.* In this case, gains net of taxes. "The performance you see in the newspaper or on your statement is not what you actually earn," says Colin Ferenbach, co-manager of the $85 million Haven fund. "The return that matters is what you have left after April 15th."

To help you gauge a fund's returns after taxes, the fund-tracking firm Morningstar calculates a so-called tax-efficiency rating for all portfolios that have a track record of at least three years. In the past, Morningstar arrived at that figure by calculating the percentage of pre-tax gains that are left after an investor pays federal tax on income and short-term gains distributions at the maximum rate of 39.6% and long-term gains at the old top rate of 28%. Morningstar also factors into its ratings the new top rate of 20% for capital gains on assets held longer than 18 months.

The average diversified equity fund had a tax efficiency ranging from 84% to 88% over the last three, five and 10 years, according to Morningstar. In other words, shareholders typically handed over to Uncle Sam 12% to 16% of the annual gains their funds paid them. The tax tab is even higher in high-tax states, such as California, where investors fork over as much as another 9.3% to the state taxman. You can check out your funds' tax-efficiency rating in *Morningstar Mutual Funds* , a compendium of fund performance statistics available at most public libraries. The annual fund performance rankings in *Money Mutual Fund Finder*, the supplemental booklet you get with this *Money Adviser 1998*, also lists tax-efficiency ratings for all funds in Morningstar's database that have track records of at least three years.

You should have no trouble finding funds in a variety of investing styles that have long track records of outrunning their peers both before and after taxes are taken into account. For example, $3.3 billion Baron Asset, which invests in fast-growing small and medium-size companies, racked up annualized gains of 29% annually for the three years to December 1, 1997, placing the portfolio ahead of 85% of its peers before taxes. Better yet, the fund's near 99% tax-efficiency rating means that shareholders have had to give back only 1%, thus pocketing net gains of 28.7% a year. Similarly, $1.6 billion Third Avenue Value manager Marty Whitman, who specializes in unearthing undervalued stocks and bonds, has delivered annual gains of 25.6% over the past three years vs. 18.5% for competitors, while maintaining a 95% tax-efficiency.

Fortunately, once you've gone to the trouble of identifying a tax-efficient fund, chances are better than even that it will maintain its tax-wise ways. A recent Morningstar study showed that two-thirds of funds with above-average tax ratings in 1994 remained highly efficient in 1997. Only 22% slipped back to average efficiency, and only 12% of those former tax stars dropped into the below-average group. Tax scoundrels show a remarkable—if unprofitable—consistency too. Morningstar found that only 26% of funds that ranked below the average in the tax-efficiency standings managed to catapult themselves into the top half of the rankings over the three years to 1997.

If a fund hasn't been around long enough for a full-fledged Morningstar rating, you can get a clue to its tax efficiency by checking out its portfolio turnover ratio—a measure of how quickly the fund trades its holdings— which is also available from Morningstar. Funds with very low turnover—

Short of plowing through all 327 pages of the Taxpayer Relief Act, what's the best way to grab the breaks you deserve? Fire up your computer. There's more help than ever to be found in the two major tax CD-ROM software packages: Intuit's TurboTax (800-446-8848; www.turbotax.com) and Block Financial's Kiplinger TaxCut (800-235-4060; www.taxcut.com.) And this year you have a third way to prepare your taxes electronically: File on the Web with Intuit's TurboTax Online (www.turbotax.com).

You should select tax software based on the complexity of your finances. We offer these recommendations for taxpayers with different needs:

▶ **Your tax return is simple.** If you want a quick, cheap way to fill it out and send it to the IRS, your best bet is TurboTax Online. The version MONEY tested was a breeze to use. You log on to the site and click your way through an interactive interview that prompts you with questions about your income, number of dependents and deductions you might qualify for. Your answers are factored into an electronic version of your return, so you never grapple with actual tax forms. Once the interview is finished, you can print out a paper copy of your return, and then zap the digital version to Intuit, which passes it along to the IRS. To prevent hackers from snooping around with your tax information, the site requires that you use a browser, such as Netscape Navigator 3.0 or Microsoft Explorer 3.0 for Windows 95, which employs encryption technology.

Unfortunately, the site can handle only the simplest tax forms: the 1040EZ (for taxpayers who don't itemize deductions) and the 1040 with Schedule A (for itemized deductions) and B (interest and dividend income). You can also file a Schedule D (for capital gains or losses on securities), as long as you're not reporting profits or losses on more than 10 stocks or mutual funds. As for state taxes, the site can only prepare state returns for California residents.

▶ **Your return is complicated.** You can't do it online—and you would also like tax-planning advice. Go with the deluxe version of Intuit's TurboTax. Both TurboTax and Kiplinger TaxCut can handle anything from the simplest to the most devilishly detailed returns. But the deluxe edition of TurboTax is superior for two reasons: It makes preparing your return far less tedious, and it's packed with tax-cutting tips and helpful resources.

One of TurboTax deluxe's most useful features is that it alerts you to possible tax credits and deductions without your having to ask about them. Once you list children under age 18 as dependents, for example, the program automatically tells you that the new tax law allows for a per-child tax credit of as much as $400 a year. Similarly, the program calculates, without prompting from you, the maximum tax-deductible contribution, if any, you and your working spouse can make to your Individual Retirement Accounts. TaxCut, by contrast, simply asks whether you invested in an IRA and then refers you to its electronic copy of IRS Publication 590.

those that hold their securities 18 months or more vs. 14 months for the average fund—tend to be more tax-efficient because the manager isn't realizing a lot of gains. Some of the lowest turnover rates can be found in index funds, which sell securities only when there is a change in the underlying benchmark or when the fund must meet shareholder redemption requests. As a result of its minimal trading, the $45.9 billion Vanguard Index 500, for example, has a 95% tax efficiency for the past three years.

Be careful, though; a low turnover ratio can be misleading. In fact, many funds with low turnover have below-average efficiency ratings. The $7.7 billion Mutual Shares fund, for example, earned a below-average efficiency figure of just 79%, even though it held its stocks for 20 months on average vs. just the 14 months for the typical stock fund. That's because roughly 10% to 20% of the fund's 25% annualized gain over the past three years came from dividends, which are taxed at a maximum rate of 39.6%.

And don't assume high turnover will automatically generate huge taxable gains. In fact, many hyper-traders are highly efficient because they are adept at using losses in some holdings to offset gains in others. Even though $6.7 billion Aim Value A held stocks for less than nine months on average during the past three calendar years—or about five months less than the average fund—the fund has a lofty 92% tax-efficiency score. Rather than judge a fund solely by how long it holds on to its securities, check out how often its trading translates into dividend and capital-gains payments to shareholders. *Morningstar Mutual Funds* lists the annual capital gains and income distributions for 1,500 funds. To see how often a fund you already own pays out taxable gains, simply scan your end-of-year account statement or check the 1099 form your fund sends you each year it distributes taxable gains.

Consider funds that minimize taxes. Only about 15 so-called tax-managed funds are now available, although they do come in a variety of choices, ranging from funds that specialize in large-company stocks to small-cap shares to balanced portfolios that invest in a mix of stocks and bonds. All have the common aim, though, of doing everything possible to minimize the taxable gains they pass on to shareholders.

In November 1997, for example, Dreyfus debuted its Premier Tax-Managed Growth fund, which will aim to keep taxable distributions to a minimum—and snag the low 20% gains tax—by holding its large-company stocks for at least five years. And in June 1997, T. Rowe Price launched its $11.5 million Tax-Efficient Balanced fund, which seeks to boost after-tax returns by mixing growth stocks and tax-exempt municipal bonds.

These newcomers join a small group of tax-managed portfolios that have been delivering tax-efficient returns for years. The $2.7 billion Schwab 1000 fund, which was launched in 1991, operates much like an index fund in that it invests in the securities of a benchmark, in this case the 1,000 largest companies in the U.S. But unlike conventional index funds, which slavishly stick to the securities in their benchmarks, Schwab 1000 manager Geraldine Hom has the leeway to sidestep taxable gains by, among other things, taking losses in some holdings to offset gains in others. As a result, the fund operates at 98% tax efficiency, which means investors have pocketed nearly all of the fund's 26.2% annual gains the past three years.

Vanguard's $852 million Tax-Managed Capital Appreciation, $500 million Tax Managed Growth & Income and $110 million Tax-Managed Balanced are also quasi-index funds that operate much like the Schwab 1000 by offsetting gains with losses and keeping turnover to a bare minimum.

In the wake of the changes in the tax law, fund experts such as Ed Goldfarb of Kobren Insight Funds in Wellesley, Mass. believe we could see a spate of more tax-managed funds over the next year or so.

Hold your funds for the long term. You can blame managers
for most of your fund tax headaches. But it is up to you to control another tax threat—namely, the IRS tab you trigger every time you sell fund shares at a profit. Just how much of your gains might you give up by cashing out of one fund to buy another? Remember the Morningstar stat that showed that the average diversified equity fund's three-year gains after taxes amounted to just 88% or so of the manager's pre-tax return? Well, it gets a whole lot worse if shareholders also sold their fund after three years. According to Morningstar, after paying taxes on the gains the fund distributes and then paying the tab on the profit you would earn from the rise in the value of the fund shares themselves, your gain sinks to an abysmal 77% of pre-tax return.

Now, of course, there is no way completely to avoid paying a tax on the appreciated value of your fund shares. The IRS will exact its toll eventually when you or your heirs cash them in. But aside from dumping funds that prove themselves to be laggards, it makes no sense to trade funds and let taxes dilute your gains. Instead, hold on to your funds for as long as possible, and let your gains compound.

Don't be a tax-efficiency fanatic. While limiting taxable gains
from your funds is important, you shouldn't make tax efficiency your sole criterion for choosing funds. "You don't want the tax tail to wag the dog,"

says Daniel Wiener, editor of the monthly *Independent Adviser for Vanguard Investors.* "Taxes should be part of your decision-making process, but don't lose sight of other important goals like building a diversified portfolio that can reduce risk."

So you would be making a mistake, for example, to purge your portfolio of bond funds and balanced funds, both of which are intrinscially tax-*inefficient* because interest and dividend payments that these funds throw off to shareholders may be taxed at a maximum rate of 39.6%. But these types of funds also typically deliver solid long-term gains with below-average risk—a definite plus in today's highly volatile market. When the S&P 500 fell 3.4% in October, for example, balanced funds slipped only half as much, 1.7%, while high-quality corporate bond funds actually posted a 0.9% gain. So it may be worthwhile to give up a few percentage points in tax efficiency to gain a bit of ballast to ride out market downdrafts. Besides, chances are you can shield at least some of these high-income producers from the confiscatory tax rates that apply to dividends and interest by holding such funds in tax-sheltered vehicles such as 401(k)s, Keoghs and Individual Retirement Accounts.

Finally, in your drive to minimize taxes, don't forget that a few notable tax-inefficient funds generate such powerful pre-tax gains that shareholders come out ahead even after deducting hefty taxes. For example, taxes typically lop 20% or so off the gross returns of Ken Heebner's $732 million CGM Capital Development fund. But his three-year annualized *after-tax* gain of 24.5% still beats 87% of his peers. So don't automatically reject a top-performing fund just because it's weak in the tax-efficiency department. After all, your ultimate goal isn't simply to slash your taxes—it's to wind up with the biggest gains possible after paying them.

SHRINK INCOME FOR BIGGER TAX BREAKS

The new Taxpayer Relief Act creates new incentives for an old gambit: reducing your taxable income to cut your tax. Because most of the new write-offs are available only to people earning less than certain proscribed amounts, upper-middle-income families who find ways to reduce their Adjusted Gross Income could save thousands of dollars in taxes.

If your income tops the $75,000-to-$110,000 ceilings for the tax goodies, you'll want to try to grab deductions that reduce your income and may let you qualify for the breaks. Almost all key income-cutting deductions are tied to employee-benefits programs. Specifically, the money you contribute to a 401(k) or 403(b) retirement account, deferred-compensation plan, flexible spending account, dependent-care account or medical savings account can be subtracted from your wages before determining your so-called modified Adjusted Gross Income—the number that determines if you qualify for the new tax breaks.

Consider the Afflues, a hypothetical two-income couple with four children. John, 42, earns $60,000 annually, and Jane, 43, earns $53,000. John Jr., 18, starts college this fall. There's also Jenny, 15; Josh, 13; and Susan, 3. (For simplicity's sake, we'll assume all earnings come from wages.) Both John and Jane have 401(k) plans available at work, but neither contributes. Nor does John fund his employer's dependent-care account, which lets him put as much as $5,000 in pre-tax earnings each year into a savings plan that can be used to pay Susie's day-care bills. He was spooked by the federal rules saying that any money left unspent at year-end is lost.

So the Afflues are making a total of $113,000 and passing up a chance to boost their tax savings by more than 50%. Not smart. By doing that, they are losing out on three tempting tax breaks in 1998. There's the child-care tax credit of $400 per child under 17 (the credit rises to $500 in 1999 and after); it begins to phase out for couples who earn more than $110,000, which means the Afflues would lose $150 of the benefit at their income level. There's the Hope tax credit, which could reimburse them for up to $1,500 of John Jr.'s '98 college costs. But this credit is unavailable if your joint AGI exceeds $100,000. Interest on Jr.'s student loans could be written off too, although student-loan interest is deductible only for joint filers with income under $75,000 or singles with income under $55,000.

A few simple moves will let the Afflue family take advantage of these three tax breaks. Here's what they should do:

John and Jane need to contribute $7,500 each to their retirement plans, and John should put $5,000 in his dependent-care account. That will reduce their Adjusted Gross Income by $20,000, making them eligible for the full child-tax credit and a partial Hope credit. Their tax savings under the new law would jump to $1,725—$675 more than if they hadn't reduced their AGI. Better yet, these moves would also slice the Afflues' taxable income, saving them even more in taxes. Pre-tax contributions to 401(k) and dependent-care accounts will lower their federal tax tab by roughly $6,200. So all told, this little game of benefit bingo will let them pay $6,875 less to the IRS.

It's unlikely that the couple could reduce their AGI enough to qualify for the new student-loan interest deduction. John Jr. can pay back the debt and get the interest writeoff himself, though.

To be sure, the Afflues will have to live a bit more frugally to put aside an additional $15,000 annually. But since nearly half their new retirement savings will return to them in federal tax breaks—and they're likely to get state income tax breaks as well—the pinch probably won't hurt a bit.

You may not have all the options the Afflues do. If your income somewhat exceeds the thresholds for the tax breaks, however, take advantage of any employer-sponsored benefits that will help you get the new writeoffs.

WIN MORE AT THE NEW IRS

Pressure from angry taxpayers—like those at last September's Senate hearings into abusive tactics by Internal Revenue Service agents—has exposed the agency's fault lines and suggests a political earthquake could be near. Already, President Clinton has responded by appointing a new commissioner, former computer industry executive Charles Rossotti, who promises to transform the IRS into a "taxpayer advocate." And in November and December, agents in more than 50 cities put on smiley faces and made themselves available to solve taxpayer problems at first-ever open houses. Meanwhile, on Capitol Hill the House has passed legislation to rein in the agency, while over in the Senate, Finance Committee Chairman Roth is working on a bill that will provide even stronger taxpayer protection.

Below, we take a closer look at what current and proposed IRS reforms will *really* mean to taxpayers, and why all taxpayers should ultimately come out ahead as a result of the changes.

The commissioner is a modern manager. IRS will finally have a commissioner from the business world who understands computers *and* customer service. Rossotti told MONEY that it will take the better part of a decade to reengineer the IRS' troubled computer modernization program, which is the key to reducing costly errors and enabling IRS employees to provide first-class customer service. But as the former chairman of American Management Systems, an $812 million computer consulting firm with 7,000 employees in 53 offices worldwide, Rossotti is the IRS' first top tax collector with hands-on experience building and managing complex computer systems. To help him are two experienced new lieutenants: Arthur Gross, who modernized New York State's collection system and is now heading up the IRS modernization effort, and Robert Barr, former vice president of government programs at Intuit, the nation's leading developer of tax software.

Agents may have to tell you your rights.
Currently, tax practitioners say IRS agents frequently coerce taxpayers into signing away rights, such as the three-year statute of limitations on back taxes, by, say, threatening to disallow all deductions. "This is the most frequent audit-related taxpayer abuse," says Robert Schriebman, a Los Angeles tax attorney who's written 11 books on the IRS. "The practice is so pervasive as to be perversive." A provision in the House-passed bill likely to be included in final legislation would require IRS agents to notify taxpayers of their rights to refuse such requests. Schriebman calls this provision "the single best part of the bill."

Taxpayers could get new protections.
Since 1976, the agency has operated a so-called problem resolution program to help taxpayers resolve thorny disputes. Problem is, the program has never had enough power to protect taxpayers from overzealous IRS agents. Now Congress wants to make the office more independent by prohibiting the top taxpayer advocate (if he had been employed by the IRS before being appointed) from taking a job within the IRS for five years after his stint ends. This is so he or she won't hold back on taxpayer-friendly actions out of fear that a future IRS career could be hurt as a result. The House bill would also make it easier for employees in the advocate's office to provide relief by instructing them to consider whether there will be or has already been an unreasonable delay in resolving the problem and whether the taxpayer will suffer significant professional fees or irreparable injury if assistance is denied.

Roth wants to further protect taxpayers by giving them a new right to appeal IRS liens, levies and seizures before an independent body with real power to stay or reverse an IRS order.

Innocent spouses get some help.
Every year thousands of women—and some men—who signed joint returns are hit with tax bills generated by their former or current spouse. Under current law, so-called innocent spouses can get relief if they can prove they did not know nor had any reason to know of the underpayment and that it resulted from a "grossly erroneous" entry, such as a bogus tax shelter, on the return. As you can imagine, few innocent spouses can meet those requirements, because most underpayments stem from common mistakes such as omitted income or unapproved deductions. And it's virtually impossible to prove a spouse had no knowledge of or reason to know of the other's actions.

The House bill would help innocent spouses by eliminating the "grossly erroneous" requirement, so that relief might be granted in situations where underpayment resulted from an inadvertent mistake. However, that relief would be limited to innocent spouses hit with tax bills beginning in 1998. What's more, for the first time, the tax bill could be divided on the basis of the benefit the IRS says the innocent spouse received. Warns Schreibman: "This could encourage judges to split the difference, leaving the innocent spouse with a bigger bill than if they won innocent spouse relief under current law." To strengthen the measure, the Senate is being urged to drop the apportionment provision and make the bill retroactive to all outstanding assessments, so that current victims can get some relief too.

IRS oversight figures to improve. Much as citizen review boards have helped make police departments more accountable, Congress' proposed 11-member IRS oversight board should help make the agency more responsive to the Congress and public. But Roth says it won't stop abuses unless Congress enacts his plan to give the board authority over IRS enforcement actions. He would also like to establish an independent Inspector General within the agency that will report directly to the board.

TAX COLLECTORS WILL SERVE TAXPAYERS

What are the new commissioner's goals for the IRS? In an interview with us, Commissioner Charles Rossotti spoke about his plans to transform the agency.

Q. How does your new job feel?

A. It feels like stepping from a wonderful fall day into a blast furnace. There is a lot of stuff that needs to be dealt with here—and fast. My goal is to move the IRS to a point where it is not viewed as an adversary but predominately an agency that helps taxpayers figure out the best way to meet whatever obligations they have under the tax law.

Q. What will you do to prevent taxpayer abuses?

A. We are trying to get rid of statistical performance measures for auditors and collection agents that were possibly driving people to be a little too aggressive. Longer term, we need a set of more positive measures. Every good service organization measures three things: what the customer thinks of it, what the employee thinks of it and some sort of business results. Unfortunately, our measures tended to focus just on business results.

Q. What are you doing to improve access to your 800–line?

A. I have to be honest: Our phone system is just not good. It's something that grew up topsy-turvy, and now we are trying to improve it as fast as we can. But I don't want to give your readers false expectations. We will not [be providing phone service] in the next filing season that's up to par with their best experiences in the private sector. But that's our goal. It will take us a few years to get there.

Q. What about the IRS' badly bollixed computer modern‐ization effort?

A. If we are ever to provide first-rate customer service, we need to rebuild the whole technology base from the ground up. To do the whole thing will take the better part of a decade.

Q. What mark do you hope to leave on the agency?

A. I hope the IRS will not only have a taxpayer advocate but eventually everyone here will be a taxpayer advocate.

TRAPS THAT CAN TRIP UP TAX RETURNS

In its seventh test of the knowledge and ability of tax preparers across the country, MONEY reported alarming results last year. No two pros among the 45 who took the test came up with the same tax total or calculated what we believed to be the correct federal income tax for the hypothetical couple, Curt and Ann Baker, whose 1996 return we asked them to prepare. Depending on who prepared their return, the Bakers would have overpaid by as much as $52,102, or all but begged for an audit by underpaying as much as $6,014.

Learn from the tax pros' mistakes. Here's what tripped up the tax pros. They could be trouble spots for you too.

▶ **Making outright errors.** Most of the returns were marred by them. Mistakes ranged from seemingly simple matters, such as overlooking taxable dividends or miscalculating the child-care credit, to complex ones like determining the taxable portion of stock options and inheritances.

▶ **Choosing the proper tax filing status.** Four preparers incorrectly decided the Bakers should send in separate returns rather than file jointly.

▶ **Calculating mutual fund gains**

▶ **Paying the nanny tax**

▶ **Figuring Keogh writeoffs**

▶ **Computing the tax on stock options**

▶ **Getting a refund on Social Security tax**

▶ **Avoiding 401(k) penalties.** Nine preparers kneecapped Curt with a 10% early-withdrawal penalty on his $60,000 401(k) payout. They didn't realize that the tax law waives this penalty before age 59 1/2 if you take your money as part of an early-retirement package and are at least age 55.

▶ **Determining dependents.** In 1996, the Bakers paid $10,520 to help support Curt's 80-year-old father, Lester. But 23 tax pros mistakenly failed to claim the $2,550 dependency exemption. One criterion in claiming a parent as a dependent is that you must provide more than half his total support. A parent living in his own home, as Lester did, is deemed to have contributed to his own support an amount equal to the fair rental value of his house ($6,000 a year in his case) minus any amount others pay to maintain the home. Since the test stated that the Bakers paid $3,600 to help maintain Lester's house, the fair rental value came to just $2,400 ($6,000 minus $3,600). In fact, the Bakers did provide more than half Lester's support and therefore were entitled to claim him.

HOW TO CHOOSE A TAX PRO

What else can you learn from the pros' disappointing performance? Follow these steps to determine whether you need professional tax help and, if so, how to choose the right preparer:

▶ **Get up to speed yourself.** You need to understand the gist of your own tax issues so you can direct your pro to problem areas. Read the sections that apply to you in tax tomes such as *The Ernst & Young Tax Guide* or *J.K. Lasser's Your Income Tax.* Or take a stab at completing your return by using tax software such as the programs recommended in "Let Your Computer Solve Tax Problems" on page 60.

► **Seek expertise in your thorniest tax areas.** Ask friends and colleagues whose finances are similar to yours for references, and talk to a handful of preparers before choosing one. Be sure to ask the pro how he or she keeps up with the tax law. Let the pro know your tax temperament as well. If you are a strictly play-by-the-rules type of taxpayer, you don't want a push-the-envelope preparer.

► **Ask for supplementary documents.** Tell your pro you will want a letter with your completed return explaining any judgment calls he or she makes in gray areas of the tax law. Your preparer should cite the sources that buttress the position taken, such as court cases or IRS rulings. Remember: You're the one who will bear ultimate responsibility for what's on your return.

► **Demand to be part of the process.** Ask your pro to call you with any questions that arise in the course of completing your return. Your aim is to deter your preparer from making erroneous assumptions.

► **Review your completed return carefully.** Ask your preparer about any figures that seem unusually large or small. Only when you're satisfied should you sign your 1040 and send it in.

Avoiding an IRS Audit

IRS computers are most apt to notice irregularities in certain specific areas of a return. For instance, if you plan to claim unreimbursed employee business expenses, are self-employed or inflated your income when you applied for a recent mortgage, you stand a greater than average chance of getting an IRS audit notice. Here are some pesky audit attractors. If, after reading about them, you think that your return might score an IRS bull's-eye even though your deductions are legit, don't cheat yourself and skip taking the writeoffs. Just make certain your records are impeccable. And always attach to your return an explanation of deductions that might raise questions.

Perennials. Here are problems that have existed for a while and remain thorny today.

► **Writing off unreimbursed expenses.** Auditing employee business deductions usually provides a windfall of extra taxes for the IRS. The chief reason is that in order to claim them, you must be able to prove that they were legitimate business expenses and your employer didn't cover them. The IRS also knows that taxpayers have a lousy track record in proving exactly how much they spent on business expenses, largely because the record-keeping requirements for entertainment and travel expenses are among the tax law's strictest. Employees who deduct personal computers used at home are also audit targets, since you can't write off a PC unless your boss tells you to buy one for the company's convenience.

▶ **Filing a Schedule C.** Sorry, entrepreneurs, but filing a Schedule C for your unincorporated small business sends a red flag to IRS auditors, yet you must send one in if you're a sole proprietor. An alarming 5.85% of Schedule Cs with gross receipts of less than $25,000 were audited in 1995, vs. just 1.67% of all individual tax returns. Larger sole proprietors are in the IRS crosshairs too. In '95, the audit rate for those business owners with gross receipts of $25,000 to $100,000 was 3.08%; it was 3.47% if you took in $100,000 or more. Schedule C filers are also more vulnerable to so-called lifestyle audits, in which the IRS investigates your standard of living to make sure it fits with the income you report.

Here's where attaching an explanation can be of enormous help. For example, if you claim a theft loss, you should attach a statement describing the items stolen from your company and how you arrived at the amount of the deduction.

▶ **Owning rental property.** To deduct a loss, you must be able to prove that you actively managed the property by doing substantially all of the work on it last year. If you're claiming legitimate rental losses, make sure you have records showing that you took an active part in such management decisions as approving tenants and authorizing repairs on the property.

▶ **Inflating your income to get a loan.** The IRS has been comparing income on mortgage and small business loan applications with the amount borrowers show on their tax returns. A compliance study conducted in Fresno in 1995, which compared income on tax returns and loan applications, triggered nearly 500 audits.

Your 1997 return. What follows are the new tax breaks that could be audit targets in 1998. If you plan to take advantage of them, be sure to document every move you make, as suggested below:

▶ **The adoption tax credit.** It can be as much as $5,000 ($6,000 for special-needs adoptions). Safeguard your writeoff by keeping all your papers and canceled checks or receipts for adoption fees, court costs, attorney fees and other expenses directly related to legally adopting your child. For example, if you need to renovate your home to meet state adoption requirements, hold on to your fix-up bills.

▶ **Long-term care costs.** Keep a copy of any long-term-care contract, receipts or canceled checks for premiums and medical services not covered by insurance, plus, if you're paying a relative, a copy of the caregiver's professional license.

▶ **Penalty-free IRA withdrawals.** You can take one to pay for medical insurance if you're unemployed for at least 12 consecutive weeks. Save copies of your unemployment checks, the Form 1099-R from your IRA sponsor showing your distribution, and canceled checks or receipts for your health insurance premiums.

▶ **Tax-free medical savings accounts.** If you sign up for an MSA, keep a copy of the insurance policy, proof of your contributions to your account and canceled checks or receipts for medical expenses.

GET YOUR ESTATE IN SHAPE NOW

You're never too young to work up your estate plan. Yes, the problems that can come if you haven't taken proper steps to safeguard your estate can be most severe financially once you've had many years to amass your fortune. But on a personal and emotional level, the devastation can be deeper when you're young. We will explain here the dangers that poor estate planning can pose at every stage of your life. And we will tell you how to avoid them, and how to take advantage of the new estate tax laws.

Estate planning starts with a will. Jane Markey, 45, a state appeals court judge in Grand Rapids, had never before felt an emotion quite like this one. But as she and her lawyer husband Curt Benson, 37, prepared for a leave-the-kids-behind cruise, she was consumed with dread. The focus of her anxiety: her kids—daughter Caitlin, 8, and son Robert ("Bo"), 6. "What would happen to them," she recalls worrying, "if we didn't come back?"

An irrational fear? Hardly. That's because neither of these two highly educated people had ever prepared a will. Nor had they named guardians for Caitlin and Bo if the kids were orphaned. Nor had they done anything to ensure that their roughly $1.5 million estate, which includes $600,000 life insurance policies on each of them, would be soundly managed for their kids' benefit. "As lawyers, we felt especially derelict," confesses Jane.

So, belatedly, they took action. The day before they left on their trip, Markey and Benson (and the local attorney they hired to help them) put the finishing touches on a comprehensive estate plan. It includes wills for each of them and two simple trusts to maximize financial protection and flexibility for their survivors should one or both of them die. Total cost: roughly $1,500. "The guilt has definitely melted away," Markey says. "It gave both of us peace of mind on our vacation."

You're rich enough to be in need. Benson and Markey admit they were negligent in not having a will. Then again, they had plenty of company. Roughly 70% of U.S. adults don't have wills, and financial and estate-planning authorities say that even those who do often haven't done all they should to build an airtight estate plan. And no wonder. No one likes to contemplate his own death. Plus, all too many Americans figure—wrongly, of course—that they are simply not rich enough to need a will, let alone an estate plan.

The truth is that you need not be morbid to need a will. And if you have young children or other dependents, you probably ought to set up one or more trusts as well. "Estate planning," says Carol Harrington, a trusts and estates lawyer in Chicago, "is for anyone who is responsible for someone or something else." And that, when you think about it, is just about everyone—young or old, rich or not so rich.

Then too, only with a well-executed estate plan can you erase or ease the tax man's take, which in these days of $400,000 California bungalows can zap you hard and fast. In reality, says Howard Zaritsky, an estate-planning lawyer in Fairfax, Va., "the less you've got, the less you can afford to forfeit to the government, which makes planning all the more crucial."

To get started, hire an attorney who specializes in estate planning. This means the lawyer who handled your last house closing probably isn't your best choice. Expect to pay $150 to $500 for a will and $500 to $1,500 for the most common types of trust documents. You'll get a better estate plan—and potentially save time and money—if you understand these estate-planning basics.

Your family comes first. Your will is the cornerstone on which family members and loved ones will build financial security after your death. Go to your grave without one, and you could leave behind the following sorts of problems:

A judge will decide who raises your children. That's right. A will is where you nominate guardians to raise your children and manage their inheritances. Fail to do so, and a probate court judge will select the caretakers for you. She or he may choose wisely—or not. But even if the judge does make a good choice, it may not satisfy everyone. The result: possible custody fights. "The ensuing battles not only prolong the immediate trauma," says Zaritsky, "they can cause such rifts that some family members never speak to one another again, effectively depriving the children of relationships you might want them to have."

Your wealth may not go where you want it to. If you die without a will, state law determines how to distribute assets that don't have a named beneficiary or are not jointly owned. That can spell trouble for single people as well as married couples. In most states, for instance, if you're single, childless and die without a will, your parents get almost everything you own outright. Your significant other will be left out unless you state your intentions in a will.

If you are married with children and die without a will, by law half to two-thirds of your wealth generally goes in equal portions to your kids. That may not sound unfair until you consider that one child (say, one with special needs) may have greater financial requirements than another, or that your aging spouse may need the money more than your investment banker daughter. Wendy Yurachek, an estate-planning lawyer in Falls Church, Va., remembers the case of a family with four children—two out of college and two in grade school. When the father died without a will, the kids each inherited roughly $10,000. Equitable? Not really, says Yurachek: "The lack of planning has left the four kids in vastly different circumstances; the younger ones still clearly have paying for college ahead of them."

Finally, if you're married and childless and die without a will, you could leave a mess behind even if all your property is owned jointly with your spouse. Say the husband dies and the surviving wife becomes the sole owner of their jointly owned assets. When she dies, all of the former joint property goes to her family, unless she has written a will that names his kin as her heirs. Want to provide for your elderly mother or for children from a first marriage? Then say so—in a will.

The probate court will decide who administers your estate. In your will, you also name an executor. That person pays off your debts and distributes your legacy. If you don't have a will, the court appoints the executor, opting for a professional administrator if your relatives are unwilling or unable to serve. In general, fees for court-appointed pros eat up 3% to 5% of your estate; by contrast, friends or relatives may waive fees entirely or take more modest compensation.

How trusts can work for you. For all its important advantages, a will alone may not be enough to assure the smooth transfer of assets to your heirs. This is especially true if your heirs are minors. Assume, for example, that you die, having willed some of your wealth to your young children. The guardian of the children's property named in your will must annually report all major investments and expenditures on the children's behalf to a probate judge—even if the guardian is the surviving parent. Such oversight presumably guards against thievery and mismanagement. But, says Washington, D.C. estate-planning attorney Michael Curtin, it's also "a silly, ignominious way for a scrupulous guardian to manage a child's money."

It can be costly too. Case in point: Curtin once worked with a District of Columbia woman whose seven-year-old daughter inherited $322,000 from her father. By law, though, the mother had to post a bond with the D.C. court equal to that amount, plus a year's worth of interest. Her cost: $3,000 a year.

Curtin's client could have sidestepped that problem if her husband had left the money in trust for his daughter instead of leaving it to her outright. Moreover, a trust can clear away another estate-planning brier patch—namely, that children gain complete control of their legacies at the so-called age of majority (18 in most jurisdictions). "I tell my clients to picture themselves at 18," says Orinda, Calif. lawyer Paula Leibovitz. "Then they understand how someone just out of high school is usually ill-equipped to handle an inheritance."

Simple steps to secure a safe future. Setting up a trust or two is a straightforward exercise. It basically boils down to this: You appoint a trustee to administer the inheritance according to detailed instructions you set forth in a trust document. There is no court oversight and no state-mandated deadlines for distributing the money. You can say, for example, when payouts of interest and principal should be made; what financial goals you want the trustee to achieve, such as paying for your children's college education; and when any remaining money should be paid to your heirs (say, at ages 25, 30 and 35). For example, according to the plan that Benson and Markey set up, when Bo reaches the age of 21, the assets held in trust for him and Caitlin will be split into a separate trust for each child. When they turn 35, they can claim their trust's principal; until that age, they need the trustee's approval for any withdrawals.

You can appoint a financially savvy relative or friend as trustee. Or you can opt for a bank, trust company or investment management firm. The latter choices are often wise if your assets are substantial—say, $500,000 or more. That's because managing such sizable amounts often proves daunting to nonprofessionals. Expect to pay fees of 1% or so of trust assets a year.

You will need to choose between two basic types of trust. A testamentary trust, which can be drawn up for $250 to $500, is established in your will and stipulates that the property you designate be placed in the trust when you die. A revocable living trust, which costs $500 to $1,000, is created outside your will and starts to operate during your lifetime. You transfer title of your assets to the trust while you're alive, but you retain complete control of them by naming yourself as trustee. Then, on your death, a successor trustee you've named takes over and manages the money for your heirs.

The big difference between the two types of trusts is that assets in a testamentary trust pass through probate, which is the court procedure for validating a will. By contrast, assets in a revocable living trust do not go through probate. That's because they pass to your heirs outside your will, according to instructions you set forth in the trust document. Another plus: Since there's no probate, there are no public court records of living-trust bequests. You thus shield your heirs from nosy neighbors or, worse, scamsters who page through court documents scanning for potential victims. For these reasons, Benson and Markey each opted for a revocable living trust. "We like the idea of having a trust in place that will help avoid any possible complications upon our deaths," says Markey.

The combination you need. So which type of trust should you choose? Best advice: Consult your attorney. But don't buy the increasingly widespread argument—often advanced by lawyers who want to collect hefty fees—that a revocable living trust can take the place of a will. It can't. "You still need a will to name guardians for your kids," says Jonathan David, the Grand Rapids attorney who worked with Benson and Markey. "You also need a will to direct that any property you neglected to title to the trust be placed there after you die."

Shield your estate from taxes. Once your family is secure, your final mission is to shield your estate from gift and estate taxes. These so-called transfer taxes are essentially one and the same: Gift tax is imposed on transfers you make during your lifetime; estate tax is levied on property you leave at death. Happily, fewer than 2% of all estates are subject to federal tax. That's because of a variety of exclusions and deductions. One of them, called the unlimited marital deduction, lets you leave any amount of money or property tax-free to your spouse, provided the recipient is a U.S. citizen. Another permits you to pass as much as $600,000 tax-free to your heirs—an amount that will rise to $1 million by 2006.

If you plan ahead, you can take advantage of trusts that can often completely shield your wealth from death taxes. That's what Benson and Markey did. In their fairly typical setup, they each take advantage of the $600,000 they can leave their kids or other heirs tax-free. On Benson's death, for instance, assets in the revocable living trust he established will be split into two separate trusts. One trust, called a family trust (also known as a bypass or credit-shelter trust), will be funded with as much as $600,000 worth of assets. That full amount will escape estate tax, since it's covered by the $600,000 transfer-tax threshold. Any assets above that amount will spill into the other trust, called a marital deduction trust. The assets in this trust will also escape tax, since you can leave an unlimited amount to your spouse tax-free. Markey (whose trust setup is a mirror image of Benson's) will receive all of the income from the marital deduction trust and has the option of pulling out principal equal to $5,000 or 5% of the trust's value annually, whichever is greater.

When Markey dies, all of the assets remaining in the marital deduction trust will automatically flow into the family trust for the benefit of Caitlin and Bo. Result: Assuming the sum that's transferred to the family trust is less than the amount you can pass tax-free to your heirs, Benson and Markey's worldly goods will have made the trip from Benson to Markey to Caitlin and Bo free of estate tax.

Benefit from estate-tax changes.
An increase in the estate-tax exemption—the amount of money you can leave any heir free of federal estate taxes—could save your heirs as much as $400,000. Previously set at $600,000 per person, the exemption, as we just said, will rise in steps to $1 million by 2006.

You can also make larger tax-free gifts starting in 1999, an advantage if your strategy calls for you to shrink your estate below the exemption limit. For the past 15 years, the most you have been able to give each of your intended heirs without triggering the gift tax is $10,000 a year ($20,000 if you give jointly with your spouse). From 1999 on, that figure will increase with inflation, but only in $1,000 increments. Thus it would take three years of 3.5% inflation before the limit would jump to $11,000.

If you are married with an estate of more than $1.2 million, including your home and any other property, your heirs stand to benefit from these new rules, although the mechanics of the matter have not changed much. Your spouse can still inherit any amount estate-tax-free (under the unlimited marital deduction), but other heirs must pay tax on any amount above the exemption. So to avoid making Uncle Sam your biggest heir on the death of your surviving spouse, you must set up a bypass trust, as the Markeys did. If you already have a bypass trust, check that its language is flexible enough to accommodate the rising exemption amounts in the new law.

Additionally, don't be deceived by the incremental increase in the amount of property you can leave to heirs estate-tax-free. Even though it hits $1 million in 2006, don't mistakenly think that this means you'll never have to worry about federal estate tax, which currently starts at 37% and tops out at 55% on anything above $3 million. For example, unless you give up ownership of your life insurance, say, by placing the policy in a trust, the payout will be part of your taxable estate. This alone can put many people who don't consider themselves rich within the tax man's reach. Your taxable estate will also include your share of jointly owned property, such as your house; investments in 401(k)s, IRAs and other retirement plans; cash, bonds, stocks and other investments; and personal property like art, automobiles and jewelry. "I know $1 million sounds like a lot," says Kevin Flatley, director of estate planning at Bank Boston's Private Bank. "But when my clients start looking at what they own, they're usually amazed at how quickly it adds up."

Making gifts while you're alive is one of the easiest ways to reduce the size of your taxable estate. But for maximum tax cutting, you must follow a well-thought-out strategy because, as just noted, there's a cap as to how much you can give away annually tax-free. The amount of any gift exceeding the limits you can give to each of as many people as you like in a year (currently $10,000 for an individual, $20,000 for a married couple) is taxable to the giver. The tax doesn't apply in two situations: You can give a spouse who is a U.S. citizen any amount tax-free, and you can pay any amount of tuition and medical bills for as many people as you want tax-free, as long as you make the payments directly to the school or health-care provider.

If you make a taxable gift, you typically don't pay the tax out of your own pocket. Instead, after you die, your executor will subtract the value of your lifetime gifts from your estate's exemption. Say, for example, you give

$100,000 worth of stock to your daughter in one year. The law figures that you have made a $90,000 taxable gift ($100,000 minus the $10,000 gift-tax-free amount). Accordingly, your estate's tax exemption would be knocked down to $510,000 under current law. If the total taxable gifts you make during your lifetime top the exempt amount, you will have to pay tax—at estate rates—on the excess.

The kind of property you give away can have a big impact on your estate's tax bill. In general, lawyers recommend that you give away assets that haven't yet grown much in value but have excellent prospects for appreciating. That way, you remove the current value of the asset from your estate as well as all subsequent growth.

If you own highly appreciated stock shares and equity mutual fund shares, you might want to keep them. Reason: If you give away the shares, the recipient will owe capital-gains tax on all the appreciation since you bought them. In contrast, if you bequeath the stock, your heir will usually owe that tax only on the appreciation from the date of your death to the date of the sale—a potentially humongous tax saver known in tax law as "step-up in basis."

KEEP YOUR BUSINESS IN THE FAMILY

If you own a business, figuring out where your company's finances end and your family's finances begin is like trying to find the dividing line between ocean and sky on a dark summer night. But without a separate estate plan for your business, you could jeopardize your family's financial welfare as well as your company's. Here are three ways to avoid the problem.

Life insurance. When you die, your family may have to pay estate taxes on the company's value, overtime to employees who temporarily fill in for you, and a headhunter to find a new boss. The business may also experience a period of falling profits—which could mean less cash flow for your heirs.

To make sure your family has enough money for these contingencies, financial planners recommend that you buy two life insurance polices. The proceeds from the first one will cover the estate taxes. The payout from the second policy, called key-man insurance, will keep your company financially afloat until a new boss takes over.

A buy-sell agreement. In a typical deal, your partners or co-owners agree on a formula for setting the price they will pay for your stock in the company when you die, become disabled or retire. This ensures that you or your survivors will get a fair price for your ownership interest and that your business associates won't have to negotiate a price with your spouse, children or anyone else who might lay claim to your share of the firm.

A *family limited partnership.* This arrangement lets you control the business as a general partner while you gradually transfer your ownership to your children as limited partners. Because the kids don't control the business, the value of the shares you give them will be heavily discounted.

Let's say that you make your daughter a limited partner and over several years give her 75% of a $1 million business. A professional appraiser might estimate the value of her shares to be $600,000—not $750,000. That $150,000 discount would save you some $75,000 in estate tax, assuming your total taxable estate is worth less than $2.5 million. Even better, if the value of the business grows to, say, $10 million by the time you die, only your 25% ownership share, or $2.5 million, would be included in your estate.

In setting up a family limited partnership, estate-planning lawyers warn you to be careful: The Internal Revenue Service routinely challenges discounts that appear to be excessive. So use an attorney with extensive experience in establishing such partnerships, and instruct your appraiser to err on the conservative side in estimating the value of the shares that you give to your children.

CHAPTER 3

PUMP UP AND PROTECT A NEST EGG

O ver the years, the *Money Adviser* has presented a fundamental comparison to set readers on course for smart saving. Equally important as a fresh piece of information or as a reminder, here is our example once again:

Let's say you're able to put aside $500 a month for 30 years. If you put it in a safe money-market fund that earns an average 6% a year, you'll end up with roughly $553,000. But what if you stash that money in a growth-oriented blend of mostly stocks, plus bonds—or mutual funds that invest in these securities? With an average return close to 10% annually, a reasonable expectation for that portfolio over 30 years, you'll build a nest egg of $1 million. Sounds like a no-brainer, right? Why not go for gains that will just about double the money you'll have available in your retirement? What's the catch? One word: risk. The price for nearly doubling your return would be much greater uncertainty in the short run. With only a moderately risky growth portfolio, you should still be prepared to ride out market drops that could be as chilling as 20% over the course of several months or even weeks.

Whether you're just beginning to build your nest egg or close to retiring with it, the strategies in this chapter will help you get the most out of your money. The important decisions you'll be implementing over the years will rest largely on your age, where your financial assets are concentrated, the state of the economy and your tolerance for risk. The ups and downs of the stock and bond markets are two factors you should consider in investing your money. But you should also make gradual adjustments in your asset mix to match your changing needs for capital growth, steady income or a combination of both.

LEARN HOW MUCH RISK TO TAKE

You need to know not only your own level of tolerance for taking chances, but what makes sense at various stages of your life. Want a key to savvy asset allocation? It's simple: Begin by carefully analyzing your investments and other aspects of your financial life to determine the degree that each exposes you to the following types of risk.

Risk from inflation. When prices go up, the purchasing power of an investment goes down. For example, an annual inflation rate of 5% over 15 years will reduce the value of $1,000 to $480. Therefore, investors who are overcautious and hoard assets in low-yielding vehicles such as savings accounts and money-market funds may not earn enough to outpace rising prices. Rising inflation also lowers the value of future income generated by investments with fixed payments, most notably long-term bonds.

Risk from interest rates. Rising interest rates will cause investments to drop in price. Higher rates make yields on existing bonds less attractive, so their market values go down. Rising rates also hurt stocks by making their dividend yield less appealing. Moreover, risk will increase for people who invest borrowed money through margin accounts or have other kinds of floating-rate debt, because higher interest rates cut into their net profits.

Risk from the economy. Slower growth in the economy will cause investments to fall in price. It will have an impact on shares of small growth companies because they neeed a booming economy to maintain robust earnings gains. Cyclical companies, such as automakers and chemical producers, can't easily cut costs during a recession, so their stock prices may fall. And economic slumps can undercut junk bonds issued by financially weak companies that might default.

Market risk. Political developments and Wall Street fads are among the factors that can hurt investment markets. Other contributors to market risk include tax law changes, trade agreements, program trading and the idiosyncracies of investor psychology; each helps account for much of the stock market's day-to-day volatility. Gold also carries considerable market risk because its price moves sharply when political or military upheavals in other nations encourage the flight of capital.

Specific risk. This covers occurences such as poor management or bad luck that may affect only a specific company or industry; high-flying growth stocks are particularly vulnerable to earnings disappointments. You amass considerable specific risk when you buy stock in a company with a heavy debt burden or invest in specialty stock funds, often called sector funds because they concentrate their holdings in a single industry such as technology. Specific risk also includes the chance that government regulation will hurt a particular group of companies.

ASSESS YOUR ASSETS FOR TOP RESULTS

It's important to figure out the big risks in your portfolio because then you can correct problems by redeploying assets. When you take inventory, don't confine it to investments in your brokerage account. Your most valuable asset, for example, may be your earning power. Your equity in a home may be second best. And don't forget your assets invested in a company pension plan or insurance policies with cash value. If you own a small business, be sure to examine the risks that could reduce its value.

Risk can sneak up on you. Your retirement plan assets can grow more than you realize, especially if you make regular contributions or reinvest your returns. That increase in value is wonderful, but it can create a problem. Why? Because growth in one asset can disrupt the balance of your portfolio if other investments don't keep pace. Suppose a prolonged bull market, like the one we recently experienced, revs up the value of your stocks. You may have to sell some shares to restore the balance between your stock and other assets. Along the same lines, if one of your stocks zooms up in price, it might be time to sell some shares. Be especially wary of loading up on your company's stock through retirement and savings plans. If the company hits hard times, both your job and your stock holdings may be in danger simultaneously.

To assess your own asset mix, take a close look at all your investments and other aspects of your finances. Here's a rundown of strengths and weaknesses of various assets.

Stocks and stock funds. They are vulnerable to the possibility that nervous investors will panic for some reason and drive down share prices. That's an example of market risk. But there are other risks, too. Inflation, interest rates and the economy can affect different stocks in different ways. A boost in the inflation rate lowers stock prices because it may cut the purchasing power of future dividends to stockholders. Also, inflation usually coincides with higher interest rates, and they move investors from stocks to bonds. What companies are your best bets during inflation? Generally, you might consider firms such as retailers, consumer product manufacturers and service companies. Reason: They can pass along cost increases to consumers relatively easily, so they are more likely to prosper during periods of high inflation.

Slowing economic growth tends to hurt some firms more than others. Manufacturers with high overhead, known as cyclicals, cannot easily cut costs when a recession slices sales. So their earnings quickly tail off. Many small growth companies also require an expanding economy to sustain their earnings growth and stock prices. By contrast, firms that sell necessities such as food or clothing often shine in a lackluster economy, and their shares tend to hold up relatively well. Since overseas stocks are partly immune to changes in the American economy and markets, they may stand firm while U.S. stocks sink. Unlike domestic issues, however, foreign shares carry currency risk. A weaker dollar abroad helps to inflate returns that are earned on overseas assets, while a stronger dollar deflates them.

Bonds and bond funds. Their prices go down when interest rates go up. But the extent of the drop depends on a bond's maturity and the amount of its coupon. Short-term bonds fall slightly when interest rates rise, and a high coupon also offers some protection against climbing rates. At the opposite extreme, zero-coupon bonds fall sharply when rates head higher. A recession generally brings lower interest rates, which boost bond prices. But some issues react negatively to the threat of an economic slowdown. So-called junk bonds, in particular, may lose ground because investors fear that financially weak firms will default and fail to make payments of interest and principal to bondholders on time. U.S. Treasury and high-grade corporate bonds gain the most during hard times because income investors seek them out as safe havens.

Real estate investments. Over time they tend to keep pace with inflation. But they present other hazards. If you own a rental property, you might not be able to find a tenant. A real estate partnership that owns several properties in different regions can reduce such risks through diversification, but it may lose value if tax changes or a recession drive down property values across the country. REITs (real estate investment trusts) and the funds that own them can fluctuate with the stock market as well as with property values.

RATE YOUR NEST EGG'S RISK EXPOSURE

Most people shield some of their fund investments against different types of risk. But few balance all of their assets so that they are well protected. This quiz can help you identify your points of vulnerability. With each question, you will accumulate points for one or more of the five major investment risks that are described in the main text. Write the points in the boxes below. Then total the points for each risk and interpret your scores as follows: Fewer than five points is low. Five to 10 points is moderate. Above 10 points is high. While you may want to vary your exposure to different categories of risk, depending on your personal circumstances and outlook for the financial markets, any score that comes in above 10 points should set off alarm bells.

Once you have identified vulnerabilities, you can take steps to shore up your defenses. Say that you score high for inflation risk and low for market risk. You might balance your portfolio better by switching some cash from money-market funds to those invested in stocks or gold-mining shares. While your risk of a temporary decline in the value of your portfolio will increase, you will have a better chance of outpacing inflation.

In answering the questions, don't make the mistake of overlooking funds located in 401(k) accounts, IRAs or any other savings or deferred-compensation plans. It may be difficult to pin down the value of some assets. For instance, you may have a universal life policy with an important investment component. Just make the best estimates that you can. It isn't necessary to be exact. But it is important that your inventory be as complete as possible.

QUESTIONS

	INFLATION RISK	INTEREST RATE RISK	ECONOMIC RISK	MARKET RISK	SPECIFIC RISK
▶ Are your assets diversified among fewer than four of these five categories—stocks, real estate, gold, bonds and cash? If yes, score one point for each risk.					
▶ Are more than 35% of your assets invested in any one of the five categories? If yes, score one point for each risk.					
▶ Is at least 10% of your portfolio in assets such as gold, natural-resource stocks or high-grade collectibles such as rare stamps? If no, score one point for inflation risk.					
▶ Is at least 30% of your portfolio in investments such as growth stocks and real estate, which are likely to produce long-term capital gains that can outpace inflation? If no, score two points for inflation risk.					
▶ Are your real estate and gold investments held primarily in assets such as gold-mining shares and REITs (real estate investment trusts), which tend to fluctuate with the stock market? If yes, score one point for market risk.					
▶ Do you generally keep at least 15% of your portfolio in cash equivalents such as Treasury bills or money-market funds? If no, score two points for interest rate risk.					
▶ Is more than 30% of your portfolio composed of assets such as long-term government bonds, CDs (certificates of deposit) or annuities that promise to pay investors fixed payments over a period of many years? If yes, then score three points each for inflation and interest rate risk.					

	INFLATION RISK	INTEREST RATE RISK	ECONOMIC RISK	MARKET RISK	SPECIFIC RISK
▶ Do highly volatile zero-coupon bonds account for more than 30% of your fixed-income assets? If yes, score two points each for inflation and interest rate risk.					
▶ Do small growth stocks or junk bonds, which may fall sharply in a recession, account for more than 25% of your portfolio? If yes, score three points for economic risk.					
▶ Do you switch money among different assets to try and catch the highs and lows of different investment markets? If yes, score two points for market risk.					
▶ Do you use dollar cost averaging or a similar plan that involves adding money to your investment portfolio at regular intervals? If no, score two points for market risk.					
▶ Is more than 20% of your portfolio concentrated in a single industry? If yes, score three points each for economic risk, market risk and specific risk.					
▶ Do stocks or bonds issued by one company (including the one that you work for) or shares in a single mutual fund or limited partnership account for more than 15% of your assets? If yes, score three points each for economic risk, market risk and specific risk.					
▶ Does your share in a privately held business account for more than 30% of your portfolio? If yes, score one point for economic risk and four points for specific risk.					
▶ Does a rental property account for more than 30% of your portfolio? If yes, score one point for economic risk and three points for specific risk.					
▶ Do foreign stocks and shares of domestic companies with significant overseas sales account for less than 10% of your portfolio? If yes, score one point for economic risk.					
▶ Will you need access in the next three to five years to principal in volatile assets such as stocks or long-term bonds? If yes, score one point each for inflation, interest rate, economic and market risk.					
▶ Do you have variable-rate loans such as mortgages or credit-card revolving debt that recently has amounted to 30% or more of the market value of your portfolio? If yes, score four points for interest rate risk.					
▶ Is 20% or more of your portfolio financed by loans or invested in highly leveraged assets such as options? If yes, score one point each for interest rate and market risk.					
TOTAL					

Gold and other hard assets. The price of gold can zoom upwards during periods of rising inflation. Example: Between 1968 and 1988, the consumer price index showed nine annual spurts of 6% or more. During those years, gold rewarded investors with an average gain of 34%. Gold-mining stocks are more volatile than the metal itself and expose investors to other risks. A miners' strike might boost the price of bullion but cut profits at mining companies. Other tangibles present their own problems. While antiques or rare stamps may outpace inflation in the long run, prices of items such as baseball cards are largely subject to collectors' whims.

THE BEST MIX FOR STAGES OF YOUR LIFE

Why does asset allocation determine most of an investor's return? According to researchers, the basic reason is that different types of investments don't rise and fall at the same time. By diversifying among stocks, bonds or cash, you can usually offset losses in one asset category with gains in another. For example, in October 1987, when stocks plummeted nearly 22%, long-term bonds rose 6%. The opposite was true in 1994. Bonds fell 3%, while the S&P eked out a 1% gain. While diversification can't guarantee that you'll never lose money, it can reduce your portfolio's overall risk and dramatically improve your odds of reaching your investment goals.

To determine the most efficient mix of investments for a retirement port-folio, experts first look at the correlation between various asset classes. Correlation is the technical term for comparing how different assets perform relative to one another over varying market cycles. You ideally want to build a portfolio of assets that are not closely correlated to one another. That way, you won't get clobbered by all your investments dropping in value at approximately the same time.

What's more, a properly diversified portfolio lets you put some of your money in potentially high-paying assets that otherwise might be too risky. You perform this alchemy by combining them with investments to which the high flyers are only weakly correlated. For example, a portfolio entirely invested in the large domestic stocks that make up the S&P 500 would have gained over 14% a year over the two decades from 1977 to 1997. But you could have earned 16% a year over the same time with a portfolio invested 65% in S&P 500 stocks, 20% in overseas stocks and 15% in small-company shares. In allocating assets, the pros rely not only on stocks' and bonds' past performances but also on estimates of their potential future returns. These predictions are based on forecasts of how market cycles will affect the performance of different asset classes.

Achieve your goals as your life changes. As you grow older, start a family and move closer to retirement, your investment goals and taste for risk change. Your portfolio should change along with you. Younger people, for example, can afford to aim for high returns with aggressive portfolios because they have many years to recover from market slumps. But as you get closer to retirement, you need to shift to a more cautious allocation that will preserve your gains. There's a second, equally powerful argument in favor of asset allocation. Academic studies show that about 90% of investors' returns come from the right combination of assets, with the remainder derived from their skill in picking securities and timely trading. To help you design your own allocation, MONEY surveyed many experts to devise a model portfolio for each of the four major stages in most people's working lives—starting out, building a family, peak earning years and nearing retirement (depicted on pages 90 to 93). Of course, the portfolios described here are only rough guidelines. You should customize your allocations to meet special needs.

Aim high in your 20s to early 30s. At this freewheeling stage, you have about 30 years before early retirement. So you can afford to gun for growth by stashing at least 80% of your portfolio in stocks and stock funds. Go for as much as 100% if you feel comfortable riding out market swings. Those who tend to get queasy in roller-coaster markets might put as much as 25% of their money in bonds and bond funds, which pay interest income that will help stabilize their portfolios. Based on long-term performance, this 75-25 lineup has the potential to return 9% annually.

For beginners with small savings, a single mutual fund that buys large-company stocks is a sound choice. Blue chips tend to offer solid capital appreciation with less volatility than smaller stocks. Nervous investors might want to opt for a balanced or asset-allocation fund instead. These all-in-one fund portfolios will typically keep about 60% of their assets in stocks and the rest in risk-cushioning bonds and other fixed-income investments. Investors who have $10,000 or more ought to assemble a diversified portfolio of funds. Allocate about 30% of your assets to large-company stocks, 25% to small-company stocks and 20% to overseas stocks. Small stocks historically have outpaced their bigger brothers, though with greater volatility. Overseas stocks can spice up your portfolio because many foreign

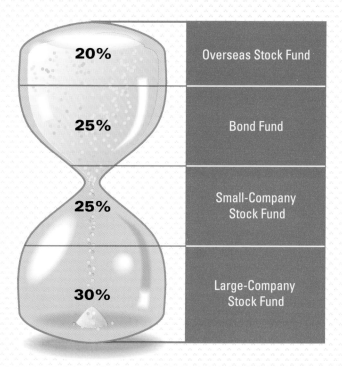

Single person, late twenties, with $10,000 saved

20%	Overseas Stock Fund
25%	Bond Fund
25%	Small-Company Stock Fund
30%	Large-Company Stock Fund

economies, particularly developing ones in Asia and Latin America, are likely to grow much faster than ours over the next decade. The risks you face are political instability and adverse swings in the value of the dollar. But if you can hold on through the downturns, your retirement fund could benefit greatly in the long run.

For a smoother ride to those higher returns, you might include both value and growth–stock funds in your portfolio. Value managers look for out-of-favor companies with share prices that do not fully reflect their earnings prospects or asset values. By contrast, growth–stock managers, as the name suggests, prefer companies with rapidly accelerating revenues and earnings, even though their shares typically will command premium prices. You can't really predict which investing style will be more successful in any given year. Studies show that over periods of 20 years or more, however, value has a slight performance advantage over growth.

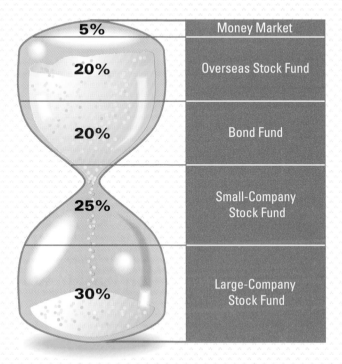

Couple, thirties, two preschoolers, $50,000 saved

5%	Money Market
20%	Overseas Stock Fund
20%	Bond Fund
25%	Small-Company Stock Fund
30%	Large-Company Stock Fund

As for your fixed-income holdings, put about 15% to 20% of your money in investment-grade bonds with intermediate maturities of five to 10 years. Studies show that five-year issues produce 96% of the return of 30-year issues with only half the volatility. About 5% of your money should go into a convertible bond fund, which will give you a shot at capital gains, or to a high-yield fund, which takes on extra risk in pursuit of the fatter yields paid by junk bonds. But steer clear of bond funds that carry sales charges or fees that total more than 1% of net assets. Their managers generally can't overcome those high expenses with superior performance. Fees are listed in a fund's prospectus.

Bankroll a family in your early 30s to 40s. With young families to provide for and mortgages to pay off, many investors in this age group prefer to reduce their portfolios' risk level. Just don't overdo it. You

Couple, early fifties, three teens, $200,000 saved

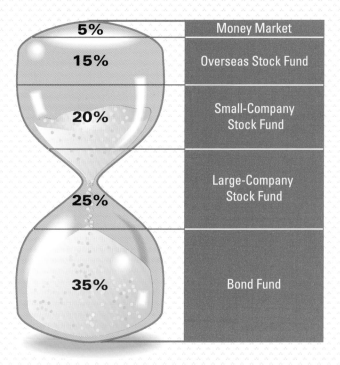

5%	Money Market
15%	Overseas Stock Fund
20%	Small-Company Stock Fund
25%	Large-Company Stock Fund
35%	Bond Fund

will be working for another 20 years or more, so you should keep at least 75% of your money in stocks. You can achieve that balance by gradually trimming back your stock funds and moving the excess cash to a money-market fund. Overall, our model is designed to give you average returns of about 8% annually. At this stage, you should further diversify your bond holdings. High earners should consider transferring the money in their convertible or high-yield corporate bond fund to a tax-free municipal bond fund and adding enough money so that it becomes 10% of the portfolio. A taxable alternative is an international bond fund. Fixed-income markets in the U.S. and abroad generally move in different directions, so you will offset a falling market with one that is on the rise. Foreign bond funds, of course, can respond sharply to currency fluctuations. But the swings will likely even out if you can let your money ride for at least 10 years.

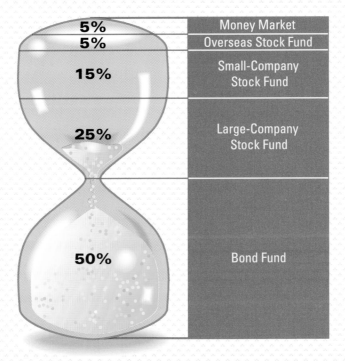

Couple, mid sixties, empty nesters, $400,000 saved

5%	Money Market
5%	Overseas Stock Fund
15%	Small-Company Stock Fund
25%	Large-Company Stock Fund
50%	Bond Fund

Hit stride in your early 40s to 50s. You have reached your peak earning years—just in time to pay your kids' college bills. Don't let that serve as an excuse to neglect your savings. Stocks should still be the center-piece of your portfolio. But ease back on risk by reducing your exposure to large-company stocks to about 25%, small caps to 20% and overseas stocks to 15%. This model aims to provide you with average returns of around 8% annually. You can add greater stability to your portfolio by emphasizing value funds. Since value funds focus on bargain-priced companies, they tend to fall less far than their high-flying growth peers during market cor-rections. And the stocks in value funds tend to pay dividends that will bol-ster your returns in down years. In the fixed-income portion of your port-folio, you might seek additional security by cutting international bonds to 5% and exchanging any intermediate-term corporate bond fund for one that holds government issues. Investors in high brackets, however, will probably do better with tax-exempt bonds. To earn high returns with minimum risk, look for muni funds with annual fees of less than 1% that hold mainly bonds rated A or higher.

Kick back in your early 50s to 60s. With retirement around the corner, you may be tempted to cash in your stock funds and tuck the proceeds into principal-preserving bond funds or bank CDs. That could prove to be a bad move for most MONEY readers. At 50 you still have a lifetime of at least 30 years ahead of you. If inflation were to hold steady at 3% a year, that would cut the purchasing power of today's dollar in half in only 12 years. Thus you should still hold a roughly 45% stake in stocks. Such a model portfolio should produce average returns of around 7% a year. In addition, now is an excellent time to move out of international bonds entirely and into U.S. government issues for greater safety. Truly risk-adverse investors might anchor their portfolios with Treasury notes, which mature in two to 10 years, because their principal and interest payments are federally guaranteed. You can opt for a Treasury-only bond fund. But odds are you can do just as well purchasing the Treasuries directly from the Federal Reserve Bank with no fee. We think that's a good deal for investors in any phase of life.

WAYS TO PICK WINNING STOCKS

All successful stock-picking strategies are variations on two themes: growth and value. As we said earlier, value investors are those bargain-rack shoppers who snap up stocks selling at a discount to what they believe is the stocks' real worth. Growth investors, on the other hand, favor companies with market-beating earnings growth, which they expect will propel the stock price upward.

But while those by-the-book definitions might be good enough to distinguish between types of mutual funds, they are not much use in picking stocks that can beat the market. How do you know a stock's "real" worth, for example? If a question like that has ever occurred to you when sizing up a promising stock, then this information is for you. We will walk you through the key attributes of top-performing value and growth stocks..

Value investing requires the courage to buy unloved stocks, as well as the patience to hang on to them for three years or more until the market recognizes their value. This is the buy-it-and-stuff-it-in-the-sock-drawer school of investing. Says David Schafer, manager of Strong Schafer Value fund: "Value players have got to keep their emotions in check because they invest against the grain."

Growth investing, on the other hand, appeals to quick-change artists. Sig Segalas, manager of Harbor Capital Appreciation, says: "You need to be optimistic but willing to move fast if things don't work out." The risk is that your companies won't deliver on their anticipated earnings. Because shareholders of growth firms often pay quickly and dearly for any earnings disappointment, you should accept the risk that your stock could tumble 20% or more on bad news.

All of the financial data that is discussed below can be found in reference books such as the *Value Line Investment Survey*, which is available in most major libraries. If you are wired into the Net, you can find similar information at investing sites such as http://www.wsrn.com. You can also find it at America Online's personal-finance site (keyword: finance).

Going for gains from growth. The easy part of investing in growth stocks is finding companies growing at 15% or 20% a year. The tough part is finding those that can continue their earnings streak into the future. Ideally, a growth stock should clear all five hurdles below. If it doesn't score on at least three, look elsewhere.

1. A five-year history of 15% earnings increases. Your starting point is the company's past profit growth. A five-year record of 15% gains—which would put the company in the top 25% of the S&P 500—shows you that growth is no fluke. Companies with these sterling records typically have dominant market share in an expanding industry like technology, health care or consumer products.

2. Projected earnings growth of 15% or more for five years. With most forecasters looking for the S&P's profit growth to slow, a reliable large-cap grower should be expected to deliver 15% or more profit growth next year and average the same amount over the following four. Because they are subject to frequent revision, however, earnings predictions are the shakiest pillar supporting the case for any growth stock. To minimize that uncertainty, stick with companies where the business plan expected to drive future growth is already securely in place.

3. A five-year record of 10% or better sales growth. If the bottom line is growing but sales are not, it may be an indication that earnings growth is coming entirely from cost cutting. Conversely, booming revenues and decreasing profits say the company is losing control of its outlays. Both mean that earnings will eventually stop growing. An ideal pick will show five-year growth on both the top and bottom lines.

4. A return on equity (ROE) of 20% or more in the past three years. This ratio, expressed as net income divided by shareholders' equity, measures the company's overall profitability. The higher the better—as long as the company hasn't leveraged its profits too much by taking on debt. In general, debt should not exceed 50¢ per $1 of shareholders' equity. Dave Fowler, co-manager of Vanguard U.S. Growth, looks for low-debt stocks whose ROE ranks in the top third of Standard & Poor's 500-stock index, which means 20% or better.

5. A price/earnings multiple that does not exceed the growth rate by more than 25%. Sometimes investors' expectations (as reflected in the stock's price) can be so high that even the sturdiest growth machine is bound to disappoint—with ugly consequences for shareholders. You can reduce that risk by comparing your stock's P/E based on its estimated next 12 months' earnings with its projected five-year earnings growth rate. If the P/E is more than 25% higher than the growth rate—for example, the P/E is 23 and the company is expected to grow 15% a year—the stock is in dangerous territory. Ideally, you would like to find a fast-growing company trading at a P/E less than its growth rate.

Profiting from undervalued firms. Value investors reject the growth buyer's obsession with predicting the future. They prefer to uncover undervalued assets in a company's here and now, even if it's not entirely clear how and when the market will ever realize that value. As Warren Buffett, the nation's most famous value investor, summed up his philosophy: "If I can buy a dollar for 50¢, something good might happen to me." The problem is that undervalued assets tend to reside only in companies that have run into difficulty or that are part of unpopular industries. So to protect yourself, look for:

1. A P/E lower than that of its peers. "If a stock is selling at a significant P/E discount to others in its industry, then it's worth a close look," says David Schafer.

2. A price-to-book-value ratio of less than 2.5. Book value, as you know from Finance 101, equals a company's assets minus its liabilities. So if the stock trades at less than its per-share book value, you can essentially buy the company for less than the value of the things it owns.

3. A debt-to-equity ratio of less than 50%. Investors don't buy value stocks, they marry them. So make sure that debt won't destroy your relationship. Value buyers, like many growth investors, usually consider 50¢ of debt for every $1 of shareholders' equity an adequate margin of safety. The lower the ratio, the less risk.

4. Consistent earnings growth over the past five years. To minimize their risk still further, bargain-hunting value investors also want steady or expanding profits.

DON'T OVERLOOK DRIPS

Even in a high-anxiety market, you still need to own equities. They remain the best way to keep your portfolio growing for a decade or more to meet such long-term goals as college for your kids and a comfortable retirement for yourself. Fortunately, at times when the market looks uncertain, a good way to buy such stocks is through the increasingly popular dividend-rein-vestment plans known as DRIPs. Their lash-yourself-to-the-mast investing discipline provides an almost painless way of piling up equities that works especially well when stock prices begin to dip and your dollars buy even more shares. About 1,100 companies now offer DRIPs, and experts predict that about 400 more will within four years.

Here's a short course on how DRIPs work: After you buy one or more shares of a company's stock, you can automatically reinvest your quarterly dividends in more shares through the firm's DRIP, often with no commissions. You can also buy additional shares through the same program either regularly or whenever you have some extra cash. Charles Carlson, a chartered financial analyst and editor of the monthly newsletter *DRIP Investor*, cites this example to demonstrate a DRIP's ability to build up your wealth: "If you had invested $10,000 in Standard & Poor's 500-stock index at the end of 1985 and not bothered to reinvest your dividends, you would have had $29,150 by the end of 1995. Had you reinvested the dividends, your total would have been more than $40,000."

As interest in DRIPs has swelled, many companies with the plans have been adding a wrinkle called direct investment. In a traditional DRIP, you acquire the initial share or shares through your broker, paying commissions of $25 to $45 at a discount firm and as much as $75 at a full-service broker. (You guessed it: The commissions can cost as much as your shares.) Then the broker must register the stock in your name while you find out how to enroll from the company's investor relations department.

To avoid this cumbersome, costly process, many companies will sell you shares directly, bypassing brokers. Since the Securities and Exchange Commission approved this kind of direct-investment plan at the end of 1994, the number of companies offering them has risen from 52 to more than 300.

However, as DRIPs and direct-purchase plans have grown more popular, companies have increasingly begun to charge stiff fees for their investment services. High fees aren't the only problem with some DRIPs; another is slow execution of orders to buy or sell shares. Many companies batch orders into round lots of 100 shares and fill them when it is convenient. Or they may fill them only once a month, thereby trading shares for you even if the price has moved temporarily against you. Because of these drawbacks, don't invest through a DRIP unless you can answer yes to the following questions:

First, are the fees low? Next, do you plan to hold the stock for five years or longer? You might not emulate billionaire investor Warren Buffett, who likes to say, "My ideal holding period is infinity." But direct investing makes the most sense if you expect to own the stock for at least five years and preferably longer. Over shorter periods, you lose the compounding effect of reinvesting dividends in additional shares.

Finally, would you buy the stock even if there were no DRIP? A dividend-reinvestment plan is an attractive perk for a stock you want to own anyway. But a DRIP isn't a sufficient reason by itself to buy shares, mainly because you can't usually count on the timely execution of your order. Thus the best DRIP candidates are stocks with steadily growing earnings and bright long-term prospects. Regularly rising dividends are also a plus. That's because over five years or more, a sensible investor wouldn't mind buying such stocks at increasingly high prices in a rising market—or picking up more shares in a downmarket—since he or she would almost certainly make a substantial profit in the end.

RISKS AND REWARDS OF SELLING SHORT

How can you hedge against loss in a sliding market? One strategy is to go short—that is, borrow shares from your broker, sell them and then buy them back for less money after the price of the stock has fallen. Your profit is the difference between what you received when you sold the borrowed shares and what you paid to replace them, minus brokerage commissions. Though short-selling can be an extremely high-risk move for reasons we'll explain in a minute, used properly and limited to no more than 5% to 10% of the value of your portfolio, it can also be an effective hedge.

You must, however, consider the risks. First tip: This is not a strategy to be pursued by anyone who is afraid of getting gored. You can lose many times the value of your initial investment when you go short. "Your losses are potentially unlimited," says Harry Strunk, a Palm Beach, Fla. broker who keeps data on the performance of short-sellers.

Here's why the risk is high. Suppose you buy 200 shares of a $50 stock. What's the worst that can happen to you? The company files for bankruptcy, and you lose your entire $10,000. Yes, that's very painful. Now suppose that you short 200 shares of a $50 stock. But instead of falling, the stock triples. The $50 stock becomes a $150 stock. To replace the 200 borrowed shares and close out your position, you've got to pay $30,000. That's not painful—that's excruciating. It's also the reason why Gerald Kuschuk, a senior vice president with Prudential Securities, calls shorting "the most hazardous strategy out there for the individual investor."

Before you embark on your first short sale, most experts recommend that you have securities or cash in your account worth 100% of the value of the shares you are shorting. Brokerage rules call for 50% when you make the trade and at least 25% to 30% in your account as collateral after that. Put up just 50%, however, and you could be forced to cough up more cash or securities as collateral if the stock rises more than 10%. Fail to come up with the green, and the firm can close your position without telling you, saddling you with hefty losses.

You can minimize your risk by observing the following rules:

Start small. Begin by shorting 100 shares to see how the process works. And keep your short holdings small in relation to your total portfolio, and varied. Says Paul McEntire, chairman of Skye Investment Advisors, a Los Gatos, Calif. money manager who specializes in short-selling: "If you allocate 10% or 15% of your portfolio to a single short position and the stock quadruples, you can wipe out years of good investing."

So, diversify among three to 10 stocks. When a shorted stock moves against you, it becomes a bigger part of your portfolio and the risk gets greater. Use at least a handful of shorts to prevent one from overwhelming your portfolio.

Set a limit to your losses. Most experts suggest that you close out a short position if a stock rises roughly 25% above where you sold it. Once the stock reaches your limit, close out your trade. Otherwise, you can take a pounding from so-called momentum investors, who jump into stocks on the rise, pushing their prices (and your short-selling losses) even higher. You can short the stock again once it ceases its upward spiral.

Do your own homework. You can't expect your broker to help you pick a short candidate. Says Sal Campo, a managing director at Smith Barney: "A broker might call you up and say that a company is a good buy, but he's not going to call and say: 'This company's overvalued. Why don't you short it?'" That's because analysts at big brokerage firms are loath to write negative reports on the companies they cover for fear that the brokerage will lose the outfit's investment banking business. And firms usually prohibit their brokers from initiating discussions on companies that aren't covered by their analysts.

That means you'll have to come up with your own ideas. One strategy is to piggyback on the work of more sophisticated investors by putting money in the most heavily shorted stocks. These are listed in monthly tables that appear in *The Wall Street Journal* and other newspapers, usually under the heading "Short Interest Highlights." But be sure to ask your broker whether the stock is hard to borrow; if he says yes, stay away. Another option is to subscribe to a stock rating service such as Value Line Investment Survey, which ranks stocks in terms of whether you should buy them from 1 (best) to 5 (worst). Look at the bottom end of those lists instead of the top end.

STAY AWAY FROM ANNUITY TRAPS

You have undoubtedly heard the pitch for those endearingly complex insurance-company-sponsored contraptions called tax-deferred annuities. The devices work something like this: You put in as much cash as you want at one end, then watch the gears mesh, the wheels whir and—presto!—out from the other end comes a great deal more money. No wonder, then, that at the end of 1995 annuity assets had reached $536 billion, up 450% in a decade, according to the American Council of Life Insurance. But unfortunately, for most investors the annuity machine—part investment, part insurance—doesn't work nearly as well as promised.

To be sure, there's nothing Rube Goldbergish about annuities' central advantage, tax deferral. As is also true with 401(k)s and Individual Retirement Accounts, your money compounds without being taxed, so that over time you come out with much more than if you had to share your gains with Uncle Sam year after year. When you withdraw your money, the investment earnings are taxed as ordinary income, and if you cash out before age 59 1/2, you have to pay an additional 10% tax penalty. Unlike many other tax-deferred plans, however, annuities don't give you a current tax deduction on the money you invest; on the other hand, there are no annual limits on the amount you can contribute.

But what really makes annuities iffier than their tax-deferred cousins is the other baggage they come with. There are three kinds of annuities: fixed, which offer a fixed rate of return (recent average: 6%); index, whose returns are pegged to some market measure like Standard & Poor's 500-stock index; and variable, essentially a collection of mutual funds wrapped in a thin layer of insurance. All have their own problems, as you will see.

In fact, our objections to index and fixed annuities are serious enough that we're going to cut to the chase: Forget 'em. Most index products limit your returns to about 80% of the price gains in the index they are tied to, and dividend income is not included in the calculations. As a result, your earnings will pale next to what you could make in a regular index mutual fund.

With fixed annuities, which promise an unvarying interest rate, you face a different set of woes. Prime among them: the sponsor's own early-with-drawal charges for taking your money out before the annuity contract expires. These typically begin at 7% of your gains and decline thereafter—and they come on top of the 10% penalty that Uncle Sam extracts for early withdrawal. The effect is that you are essentially trapped in the product, and that can get mighty depressing if rates rise substantially after you invest. Asks Lisa Osofsky, a financial planner in Edison, N.J.: "Why tie up your money? There are other options for people who want a fixed return and low risk, like a short-term municipal bond fund."

That leaves variable annuities. Offering both tax deferral and a shot at market gains, variables accounted for $202 billion of annuity assets last year. The typical variable contract lets you invest a minimum of $500 to $5,000 in any of 10 or so stock and bond funds—called subaccounts—ranging from aggressive growth to conservative fixed income. Often the funds are created and managed especially for the annuity, either by the annuity's insurance company sponsor or by well-known mutual fund groups like Vanguard, Scudder and T. Rowe Price. In other cases, the annuities include funds similar to the retail funds you can buy directly from the fund companies.

Well and good so far. But the catch is that variable annuities have such high expenses that unless you can put away money for 17 years or more, you're better off investing in a no-load mutual fund and forgoing the tax benefits. When you own a variable annuity, each year you are nicked not only for standard mutual fund management fees, but also for mortality charges and expense-guarantee fees. The mortality charge (a.k.a. the insurance) guarantees that your heirs will receive at least your original investment should you die before you begin withdrawals. The expense fee protects you against an increase in your other fees. Says Harold Evensky, a financial planner in Coral Gables, Fla.: "These are long-term investments, so the chance that the account value at the annuity holder's death will be less than his investment is infinitesimal. Moreover, any fee increase is likely to amount to less than you'll pay in expense fees over the life of the contract."

The fees don't stop there. There's also the annual contract charge or service fee and, finally, surrender charges for taking your money out before the agreed-upon withdrawal date. Surrender charges run between 5% and 10% of your investment, although they typically expire after seven to 10 years. The end result is that all the fees so erode your returns that it can take as long as 17 years for the benefits of tax deferral to kick in and outweigh the expenses.

What's more, unless you annuitize—that is, start withdrawing your money on a regular basis—or pull it out all at once, your beneficiaries will have to pay income taxes in their tax bracket when they inherit the annuity. If the amount exceeds $600,000, they'll owe estate taxes as well. Other investments like stocks and bonds are valued as of the day of your death, and when the assets are sold, the beneficiaries will owe capital-gains taxes only on the difference between the inherited value and the realized price. (As with annuities, they will also owe estate taxes if the value exceeds $600,000.)

If you can afford to put money away for a very long time, then variable annuities can make sense provided you meet some other criteria:

You have maxed out on your 401(k) and IRA or other tax-sheltered accounts. "Annuities will never beat the benefits of other tax-sheltered retirement accounts like pre-tax savings and the employer match," says Cincinnati financial planner Michael Chasnoff. "So use those up first."

You want to protect assets from creditors. Depending on how your state's bankruptcy law is written, a tax-deferred annuity can shelter money from your creditors. But this is also true for IRAs and 401(k)s.

Finally, a last word of advice: Don't gild the lily by putting an annuity in another tax-sheltered account like an IRA. "This is one of the biggest mistakes annuity investors make," says David Bugen, a financial planner in Chatham, N.J. The annuity's tax shelter, for which you are paying those enormous fees, becomes superfluous in another tax-sheltered account.

GET THE HIGHEST YIELDS FOR YOUR CASH

If you're among the 20 million Americans who keep cash in a bank money-market deposit account, you're earning a puny return, about 2.6%. You can do better than that with money-market mutual funds, which recently paid an average of 5.16%. And you can get the highest yield of all by choosing your money fund wisely. Since federal rules sharply limit the risks that such funds can take, they all invest in similar securities. So the only surefire way to get above-average yields is to invest in a fund with below-average annual fees—that is, less than 0.58% of assets.

Unfortunately, you can't identify such a fund simply by looking at its yield. Funds sometimes boost their payouts about half a percentage point by temporarily waiving most fees—a marketing gimmick to attract new deposits. When the waivers expire, possibly within the next six months, the yields drop.

Instead, use this strategy: Go for a money fund with a low deposit limit and permanently low fees. If you're in the 36% tax bracket or higher—1998 taxable income above $155,950 for married joint filers; $77,975 for singles— you can pocket even more by putting your cash in a tax-exempt money fund. If a tax-exempt fund doesn't make sense for you, you might consider putting your cash in a short-term bond fund. But beware: Unlike money funds, whose shares stay fixed at $1, the value of your assets in a short-term bond fund will drop—albeit only slightly—when interest rates rise.

DON'T GET SUCKERED BY STOCK SCAMS

Suppose you pick up the phone and this is what you're told: "I probably hear more ideas in the morning going down to have coffee than your broker hears in an entire week. By the time we go home here on Wall Street... I'm showing you 30 to 40 to 50 percent on your money...I want to see you own the stock...You take 300 shares now, on my timing and pricing." Then you're addressed by your first name and asked, "How do you typically title your accounts?"

A broker did deliver that cold-call telephone pitch last July, trying to convince an individual investor he'd never met to buy 1,000 shares of a small software firm, based on a promise that the stock's price would triple within three months. Unfortunately for the broker, he hooked the wrong fish. At the other end of the line was J. Matthew Jenkins, a director of the Utah Division

SHOULD YOU BANK WITH YOUR BROKER?

Fed up with your bank's niggling fees and low rates on deposits? If so, America's major brokerage houses are eager to cash in on your ire by signing you up for an asset management account. Launched 20 years ago as a pricey perk for wealthy investors, today such accounts offer everything from no-fee check writing to debit cards and online bill paying, so you can pay the plumber and get money from an automated teller machine (ATM) as easily as you can with a bank checking account. And brokers will pay you higher interest rates on your idle cash than banks do.

Asset management accounts make most sense for people who already invest with a broker and don't often need to visit a bank branch to make deposits or conduct other business. But an asset management account won't save you from fees. For example, some brokerages charge annual account fees of $50 to $100.

To help you decide whether an asset management account is right for you, here is a look at how brokerages compare with bank accounts in key areas.

▶ **Account minimums.** To get unlimited free check writing, you'll need to keep $5,000 to $20,000 at a brokerage. True, that's well above the typical $2,000 that banks require you to have on deposit to qualify for free interest-bearing checking. But at a brokerage, the entire value of the stocks, bonds, mutual funds and cash in your brokerage account is counted toward the minimum. Moreover, the cash portion of your brokerage account—against which you write your checks—sits in a money-market fund, with a typical yield slightly higher than 5%, compared to less than 3% for the average bank money-market account.

▶ **ATM transaction fees.** You may wind up paying as much as $2 for each ATM withdrawal you make from an asset management account. Reason: Most of the brokerages we surveyed charge as much as $1 for each ATM withdrawal. In addition, because brokerages don't run their own ATMs, you run a high risk of paying a $1 surcharge to the ATM operator. By comparison, at least 90% of banks don't charge their customers for withdrawals made from the bank's own ATMs.

▶ **Overdraft protection.** To get overdraft protection with your broker, you need to establish a margin line of credit. Your coverage will generally equal up to half the value of the securities in your portfolio. If you're ever overdrawn, your brokerage will typically charge you interest of 9% or so on the amount of overdraft protection you need. To compare, your bank will generally charge you 18% for overdraft protection.

▶ **Deposit insurance.** The Securities Investor Protection Corporation (SIPC), an industry-funded group, provides insurance for as much as $100,000 of the cash you hold in your brokerage account. The Federal Deposit Insurance Corporation covers all individual bank checking accounts for $100,000 per person at each institution.

▶ **Canceled checks.** Instead of returning your canceled checks, a brokerage will simply list your transactions on your monthly statement. For a copy of the draft, you'll have to pay $2 to $3. Most banks still return your originals each month.

of Securities, who recorded the call, capturing what he describes as three classic elements of a stock scam: the lure of lofty returns, a claim of inside connections, and a pressurized pitch to open an account on the spot.

Utah authorities filed administrative charges against the broker, alleging that, among other things, he gave false and misleading information to an investor. But they knew that even if the charges stuck, he likely would face only a few thousand dollars in fines or a few months' suspension. The penalties are hardly severe enough to stop such hustles.

So if you haven't already been targeted by a fast-talking salesman reading a script, chances are you will. State securities regulators contend that stock fraud has tripled since 1989.

Regulators add that they are facing cagier crooks. For example, responding to rampant ripoffs in low-priced shares known as penny stocks, Congress passed legislation in 1990 requiring rigorous disclosure for stocks selling for less than $5 a share. Deceitful brokers have adapted by hawking equally problematic stocks priced at just over five bucks. Another recent ploy is The Name Drop. To put skeptical investors at ease, a slippery broker implies that his tiny, little-known shop is associated with a Wall Street powerhouse. In reality, the prestigious firm typically is acting only as a clearing agent—that is, executing trades and sending out account statements for the small brokerage.

Problem brokerage firms often manage to avoid being drummed out of the business for years. So to help you protect yourself from scamsters, MONEY gathered advice from state securities regulators, attorneys general and officials at agencies like the Securities and Exchange Commission (SEC) and the National Association of Securities Dealers (NASD). What follows are four of the latest pitches that sleazy brokers are likely to spring on you—followed by advice on what you should do if you are targeted.

Promising an inside deal.
At the heart of virtually every stock scam is a promise of huge, quick gains—often 50% to 100% over a period of a few days or weeks. If investors express skepticism, rogue brokers often claim, falsely, that they are privy to special deals or inside information, or are able to grab stocks at below-market prices.

Denver investor Carol Reed, 54, let a broker convince her to sink $50,000 into an investment that could supposedly provide a substantial profit within two or three days. Reed admits she didn't know exactly what he wanted her to invest in. But, she says, "I trusted him because he worked at a major brokerage firm and was a friend of my sister's." Reed didn't even get suspicious when the broker told her to wire her $50,000 to his personal bank account.

He claimed that to take advantage of this special opportunity, he had to invest the money with another brokerage.

Months passed, but the great returns never materialized. In addition, the broker talked Reed into investing more of her money in a variety of tiny speculative firms. Eventually, with her losses totalling $86,000, Reed hired an attorney to look into her investments. Through Denver District Attorney William Ritter, she found that she was one of at least 10 investors who had been taken by the broker for more than $436,000.

To protect yourself, never invest with a broker who touts quick gains that are double or triple the gains of reputable stocks. Legitimate investments don't provide those kinds of profits. Be wary if a broker suggests buying investments outside your regular brokerage account. That tactic, known as "trading away," is almost always a tip-off that the broker is pushing a phony investment and doesn't want his firm to know. If your broker proposes such an arrangement, call the brokerage's compliance department. If that doesn't bring action, contact your state securities regulator, whose number is available from the North American Association of State Securities Regulators (888-84NASAA; www.nasaa.org) or the NASD (800-289-9999; www.nasdr.com).

Bait-and-switch. When agents from a task force of securities regulators from four states raided five suspect brokerage firms last February, they turned up more than 100 cold-call scripts. One insidious sales tactic that shows up again and again in these scripts is a version of the old bait-and-switch. Essentially, a dishonest broker convinces you to invest a relatively small amount, say $1,000, so he can prove how good he is. Within weeks, the stock he's peddled appears to climb to big gains. (In fact, in the case of a penny stock, the broker has usually driven the share price up by pushing it on other investors.)

Having won your confidence, the broker then calls back and tells you it's time to make some real money, and pressures you to invest $10,000 or more. The second stock is usually one the broker bought for himself, sometimes for pennies a share, before pushing up its price by reeling in other investors. Once you invest at the inflated price, the broker will begin dumping his shares, driving the price down and leaving you with big losses.

To protect yourself, don't go along when a broker asks you to start small and then asks for a much larger subsequent investment. To avoid stocks that brokers can manipulate easily, stick with issues that trade on the New York Stock Exchange, the American Stock Exchange or the Nasdaq National Market.

Trading without your permission. Virtually all brokers are compensated by the commissions and other fees they generate when they trade securities for customers' accounts. That arrangement creates a powerful incentive for them to induce you to buy and sell stocks. In some cases, brokers go further and trade without informing you, or even against your wishes.

To protect yourself, before doing business with a broker, especially with a little-known firm, check his and his firm's record with state regulators and the NASD. If you feel a broker is unduly pressuring you, complain to the compliance officers at the brokerage, as well as regulators. If the brokerage doesn't act, or if you find that others of its clients have complained about similar tactics, move your account to another firm.

Promising safety but delivering risk. Leona Svogar, 70, met a broker shortly after her husband died. Having no experience in financial matters, she was looking for someone to help her manage her money in retirement. "All I wanted was a place to put my money that would allow me to take so much out a month and keep the rest of it growing steadily," she says. She claims that the broker agreed to help her do that, and she eventually invested nearly $400,000 with him.

But the broker immediately began investing Svogar's stash in small companies, including a Canadian telecommunications firm. Even as that telcom stock began to slide, he continued to buy and sell more shares over a 15-month period, generating $49,000 in losses for Svogar. "I was getting concerned, but he always told me not to worry—that he'd take care of it," Svogar says. After racking up $211,000 in losses in the Canadian telcom company and other stocks, Svogar filed a complaint with the NASD, alleging, among other things, misrepresentation and negligence. That same month, the brokerage house fired the man and ultimately paid Svogar $200,000 to settle the matter.

To protect yourself, make sure that you and your broker agree on how your money should be invested. Prepare written investing goals together, including examples of holdings that are—and are not—appropriate. If your broker then takes risks that make you uncomfortable, switch your account immediately. Accepting excuses and waiting can be the biggest risk of all.

WHAT TO ASK BROKERS BEFORE YOU INVEST

Yes, there's lots of scamming going on by cold-calling brokers. But some very profitable client/broker relationships have started with cold calls.

In fact, cold-calling is perfectly acceptable to the National Association of Securities Dealers, which regulates the activities of more than 500,000 registered brokers. But NASD has laid down specific rules for cold calls. For instance, they may not be made before 8 a.m. or after 9 p.m. A broker must tell you his or her name, the name of the firm, its address and phone number, and the purpose of the call.

Even if a broker has followed those rules, you should take a few precautions before you act on any of his or her ideas. Ask these questions:

Where did you get my name? A reputable broker will describe how she obtained your name and be willing to acknowledge she's making a cold call. She should also be willing to explain why the investment she's recommending is appropriate for someone like you. If what you hear instead is, "This is a once-in-a-lifetime opportunity, and if you don't grab it you'll be the loser," hang up.

If the idea seems to make sense, however, tell the broker that you're not ready to buy now. "You don't buy stocks over the phone from someone you've never met before," advises Nancy Smith, director of the Securities and Exchange Commission's office of investor education and assistance. Suggest that the broker call you again when she gets other ideas that she thinks might interest you. If she wants you as a client, you'll hear from her. In the meantime, you can track how her recommendations perform. Then, if she continues to impress you, make an appointment to meet her in her office.

What's your background? Some brokers are more highly qualified than others, but there are basics they all must meet. They and their firms must be licensed with state securities regulators and registered with the NASD, which administers a series of tests that qualify brokers to sell securities. Ideally, you want someone who has at least five to 10 years' experience and has been with his or her firm for at least two years, says financial planner Paul Westbrook of Ridgewood, N.J. If your meeting is the result of a cold call, however, the broker isn't likely to have had much experience, so look for a college degree in a financial field as well as the appropriate registrations.

Don't be shy about inquiring if the broker has ever been disciplined by the SEC, a state securities regulator or any other organization. Next, double-check whatever the broker tells you. Donald J. Reis, Nevada Deputy Secretary of State for Securities Regulation, recommends that you ask for the broker's CRD (Central Registration Depository) number, which will identify him in NASD's database. Call NASD's public disclosure number (800-289-9999) for background information on the broker, including education, where he has worked and his disciplinary history. State regulators also track brokers by CRD number, and their databases may have more detailed information. To get the phone number of your state's authority, call your state government's central number or use your computer to visit the North American Securities Administrators Association Internet directory (http://www.nasaa.org/regulator/index.html). If your search turns up allegations of churning, making unauthorized trades or failure to execute trades, take your business elsewhere.

Why is this investment for me? Any security the broker recommends should suit your age, financial circumstances and risk tolerance. For example, if you are three years from retirement and unable to bear the thought of losing any principal, you don't want to invest in flighty tech stocks. To help guide you to suitable investments, the broker should inquire about your income, financial obligations, assets, debts and investment experience. If the broker doesn't ask probing questions about your finances and your investment objectives, don't open an account. "The broker must understand who you are and why you are investing before recommending a stock to you," says Gail Wickes, a senior vice president at PaineWebber. "It's like a doctor needing to know what other medication you're taking before giving you a new prescription."

Does the tip have ulterior motives? This is an awkward question, and you won't get a straight answer from a dishonest broker. So you'll have to watch for signs of hidden motives. For instance, if the broker recommends that you buy shares of a company's initial public offering or of a secondary offering, he may be in line for an extra commission. Moreover, brokers are sometimes more highly compensated if they sell securities the firm owns. The stock might be an excellent investment even though the broker receives a bigger commission for selling it, but you should know whether that is influencing his or her judgment.

Unfortunately, brokers are not required to tell you anything about how they are compensated, nor do they have to reveal normal and standard business dealings their firms may have with a recommended company, such as an investment banking relationship. Thus Michael Jones, NASD vice president of the office of individual investor services, suggests that you ask flat out whether the broker is in line for any special financial incentive or is involved in any sales contest—say, Win a Week in Waikiki! If you doubt the answer, check with the broker's branch manager or compliance officer.

Not all discussions of risk are equally enlightening, however. Some fund companies, such as John Hancock, T. Rowe Price and Vanguard, do a fine job explaining how you might lose money. But most other prospectuses are loaded with lists of potential hazards designed primarily to protect the fund companies from lawsuits, not to inform investors. If you can't tell which risks are the serious ones, dig deeper by checking out Morningstar's free Website (www.morningstar.net) or *Morningstar Mutual Funds*, available at most local libraries.

BANK NOTES THAT COME WITH A CATCH

There is a relatively new product called retail deposit notes. They are issued by banks, are federally insured and are similar to certificates of deposit. They have longer maturities than CDs and pay higher interest rates—recently 7%. But this investment is not quite as good as it sounds.

Here's why. It's true these notes are FDIC-insured up to $100,000 and pay higher rates than conventional CDs do. But there are a few catches. The minimum investment is $1,000, vs. $500 for a typical CD. Plus, those longer maturities of seven to 15 years, vs. three months to five years for CDs, aren't quite what they seem. Unlike CDs, the notes are callable by the bank, typically after four years. So you can't be certain you're locking in your rate for the full term, as you can with a CD. And if you need to cash out early, you or your broker will have to find a buyer, which may be tough to do since there's no established resale market for the notes.

If you crave government protection for your investment and you want a seven- to 15-year maturity, you're probably better off buying intermediate-term U.S. Treasury notes. You may sacrifice some yield but they won't be called and, if you want to sell, there's a ready market.

KEY MOVES AT LIFE'S BIG MOMENTS

The money decisions you make at life's major crossroads can have a disproportionate effect on your finances. By making the right moves at watershed moments, such as having a baby or changing jobs, you can ensure that you get the most out of your money and, hopefully, out of your life. Here are some of the crucial events that occur during your life—and the key financial moves you need to make at those times:

Getting married (or remarried). Because Americans are marrying later—the median age for first marriages is 27 for men and 25 for women, vs. 25 and 22, respectively, in 1980—they are increasingly set in their financial ways before they wed. To avoid nasty surprises, Olivia Mellon, a Washington, D.C. psychotherapist who specializes in money issues, advises couples to give each other a full accounting of their debts, investments and spending patterns, and agree on a budget before getting hitched. Also, with 1.2 million couples divorcing annually in the U.S., you should consider a prenuptial agreement (which spells out how assets will be divided in case of divorce) if you or your intended has children from a previous relationship, if one partner owns a business or if one partner earns significantly more than the other or has significant assets he or she doesn't want to share.

This is a time to make sure you're prepared for emergencies. If you haven't already set aside three to six months' worth of living expenses to cover you in case of a crisis like losing your job, now is the time to do so. Stash the cash in a safe, short-term account such as the top-yielding money funds listed earlier in the chapter. It's time, too, for breadwinners who aren't covered by a disability insurance policy at work to find coverage on their own, and to be sure they're saving enough for retirement and other goals like college education and a house.

Having a baby. Save. Save. Save. According to the U.S. Department of Agriculture, the total cost of raising a child born in 1993 to age 17 is a staggering $334,000, and that's before Junior heads off to college. Today's newborn will face nearly $100,000 in tuition, room and board bills for four years at a state college, according to education financial counselors, and about $200,000 at a private school. And to be certain your growing family is adequately protected, analyze and rethink your insurance. Health insurance is a must. For guidance on other protection, see "The Insurance Most People Need" on page 115. You should write a will, too. Both you and your spouse need one to ensure an orderly distribution of assets and to name a guardian for your child if you die.

Changing (or losing) your job. Stay covered. If you're being laid off or if there is a waiting period before your new job's health coverage kicks in, tell the benefits department of the company you're leaving that you want to continue your existing coverage under the terms of the Consolidated Omnibus Budget Reconciliation Act (COBRA). This law says that companies with more than 20 employees must guarantee departing workers the right to carry their coverage for as long as 18 months, at about the same group-rate premium their employer had been paying.

Remember also to maintain your disability coverage. And keep your retirement funds shielded from taxes. According to the Employee Benefits Research Institute in Washington, D.C., an alarming 58.5% of Americans who receive a lump-sum distribution from a retirement plan upon leaving their job don't roll over the funds into a similar plan at their new company or into an IRA. Such a mistake will cost you dearly if you're younger than 59. You'll generally pay income taxes and a 10% penalty on the money, and you'll have to start saving for retirement anew.

Getting divorced. Cut your financial ties fast. New York City certified financial planner Melissa Levine says that separated or divorcing spouses should initiate independent relationships with financial service providers as soon as possible. Notify brokerage firms, credit-card companies and other lenders in writing that you are no longer responsible for newly incurred debts of your soon-to-be ex. "You want to make sure your spouse doesn't rack up debts or make investments that you're on the hook for," Levine explains.

Take the time to look before you leap into a settlement. Although divorce is costly—legal fees alone can range from $3,500 to $5,000 a person for even the simplest split—avoid the temptation to settle quickly. As Chicago financial planner Ellen Rogin notes, "Many people agree on terms that seem ideal at the moment but prove disastrous over time." One example: insisting on ownership of a house as part of a settlement, only to find that one salary is not enough to maintain the property. The smarter move: Tally your expected future income and expenses before making any decision. And take taxes into account. Rogin advises many separated couples who are not yet divorced to opt for "married filing separately" status when completing their tax returns. "Filing jointly may be cheaper," she says, "but when you sign that return, you're taking responsibility for the actions of someone from whom you want to distance yourself."

Receiving an inheritance. Hurry up and wait. Some 58% of Americans ages 30 to 59 expect to receive an inheritance worth a median $125,000, according to a 1997 study by Phoenix Home Life Mutual Insurance of Hartford. However much you receive, says St. Louis financial planner Don Kukla, "You'll be grieving for the death of a loved one, so you probably won't be emotionally prepared to make sound financial decisions

THE INSURANCE MOST PEOPLE NEED

We want to help you make sure you have all the protection you need without paying too much for it. You can compare your coverage against this handy checklist in about an hour.

▶ **Auto.** You should have liability insurance (which protects you against claims by people injured in an accident) and uninsured motorist coverage (which comes to your aid when you're involved in an accident with someone who has little or no insurance) of at least $100,000 per person and $300,000 per accident. That's two or three times more than many states require. But we think it's the minimum you need to protect your assets. To save money on your premiums, consider raising the deductible on the collision and comprehensive portions of your policy, which covers accidental damage and theft, among other things, to $500 from the standard $200. That would mean you would foot a bigger portion of any repair bills. But it could cut your premium costs $50 to $100 a year.

▶ **Life.** If you support a family, you generally need coverage equal to six to eight times your annual salary. If your spouse works, each of you should be insured for six to eight times your annual pay. The coverage won't guarantee your survivors a lifetime of luxury. But it would give them time to adjust to their new circumstances without worrying about bills going unpaid. Life insurance should be used to protect your survivors, not to build an investment stake. That's why we recommend term insurance, especially for people under 40, rather than whole life. These policies initially cost seven to 10 times more per year than term and double as a tax-deferred savings vehicle.

▶ **Homeowners.** By one estimate, 50,000 homes are totally destroyed each year by fire alone. To guard against such a disaster, you want insurance that will pay enough to rebuild. It's sometimes called a guaranteed replacement cost policy. If you simply buy coverage equal to what you paid for your home, or its current market value, you may be buying much less or much more insurance than you really need.

▶ **Liability.** Usually purchased in conjunction with auto or homeowners insurance, a so-called umbrella liability policy could provide valuable protection when you are sued. We suggest at least $1 million worth of such coverage. That's a lot of peace of mind for the price: about $200 a year.

▶ **Disability.** Four out of 10 workers will become disabled by injury or illness for more than 90 days at some point in their working lives. When you are unable to work, disability insurance provides a means of support. Many employers provide it free or for a nominal charge. If yours does not, or if you're self-employed, you'll have to purchase it on your own. The typical annual cost is $650 for a policy that will provide at least 60% of a $50,000 annual income for the rest of your normal working life (generally to age 65).

▶ **Policies you don't need.** To conclude your checkup, cancel any insurance that's not worth the cost. High on the list of dubious ones are credit life insurance and mortgage life insurance, which pay off your debts when you die. A much cheaper alternative is to buy sufficient term life insurance to cover your liabilities.

right away." Kukla advises clients to park their inheritance in a money-market mutual fund for six months or so. "By then you'll have a better idea of your long-term needs and goals," he says—and you can invest the windfall accordingly. Most important, steer clear of fast-buck financial advice. Work the new money into your overall life-long financial plan, and if you need help, consider consulting a certified fee-only financial adviser.

BOOST PROFITS WITH THE INTERNET

When you're doing financial research on the Internet do you ever feel like you waste your first hour mired in search engines or chasing dead-end leads? Well, we're about to make your life simpler. The key financial Websites we've identified below can answer many, if not most, of your Web queries. You can add these sites to your browser's bookmark file by clicking "Bookmarks" on the Netscape Navigator browser's tool bar or, if you use Microsoft Internet Explorer, the "Favorites" button. Once you do that, you're just a mouse click away from everything from the latest stock market news and mutual fund performance stats to the best rates on certificates of deposits and home and auto loans. Of course, you'll want to add more of your own favorites as you explore the more than 10,000 money-related sites scattered around the Net. But for a solid foundation of web resources, these seven—plus, of course, MONEY's own award-winning site, money.com—are the place to start.

Stock research. Whenever you're looking for timely research on a specific stock, make **Yahoo Finance** (quote.yahoo.com) your first stop. It's easily the fastest, most concise source for stock quotes and company research on the Net. You simply type in the ticker symbol of the stock you're interested in, and Yahoo instantly lays out that day's opening trading price, the previous day's close, the latest trade (delayed about 20 minutes)—and as many as ten recent news stories about the company. With a few clicks of the mouse, you can also summon additional stats, including dividend payments, price/earnings ratios, earnings estimates and share prices over the past five years. The site maintains connections to thousands of other financial sites. So after looking up a company's stock price, for example, you can also order the firm's annual report online by clicking on the hypertext link to the **ICB** site (www.icbinc.com).

Mutual Funds. An instant hit when it made its debut in early 1997, **Morningstar.Net** (www.morningstar.net) remains the single best site for serious fund investors. The biggest draw: free in-depth reports on more than 7,200 funds containing crucial data such as historical returns, risk ratings and expense ratios. Since its launch, the site has been improving steadily, primarily in its editorial features and fund analysis. However, the site's fund screening program introduced in August has been limiting you to two criteria at a time whenever you screen for funds. Until you're able to instantly view all the criteria you need on the Morningstar site, you should screen for top-performing funds at the Analysis section of **Stockpoint** (www.stockpoint.com).

Financial calculators. **FinanCenter** (www.financenter.com) has more than 100 online calculators that can help you grapple with the heavy-duty number crunching that inevitably crops up in areas ranging from investing for retirement to choosing the best home mortgage. Go to the site's credit-card calculator, for example, and you can quickly see that switching from a card with a 21% interest rate to one with a 14% rate will save you $202 in credit charges if you repay a $5,000 balance over two years. Wondering how much you must sock away beginning at age 40 to retire with $1 million at 65? The retirement planning calculator has the answer: $1,690 a month, assuming you earn 8% annually on your investments. You can even perform more sophisticated calculations, such as figuring out a bond's yield to maturity. That useful piece of information can help you determine whether those muni bonds your broker has been bugging you to buy really pay a competitive rate of return.

Savings and borrowing rates. Whether you're looking to stash some cash in a high-yielding bank CD or grab a low-rate auto or home loan, **Bank Rate Monitor** (www.bankrate.com) is the site to visit. Each week BRM surveys over 3,000 banks, credit unions and other financial institutions, and lists the best deals on its Website. Borrowers can find the lowest loan rates offered by lenders in more than 121 cities, as well as the average local rate on everything from mortgages to home-equity and car loans. In most cases, you must still call the bank's 800 number to request an application for a CD or loan. But BRM also lists 200 institutions that allow you to download the application to your computer directly from the Website.

Taxes. Whether you want to calculate how much you are likely to owe the IRS under the provisions of the new 1997 tax act or to learn how to file taxes for a nanny or other child-care provider, you'll get accurate answers fast by logging on to **Ernst & Young** (www.ey.com/tax), accounting firm Ernst & Young's site. Other helpful tidbits include lists of the 50 most overlooked deductions (No. 1, self servingly enough: fees for tax preparation services and IRS audits) and 25 most common sources of mistakes on tax forms (No. 1, not surprisingly: math errors). Of course, you will also want to take in the site's "tax toons," an assortment of cartoon strips that brings a tax accountant's touch to knee-slapping topics like the taxation of jointly owned property.

HOW TO AVOID ONLINE BROKER SNAFUS

Every back office makes errors, so it's not surprising that the 30-plus online brokerages occasionally slip up as well. Still, to judge from postings in online chat rooms and bulletin boards, the nascent Internet brokerage industry is enlisting a small army of unhappy customers. Their messages range from calm admonitions to howls of frustration.

There's probably less to all this cyberkvetching than meets the eye, however. Sure, customer amenities at online brokerages are minimal—but like other discount brokers, they were never meant to be fancy. And, yes, some online brokerages added customers before they had the capacity to serve them—but that's not surprising in an industry that grew an estimated 50% last year to 1.5 million customers. In fact, the SEC says that while complaints about online brokerages are on the rise, they are minuscule compared with those lodged against traditional brokers, making up only 1.4% of all protests filed since May.

Indeed, those who follow this burgeoning industry maintain that problems are concentrated among hyperactive investors known as day traders, whose rapid-fire strategies strain both the brokerages and the Internet's own traffic control. "Investors who aren't frequent traders have far fewer complaints," says Michael Amland, president of Benchmark Computers, an Internet consulting firm in Norfolk.

Balance the traders' laments against the real benefits of online investing for the typical buy-and-hold investor. Log on to **PC Financial Network**, for example, and you have a choice of analysts' earnings reports, real-time stock quotes and business news from Reuters. And commissions rarely come cheaper—as low as $9 for any trade at **Scottsdale**. When you consider that the least expensive order placed by phone at Charles Schwab would cost $39, it's easier to put online brokerages' growing pains in perspective.

Even so, you need to recognize that online investing has limits. "Remember that most of these firms have been around for less than two years," says Julio Gómez, a former online analyst with the respected computer market research firm Forrester Research and now president of his own Internet consulting firm in Boston. "A lot of the technologies needed for seamless trading are still being perfected." For a successful online experience, keep these rules in mind:

First, decide what you want and find a broker that delivers it. No single broker is best for every investor. To find your ideal trading partner, draw up a list of features that matter to you. Are low commissions most important? If so, consider Scottsdale (trade for as little as $9 with a $10,000 balance) or **Datek** (as low as $9.99 for up to 5,000 shares). Are you willing to pay more for a name you already trust? Then look into **e.Schwab**. Want outstanding research? According to Gómez, PC Financial Network and **E Trade** are among the tops.

Once you have a list of priorities, shop for the perfect match at **Choosing a Discount Broker** (www.sonic.net/donaldj), an exhaustive site run by Don Johnson, a retired professor of business history at Sonoma State University. Johnson lists the complete fee structure for every broker (not just the lowest possible trade price you see in advertisements) and tips readers off to special concerns.

For best results, don't be a day trader. The prospect of trading instantly on real-time price data has powerful appeal to action-obsessed investors. Unfortunately, day trading is where online hype exceeds reality by the widest margin. Blame the nature of the Internet itself: Since every bit of information you send must pass through innumerable gateways and servers en route to your broker, trading orders are bound to be delayed in the Net's routine traffic jams, especially during peak daytime hours. By the time an order finally arrives, the fleeting edge that traders look for may have passed. Says Benchmark Computers' Michael Amland: "There are too many variables that can slow you down to rely on the Internet for very active trading." Simple solution: Say no to day trading.

And, always, read the fine print. Although most brokers allow you to sign up online, don't send that check until you read your broker's customer agreement. That's where you'll find the many ways a company can disavow responsibility should a dispute arise. These documents vary widely from firm to firm, so make sure you can live with yours. For example, PCFN requires you to notify them immediately by mail if your password is stolen, although "immediately" is never defined. If a customer service agreement leaves you confused—and many are vaguely written—ask your broker's compliance officer to explain.

When to Bank With Your Computer

After a decade of catering mostly to computer fanatics and high-tech hobbyists, electronic home banking is finally gearing up for prime time online. The number of banks offering electronic banking is expected to top 600 in 1998, and that figure could double within four years, according to Dataquest, a San Jose high-tech research group. A third of the nation's biggest banks allow computer hookups, including Chase, Citibank and Bank of America. As many as 18 million households—or nearly one in five—will be logging on within five years, predicts Nicole Vanderbilt, an analyst at New York City market research firm Jupiter Communications.

Customers are being lured online in part by banks' expanding menu of electronic services. For example, in addition to offering basic fare like checking balances, transferring money among accounts and paying bills electronically, some will notify you by e-mail if your account balance drops below an amount you specify. But as attractive as online banking may seem, it's still not for everyone. Here's what you need to know to decide whether to move your accounts to cyberspace.

Ask yourself key questions. Do you frequently transfer money among your checking, savings and money-market deposit accounts? Do you keep careful track of recent transactions and balances? Do you mail out 10 or more checks to pay bills each month? If so, you will almost certainly profit from the convenience, time savings and extra control over your affairs that you can get by banking online. But if you write only a few checks a month or consider wrangling with your finances on a computer the very definition of boring, then you can probably tell them to start the electronic banking revolution without you.

Compare prices. Online prices are coming down. Just two years ago, customers routinely shelled out as much as $20 a month to tap into their accounts and pay bills by computer. But most institutions today charge a more reasonable $7 to $10 on average for those services. And a few major banks have jettisoned their online fees entirely. *Online Banking Report* newsletter publisher Jim Bruene estimates that within 10 years, as banks' online systems become cheaper for them to use, fees for banking and bill paying will disappear altogether. (You will still have to pay the banks' regular account fees, though.)

Check out your computer gear. The key item required for online banking is a modem. But even a relatively slow 14.4-kilobits-per-second model will do, since most banks' systems aren't equipped to handle higher speeds. Your computer should also have at least eight megabytes of RAM to run the software that links you to your bank, and 20MB or more of free space on your hard drive so you can download account balances and other information.

Most banks that offer online services now let you tap into their central computers through one or more of the popular cash management programs, including Intuit's Quicken, Microsoft's Money and MECA's Managing Your Money. If you don't already have such software, you can often download it for free from the bank or buy it from the bank for the cost of shipping and handling, typically $5 to $10. By hooking up through these personal-finance programs, you can automatically transfer bill and credit-card payments as well as other information into your software program's digital ledgers. That eliminates the tedious chore of entering the data manually. A handful of banks still require that you use their proprietary software, however. That may present a problem for you. Although banks usually provide their software at no charge, you may have a hard time transferring data from the bank's software to your other personal-finance programs.

In the near future most computer banking is likely to be done over the Internet, as banks set up more sophisticated sites on the World Wide Web. As long as you're using a so-called secure browser that scrambles messages (as do the latest versions of Netscape Navigator and Microsoft Explorer) and the bank site has the technology for receiving coded information, the chances of a hacker's cracking into your bank accounts are infinitesimal, says Bill Orr, publisher of *Cyberbanking*, a newsletter in Waterbury Center, Vt. (Online customer service representatives can verify whether the bank's site can handle encrypted messages.)

See what services are offered. Virtually every bank offering computer hookups will let you track account balances and transactions, transfer funds back and forth among accounts, and view your checking and savings statements online. Some banks, however, allow you to call up only last month's statements. For more flexibility in tracing your finances, try to find a bank that gives you access to all your account information from the time you began banking online. Ideally, you should also be able to check the status of all the accounts you maintain at the bank—including any credit cards, mortgages and mutual funds—not just your checking and savings.

If you hate the hassle of scrambling for stamps and scribbling out checks, you'll also want computerized bill paying. Once you've signed up for electronic banking, most banks will then also let you pay bills online, though typically for an extra monthly fee of $3 to $6. Canceled checks are not returned to you when you pay bills electronically. Instead, online payments are listed on the paper statement the bank sends you each month, as well as on the electronic statement that you can peruse online. If you need proof to settle a dispute, the bank can provide you with a canceled check or other verification. A few banks charge for this service, but most do it for free.

HIRING A FINANCIAL PLANNER

Even the most determined do-it-yourselfers can feel overmatched by their finances at one time or another. How do you know when you've reached that point? The answer, of course, will differ for everyone. But there are common money problems that can stymie a lone wolf. Recognizing when you're facing one can mean the difference between meeting your goals and falling short.

There are two primary reasons for calling in a financial planner.

One is budgeting. Getting a handle on your expenses is the first step to managing your finances. "Simply keeping track of where your money goes teaches you to save more," says Robert Tull, a Norfolk financial planner. But before you pay for budgeting guidance, try tracking your expenditures yourself. Afterward, if you decide that simply learning where your money goes isn't enough to channel your cash flow productively, consider hiring a financial planner to give your finances a bumper-to-bumper inspection.

The second key reason to seek help is investing. When you start socking money away, chances are you can manage on your own, especially if the sums are small and most of your investing is through an automatic option such as your company's 401(k) plan. Even if you want to pick your own individual stocks and funds, a pro remains fully optional (except, of course, you'll have to pay a commission to either a discount or full-service broker to place stock trades). Most libraries have stock and mutual fund research on CD-ROM or in print. So why not go it alone? For one, you may want to share responsibility for the outcome, especially if you have a lump sum to invest all at once, such as an inheritance or a company payout.

In addition, even if you enjoy choosing stocks or funds, you may be leaving holes in your strategy. For example, can you give a reason for owning your stocks or funds? Do you have a plan for selling each? Do you know what your investment allocations are? Do you even know how you did last year? If you can't answer those questions, consider paying for investment pointers.

Increasingly, brokerages and mutual fund companies such as Dreyfus and Dean Witter will structure a portfolio for you, often for around $100 and sometimes gratis—though of course they try hard to sell you their products. You also can open a wrap account at a brokerage if you have enough money in your portfolio, and a money manager will buy and sell stocks, bonds and funds for you. Another option is to seek more comprehensive financial help from a planner.

In theory, planners are the generalists of the financial services professions. Anyone can call himself a financial planner, but the real pros can help you map out a route to goals like retirement and estate planning, asset allocation, and tax and cash-flow planning; about half of them also manage clients' assets.

There is no shortage of good financial planners, but the challenge is to identify them. Unlike, say, a plumber, hairdresser or neurosurgeon, a financial planner does not necessarily have to open a book, take an exam or otherwise demonstrate any competence before hanging out a shingle. "I'm not remotely qualified to manage people's money," says Barbara Roper, director of investor protection for the Consumer Federation of America. "But nothing could legally stop me from promoting myself as a financial planner if I wanted."

You will have to be extremely vigilant to find the planner who suits you best. It's entirely up to you to ask the right questions and probe for the planner's professional qualifications. And most important, it's your responsibility to establish how the planner intends to make money from you.

Get referrals. The best leads come from friends whose financial situation is similar to yours. If you can't get any help there, move on to your lawyer, accountant or banker. As a last resort, ask planners' trade groups— National Association of Personal Financial Advisors (888-333-6659), the International Association for Financial Planning (800-945-4237), the Institute of Certified Financial Planners (800-282-7526)—for a list of members near where you live. Certified financial planner (C.F.P.) is a designation given to planners who meet educational, experiential and ethical requirements. A C.F.P. license is no guarantee of competence or honesty, but it suggests some commitment to the profession.

If you find your planner through friends or others you trust, you probably don't need to check references. Otherwise, ask the planner for names of clients in your circumstances. Planners will hardly refer you to clients who will speak ill of them, so you need to burrow down a bit. Talk to clients about the planner's strengths and weaknesses: Is he responsive to phone calls? Does he take the time to explain why his proposals are appropriate for you? Is the fee structure fair in light of the work the adviser does for you? Then go one more step, says Centereach, N.Y. planner Ronald Rogé, and ask the adviser for the names of lawyers, accountants and other professionals he has worked with. Ask those people whether the clients they've referred to the planner were satisfied with the service they received.

Check qualifications. Any planner worth considering should have a background in a financially related field, such as accounting, insurance, banking or stock brokerage. Mark Spangler, a Seattle financial planner and chairman of the National Association of Personal Financial Advisors (NAPFA), says the candidate should have at least five years of experience in a related field and actual advisory work.

If your planner is like most professionals, his walls will be plastered with proof that he graduated from college and did some kind of postgraduate study. None of this stuff says anything about his judgment or integrity, but it's reassuring to see. Look for a credential like the C.F.P. for certified financial planner—or Ch.F.C. for chartered financial consultant, another designation that shows the planner has passed a series of examinations, taken continuing education courses in financial planning and agreed to comply with the designating group's code of ethics.

Ask the planner to show you a copy of the disclosure document called the ADV. Every planner who gives investment advice about securities must file an ADV with the Securities and Exchange Commission and with most state securities commissions. The planner is obliged to show you Part II, which spells out how he is paid, his educational and professional qualifications, and any business affiliations that could pose conflicts of interest.

While planners are not required to show you Part I of the ADV, "it may be useful to ask for it," says Ken Berman, assistant director of the SEC's Division of Investment Management. This is the section that talks about past disciplinary problems. If a planner will not show you Part I or provide you with the same information in another form, move on to another adviser. And ask if the planner is bonded and for how much. Bonding is essential if you plan to give your adviser direct access to your money.

Discuss compensation. Have a clear understanding of how the planner will be compensated. Some planners make their living off commissions on the financial products they sell. If you're not in the market for products or don't like the commissioned planners' built-in conflict of interest, you may prefer a so-called fee-only planner. You pay such planners either a fixed amount by the hour (median rate: $100 an hour) or by the plan. It typically includes a full assessment of your finances and a step-by-step guide to reaching your goals. According to the planners' trade group the International Association for Financial Planning (IAFP), so-called fee-only advisers charge an average of $1,160 to create a basic financial plan. (A less detailed $300 one might tackle just a specific issue, such as buying a home.) "When you walk out the planner's door, you should usually have a concrete plan for the next two years or longer," says Kyra Morris, a Charleston, S.C. financial planner. In addition, some fee-only planners will manage your investments for an average of 1.4% of the amount under management or an hourly rate of $80 to $400.

Commission-based planners devise the plan for free and make their money selling the investments they recommend as part of it. Commissions range from 1% or less on money-market accounts and Treasury bills to 4.75% on mutual funds to 90% of the first year's premium on insurance products, reports Peggy Ruhlin, a Columbus, Ohio planner and president of the IAFP.

On the face of it, a fee-only arrangement seems more desirable, since it avoids the commissioned salesman's built-in conflict of interest. The problem is, more planners claim to be fee-only than really are. In fact, NAPFA, whose membership is confined to these advisers, has trademarked the term "fee-only." But as long as you have confidence in the planner, it really doesn't matter which type you choose—as long as you know how he is making his money.

When you ultimately decide to do business with a planner, that disclosure should be spelled out precisely in an engagement letter. The letter should also lay out the terms of your agreement, what services you should expect and how long the agreement will last.

Know what you are entitled to. Bob Wacker, a planner in San Luis Obispo, Calif., recommends that after you have selected a planner, you have several meetings to discuss your current financial picture and your goals. Only then should the adviser complete a comprehensive plan. You can then ask the planner to implement the recommendations or take them to your stockbroker, mutual fund or other adviser. You should also receive quarterly or semiannual portfolio statements, which include a list of the investments you've made through the planner, their rate of return and comparisons of these numbers to benchmarks.

If you decide to let a planner manage your investments, start slowly. Turn over only 25% or so of your assets at first and see how he does. Warns David Tysk, a senior adviser at American Express Financial Planning Services in Minneapolis: "If you hand over your life savings and you are not happy with the products you have been sold, it's going to be very expensive for you to get out of them."

CHAPTER 4

TAKE CHARGE OF YOUR 401 (K)

Tax-deferred savings plans are your best bet for long-term growth. And there's no better type to invest in than your company-sponsored 401(k) plan. For starters, the money you put into a 401(k) is deducted from your taxable income, which means you don't pay federal or state taxes (except in Pennsylvania) until you withdraw it. What's more, most companies that offer the plans will beef up your contributions with money of their own, typically half of the first 6% of your salary that you contribute.

By 2001 nearly 30 million workers at some 340,000 companies will be eligible to join a 401(k) plan, according to estimates by Access Research, an employee-benefits consultant in Windsor, Conn. People who work for non-profit groups like public schools have their own version of the plans, known as 401(b)s, and so do employees of state or local governments, who get tax-advantaged savings in 457 plans.

Here, in a nutshell, are the compelling facts for socking your money in tax-deferred savings: Say a 35-year-old saves 6% of a $60,000 salary in a taxable portfolio of funds. If that money earns 8% a year, he would have about $284,000 by age 65, assuming a 28% federal tax rate. But if he put that same amount in a 40l(k) he would accumulate $571,000, more than double the money. He'd have to pay income taxes on the money he withdraws. But since he could take the money out gradually, he'd lessen the tax bite, and he would be able to leave the rest in to grow tax deferred.

Unless you become disabled, you generally can't get your money back before age 59 1/2 without owing a 10% penalty on the amount you withdraw plus regular income taxes. But most companies let you borrow against your account without penalty or tax as long as you pay the loan back. And if you leave your job, you can take your money with you, rolling it over into an IRA or your new company's retirement plan without penalty or taxes. Depending on how long you've been in the plan, you'll be able to take along some or all of your company's matching contributions as well.

To get the most out of a 401(k), which is named for the section of the tax code that authorized it, you have to take charge. You must decide how much you want to save and where you want the money invested. This chapter will help you make wise decisions to get maximum benefits from your plan.

KNOW YOUR INVESTMENT OPTIONS

You usually can put in 15% of your salary up to the IRS maximum—$9,500 in 1997, and periodically boosted for inflation. Some employers cap contributions at 10% of salary or less mainly to comply with IRS regulations aimed at making sure plans don't disproportionately benefit a company's best-paid employees. You should get into a plan as soon as you're eligible (check with your benefits counselor to learn when that is). And even if you can't afford to invest 10% or 15% of your paycheck, try to come up with enough to qualify for your employer's top matching contribution.

The typical 401(k) offers a choice of mutual funds. The mix might consist of a money-market fund, a "stable value" account or bond fund, a balanced fund, a growth fund, an aggressive growth or small-company fund, and an international fund. Some large corporations give you a choice of 35 or more funds, but typically there are less than 10 options.

The funds available can be either retail funds (the kind open to investors) or private accounts managed by banks, insurance companies and money-management firms. The retail funds are becoming more common, because fund companies are honing in on the big 401(k) business. The advantage of retail funds is that, by law, they must provide investors with extensive information, including the name of the manager or managers and a detailed prospectus that describes the fund's expenses and investment policies. Most private funds are not required to disclose that much detail.

AVOID THE FIVE BIG 401(K) MISTAKES

Okay, getting the most out of your employer's 401(k) retirement savings plan seems simple enough. Contribute the maximum you're allowed, choose your investments carefully, and keep your mitts off the money until you hit 59 1/2.

You get a tax shelter against your current income, tax-deferred investment returns and, usually, a tax-free gift from your employer.

Trouble is, it's easy to mess up in an employer-sponsored savings plan. "A 401(k) could well become your largest asset, but people mismanage that money for all sorts of reasons," says Dee Lee, president of Harvard Financial Educators, a consulting firm in Harvard, Mass. Some blunders, unfortunately, can't be easily repaired. What follows are the five most common 401(k) mistakes and how to avoid making them:

Failing to maximize your company's match. Commonly, as
we've said, an employer will match 50% of an employee's contributions, up to 6% of salary. In other words, the most he'll kick in is 3% of your wages—and that's only if you put in the full 6% yourself. Salt away less, and so will he.

As we've also said, company plans often let individuals invest a higher percentage of their pre-tax pay, even though the match doesn't go that high. Now here's where things can get tricky. Say your gross is $125,000 and you want to earmark 10% for the 401(k), or $12,500. Figure that your boss will match your 401(k) contributions up to 3% of your pay—$3,750, or $144 every two weeks. But the law says an employee's tax-deferred plan contributions cannot exceed the federal limit—$9,500 in 1997. Odds are, your employer would simply take 10% out of your biweekly paycheck until you hit the $9,500 ceiling sometime in October. Then your contributions would stop—just the way your employer quits withholding Social Security taxes once you've hit the year's limit.

Stop the clock on your contributions, however, and you'll lose the company match for November and December—more than $500. "If you make a lot of money, you can lose out by putting in too much too soon," says Rich Koski, national director of pre-retirement and financial planning for Buck Consultants in Secaucus, N.J. The solution: Divide the $9,500 maximum 401(k) contribution by your salary to get the percentage of your pay that you can invest each pay period—in this case 7.6%. Have that amount taken out of your biweekly paycheck, and you'll extend your contributions—and the company match—over the entire year.

Ignoring investment allocations. The biggest headache for
many plan participants is deciding where to invest their 401(k), since the choices are wider than ever. According to the benefits consulting firm Hewitt Associates of Lincolnshire, Ill., 52% of 401(k) plans now offer six or more investment flavors, up from 22% with that many in 1993.

Too often, however, participants put too much money in one type of investment. That is partly because many plan sponsors inadvertently encourage them to invest too heavily in fixed-income options. The plans usually provide at least one choice that is expected to hold its value, such as a stable-value fund, which aims to preserve capital plus pay a stated rate of interest. In addition, many employees want a money-market account, where they can safely stash their contributions while deciding where to invest them. As a result, many 401(k)s with a variety of fixed-income funds have been slow to add stock funds. Employees often view these choices as a subtle message to invest more heavily in fixed income than in stocks.

Additionally, companies are increasingly funneling employees' profit-sharing bonuses into their 401(k) accounts. If yours does, be sure you don't blithely assume that this money will automatically be allocated in the same fashion as your regular 401(k) contributions. It often goes straight into a money-market account in the plan unless the participant fills out a special form for these bonuses and chooses another investment. So if you expect to get a profit-sharing bonus for 1998 and aren't sure how it will be invested, check with your benefits consultant.

We asked the Vanguard Group, which manages billions of dollars in 401(k) assets, to design three model porftfolios for people with varying time horizons and risk tolerances. For people 25 years old, Vanguard suggested an aggressive mix of 100% stocks—55% large-company stock funds, 25% small-company stock funds and 20% international stock funds. For 45-year-olds, the recommended blend was 80% stocks, 20% bonds—50% large-company stock funds, and 20% intermediate bond funds, 15% small-company stock funds and 15% international stock funds. A less risky recipe of 60% stocks and 40% bonds was prescribed for 55-year-olds. The breakdown: 40% large-company stocks, 40% intermediate bonds, 10% small-company stock funds, 10% international stock funds.

Turning into a stock jockey. Some 401(k) participants become so obsessed with the idea of riding winners that they shift in and out of stock funds, trying to time every dip in the market. They can get away with it because there are no immediate tax consequences for moving money around inside a plan and no sales charges for switching. But stock jockeys can pay a huge performance penalty. While the average U.S. stock fund returned 14.5% annually from 1984 through 1996, the typical fund investor earned just 6.1% a year because he got in too late, pulled out too soon or both, according to Dalbar, a financial services research firm in Boston.

You know you're investing herky-jerky, says financial consultant Wendy Rhodes, when you're frequently "hitting the phones at the end of the day to make transactions in your 401(k)." Instead, size up your 401(k) portfolio once a year. At that time, rebalance any allocations that a rising (or falling) stock market may have thrown out of whack and consider taking advantage of new investment choices.

Using your 401(k) as a loan window. On the surface, 401(k) loans are a sweet deal because you pay yourself back at an interest rate slightly above prime. By contrast, you could pay nearly twice that for an unsecured personal loan at a bank. But borrowing from your plan has an unfortunate domino effect on your portfolio. First, you are removing money whose sheltered earnings could be compounding. Worse, you get socked for taxes twice: You repay the loan with after-tax dollars, and your money gets taxed again when the funds are distributed, typically at retirement. So before you borrow from your 401(k), ask yourself: Will the money I receive be used to fund a future goal as important as my retirement? If the answer is no, borrow somewhere else.

Triggering unnecessary tax penalties. Suppose you leave your company and decide to roll over your 401(k) balance into your new employer's plan or into an IRA. If you do not have the check sent directly to your new employer or to the custodian of your IRA within 60 days of quitting, your former company will give you the money after withholding 20% for taxes. You can't reclaim that 20% until you file your income taxes the following year. Meanwhile, you will have lost tax-deferred compounding on a fifth of your total distribution.

Another potential pitfall: If you leave your job and roll over your 401(k) balance into a new plan before paying back an outstanding loan against it, the loan balance usually becomes a taxable distribution, warns Bill Chapman, president of the retirement plans group at Zurich Kemper Investments in Chicago.

DON'T OVERLOAD ON COMPANY STOCK

Believing in your employer is generally laudable. But millions of employees have taken a good idea to a dangerous extreme, investing more than 20% of their 401(k) in stock of the company that employs them. According to financial experts, 20% is the absolute maximum an investor should commit to a single stock. "At worst, owning too much company stock is courting disaster, because if your company goes belly up, you lose both your job and the bulk of your savings," says Roger Smith, a Sacramento financial planner with Securities America. "At best, you're taking on totally unnecessary investment risk."

But it's also foolish to turn down stock options or 401(k) matching contributions altogether. And, in many cases, if you've accumulated the company stock in a profit-sharing plan or as a 401(k) match, you can't sell it before retirement unless you quit. So your task is to understand the risks posed by excessive holdings in your company's shares and then weigh those risks against the often real advantages of not looking a gift stock in the mouth.

Diversify, diversify. Diversification—the practice of spreading your risk among a variety of securities—has long been recognized as the most effective way to reduce investment risk. Yet out of a misguided loyalty to the company, inertia or overconfidence, many employees are rejecting the principle wholesale. "It scares the bejeebers out of me," says Smith. But rather than urging moderation, some employers have made it more difficult than ever for their work force to avoid overdosing on the home team's stock. Consider:

Despite a trend toward offering more investment options within 401(k)s, some plans are still designed at least partly to push employee ownership of company shares. In 1997 a full 45% of companies with 401(k) plans surveyed by Buck Consultants, an employee-benefits firm, offered their stock as an investment choice, up from 30% in 1991. Some employers match only the employee contributions to their company's stock fund. Others use different methods to influence employees to invest in the company, including bonuses to managers who get their people to sign up.

Over long periods of time, holding a well-diversified stock portfolio—say, upwards of 10 blue chips and conservative growth stocks in different industries—helps to ensure you a return close to the market average. The big winners and losers in your portfolio will cancel one another out. With one stock, in contrast, you can't know ahead of time whether the return will be high, average, low or even negative. True, your company stock may not wind up a clunker. But if it does, the results can be devastating. Just ask Edith Thomson. The 69-year-old resident of South San Francisco retired in 1995 after 41 years as a gift wrapper for the Carter Hawley Hale subsidiary Emporium. At her company's urging, she invested her entire 401(k) in Carter Hawley Hale stock. Hammered by the 1990 recession, the company went belly up the next year, and by the time it emerged from bankruptcy in 1992, the stock was down about 90% from its level five years earlier. Thomson's ultimate take from her 401(k), which had held as much as $84,000 in the late 1980s: $9,000.

Be wary of double trouble.
Since you probably already depend on your company for much of your financial security—including your paycheck, pension and health benefits—gorging on company stock only compounds the risk of being nondiversified. After all, the same financial troubles that cause a stock to tank are likely to lead to layoffs, salary freezes and benefits cutbacks. "I don't care how solid your company is or how great its track record," says Jeff Schwartz, a consultant with Ibbotson Associates, a Chicago investment research firm. "Overloading on its stock just isn't worth the risk."

Why do some companies encourage employees to take the risk anyway? Employers say that putting more company stock in staffers' hands aligns their interests with the shareholders' and helps focus the work force on the bottom line. In addition, the companies say that stock options—in lieu of some salary—let them offer employees more generous total compensation packages than they could otherwise. Reason: While businesses must subtract regular compensation from earnings on their books, they don't have to subtract option grants—or the gains that are realized when the options are exercised. Result: By "paying" employees with options, a company appears to keep salaries low and earnings high.

Benefits experts add that company managements also have more self-serving motives. For one thing, employees are excellent shareholders from a manager's point of view. They're unlikely to make demands of the managers or the board, and in takeover battles they almost always side with their bosses.

It's important to realize, however, that when it comes to your portfolio, your interests and your employer's don't always coincide.

Figure out how overloaded you are.
Start by adding up the value of all your investments, including retirement and nonretirement savings. Determining the value of your stock options is tricky, but one easy way is to figure what you would pocket after exercising the options and immediately selling the shares. For simplicity's sake, leave taxes out of the computation. Say you have an option to buy 100 shares of company stock at $40 a share and the market price of the stock is now $50. If you exercise the options, you'll pocket $1,000 before taxes, so $1,000 is the value you should be using.

If you determine that more than 10% of your overall portfolio is now in company stock, it's time to stop voluntarily picking up more. If the compa-

Q. In the early 1980s, my company had a profit-sharing plan to which employees could contribute after-tax cash. I put in $7,884.75. Later, when the company began a 401(k), it rolled over my profit-sharing account into the new plan. I'll be retiring soon, and I expect my 401(k) to be worth around $200,000. But when I start taking withdrawals, will I have to pay taxes on the money that's already been taxed?

A. No, it's not as bad as that. But because your 401(k) mingles taxed and untaxed money, the IRS requires that your withdrawals have proportionate amounts of both. You'll need to compute the amount of your final account balance that the $7,884.75 represents. According to our back-of-the-envelope calculations, it's roughly 4%. So when you start withdrawing money, 4% of each withdrawal will be untaxed. The levy on the rest would be at your regular tax rate. For a worksheet that walks you through this calculation, call 800-TAX-FORM and ask for Publication 575.

By the way, after you retire, hang on to your 401(k) statements documenting that some of your contributions were already taxed. You never know if the IRS might ask you to prove it. If you can't, you'll have to pay tax and interest, currently 6%, on the disputed amount.

ny's shares make up 20% or more of your holdings, you need to take steps to rebalance your portfolio.

Don't be dazzled by discount purchase plans. About half of 227 large companies surveyed by compensation consultant Towers Perrin allow employees to purchase company stock at work—usually at a 10% or 15% discount to its current price. That's not such a great deal, however, if you're already overdosing on your company's stock. "In the long run, a 10% or 15% discount won't make that much difference if the market drops," says Stewart Koesten, a financial planner in Overland Park, Kans.

But don't turn down matching contributions. Accept them, even if they are in company stock. About 35% of large companies with 401(k) plans match some or all employee contributions with company stock, and many of them don't let you switch the match to another investment option within the plan. So you can wind up heavily freighted with corporate paper even if you never intentionally purchased a single share.

However, your employer's matching contribution—which effectively gives you an instant 25% to 100% return depending on the generosity of the match—is too good a deal to pass up. Your best move: If your portfolio is already made up of upwards of 10% of company stock, make sure you don't compound the problem by allocating your own contributions to the company-stock fund. In fact, it's a good idea not only to avoid investing in company stock when you exceed the 20% limit but also to avoid stocks of companies similar to yours. If you work for Chevron, for example, be cautious about buying other oil companies or even other natural-resources firms, since all tend to move along with commodity prices. Load up instead on stocks that tend to rise when oil prices fall—such as airlines, autos and interest-rate-sensitive businesses like banks.

Take advantage of the chance to jump ship. You generally can't control how much company stock you accumulate through your employer's profit-sharing plan or employee stock-ownership plan, since the money is automatically invested on your behalf. Once you reach age 55, however, many companies let you gradually transfer your shares into other tax-deferred investments, typically a stable-value fund or a money-market fund. So if you hold too much company stock and you're 55 or older, move it.

DEMAND TOPNOTCH SAVINGS CHOICES

Courts have lately grown more protective of employee assets in company-sponsored retirement savings plans like 401(k)s. Under the Employee Retirement Income Security Act of 1974 (ERISA), businesses are protected from worker suits if they offer a variety of investment options. But those choices must be prudent, according to the law. The courts decide what prudent means. Ask your benefits department for a wide range of investment choices and personal-finance education. "Companies that fail to heed these requests may open themselves to the threat of lawsuits from disgruntled employees," says David Wray, president of the Profit Sharing/401(k) Council of America in Chicago, an association of plan sponsors.

DON'T GET NICKED BY ERRORS

Even with the best of intentions, many employers don't give plan participants all the matching money they've been promised, as a result of an accidental calculation error. Indeed, Bill Karbon, a consulting actuary at National Retirement

Planning, a 401(k) administrator in Jamison, Pa., estimates that nearly 10% of participants could get as much as a third less than they deserve.

About two-thirds of 401(k) plans—generally those offered by small and mid-size companies—require that any employer match be a set percentage of the employee's total annual plan contribution. Trouble is, 401(k) administrators often calculate each matching amount by looking at how much you've contributed for only that pay period. So if you alter or suspend your contributions during the year, you might get a mismatch. Say you plan to contribute 8% of your $100,000 salary to your 401(k) and your employer promises to match you dollar for dollar, up to 6%. However, after six months you stop contributing; then, so does your employer. Sounds fair, but you've been shortchanged. For the full year, you'll have contributed 4% of your salary ($4,000), but your employer will have kicked in only 3% ($3,000). The company owes you a grand.

To see whether your 1997 match was too small, first check your W-2 form to see how much was withheld from your gross pay—and look at your 401(k) statements to make sure your company put that amount into your plan. Then, if the amount your employer gave as a match does not equal the promised percentage of your contribution, point out the problem to your employee-benefits office.

PROTECT YOURSELF AGAINST RIPOFFS

Like most American employees, 39-year-old helicopter pilot Sue Knoebel of Redmond, Wash. took it on faith that a 401(k) plan was the best retirement investment she could get. That is, until she landed a job three years ago with a small, 21-employee Seattle-based firm called Hospital AirTransport. "Ever since I started working here I had heard grumblings about how bad our 401(k) plan was," she recalls. She soon learned that the problem was not so much that the performance of the plan's mutual funds was lousy, but rather that the plan's provider was raking off up to 2.2% of employee assets each year in investment management and annuity fees. "I'm no financial wizard," she says, "but I knew that fees like that are exorbitant."

Many companies conceal the huge, hidden costs of 401(k)s from plan participants even when the fees seriously erode investor returns. Few employees know they pay any 401(k) fees, let alone how much they are. Most plans don't regularly disclose the costs in their quarterly account statements—as every mutual fund, by contrast, is required to do prominently in its prospectus. And most employers fail to protect their employees' interests. This is the system's most fundamental breakdown. One thing the Employee Retirement Income Security Act (ERISA) makes clear is that employers are fiduciaries. That means they must act responsibly to protect the workers enrolled in the savings plans. The government's top cop on 401(k)s, assistant secretary of the U.S. Department of Labor Olena Berg, says: "It is an employer's fiduciary duty to make sure the fees 401(k) participants pay are reasonable."

Unfortunately, very few do. Often, the bosses at companies with small or mid-size plans are scarcely more informed about 401(k) costs than their workers are. Worse, those who do focus on expenses increasingly are more intent on shifting them onto the employees than on reducing them. One result: Only 37% of employers surveyed in 1995 by Darien, Conn. investment consulting firm RogersCasey said they still paid the full administrative cost of 401(k)s, compared with 48% the previous year. Warns David Wray, president of the Profit Sharing/401(k) Council of America, a trade group for employers with 401(k)s, and a man not prone to publicly criticizing the industry: "High-cost 401(k)s are a lawsuit waiting to happen."

Perhaps so. But before you go running to the courthouse there are steps you can take to protect your savings. First and foremost, employees should educate themselves about their 401(k) costs and then pressure their employers to minimize fees. That approach worked for Sue Knoebel, the Seattle helicopter pilot. When she pointed out another mutual fund company that offered a 401(k) with a wider selection of funds than the one her company offered, at less than half the cost, her boss quickly realized he too would save money. So he switched.

Educated and determined employees like Knoebel may soon discover they have more power than they imagine. Time and again, the highly competitive 16-year-old 401(k) industry has responded rapidly to investor demands. For example, the average plan now offers six investment options, compared with four just five years ago, as well as such once rare amenities as a toll-free help line, an investment newsletter and simplified loan processing. Ted Benna of Langhorne, Pa., the pension consultant who invented the 401(k) plan, says that if consumers insisted on more competitive prices, the industry would have no choice but to comply.

In most cases, the company hires an outside firm to run the 401(k) plan. The outside firms hired to run the plan are typically an arm of a mutual fund family, bank, insurer or benefits consulting firm. It is these so-called plan providers who often charge outrageously high fees for their administrative and investment management services—and you pay most of that tab. Here is how you may get ripped off:

You pay big fees for little service. Your 401(k) charges break down this way: Administrative fees cover such services as keeping records, mailing quarterly statements, staffing toll-free lines, complying with government regulations and so on. The plan provider typically bills the employer for these. The charges may vary from a low flat fee of $1,000 for a small plan to $200,000 or more for a large plan. The provider often tacks on a separate charge of about $25 per participant.

The far larger part of 401(k) costs—about 83% of the total—is the provider's investment fees. As with mutual fund management fees, the money-management firm (which may also be the provider/administrator) collects these fees in return for selecting and monitoring the plan's investments. The charges, which are calculated as a percentage of the plan's assets, are quietly deducted directly from those assets. In other words, you pay them, but you do not feel the hand in your pocket. All that happens is that your investment returns are lower than they would have been without the fees.

Economics 101 says your 401(k)'s costs should depend on your plan's size and the service you get. But in truth, 401(k) costs can be as irrational as airline ticket pricing. The price you pay depends on what the market—or a particular employer—will allow. For example, a nationwide survey of 401(k) providers by the Baltimore-based pension research firm HR Investment Consultants found that total per capita costs for a 100-participant plan with $3 million in assets in 1996 ranged from a low of $219 to a high of $861—a difference of almost 300%. For a 1,000-employee plan with $30 million in assets, the spread was even wider—$141 to $755, or more than 425%.

You pay more at a small company. Smaller plans get hit with higher fees to compensate for fewer assets. Smaller firms also tend to be less sophisticated negotiators, so they accept lousy terms.

Giant insurers who hold 33% of small-company plan assets are the hungriest predators in this end of the market. Their favorite investment offering is the group variable annuity, essentially a family of tax-deferred mutual funds. Since all earnings in 401(k)s are already tax deferred, investing your 401(k) money in an annuity seems foolish. Some insurers offer low-cost 401(k) plans, but many slam 401(k) participants with so-called annuity fees that average around 1.25% on top of regular administrative and investment expenses.

Also feeding on the small-company 401(k) market: mutual fund families who have introduced new classes of shares of their most popular funds, which are designed to be sold by benefits firms that administer small 401(k) plans. What distinguishes the new shares from the fund's ordinary shares? Additional fees, and not much else.

You can't always count on your employer. Many employers could not care less about how much their workers are being overcharged. A 1996 survey by Access Research found that when plan sponsors were asked to name the most important criteria in choosing a full-service 401(k) provider, cost did not even make the top 10. (Financial stability and reliable record keeping were the leading concerns.) "About 85% to 95% of the sponsors I talk to don't know the total costs of their plans," says Joseph Valletta, a principal at HR Investments, the 401(k) plan consulting firm. "At best, they only know the administrative fees."

As a result, price competition among 401(k) providers often consists of shifting fees onto the workers by reducing the employer's administrative fees and raising the investment fees. On average, according to Access Research, the provider's administrative fee covers only 65% of its actual administrative costs. No problem. The providers more than recover by sticking their hands deeper into the workers' investment assets. Says Vanguard senior vice president William McNabb: "The trend among providers bidding for Fortune 500 company plans is to charge minimal or even zero administrative fees." That means some employees pay all the 401(k) costs. Notes David Kudish, president of Stratford Advisory Group, a Chicago pension consulting firm: "It's cost shifting, pure and simple." Not surprisingly, as administrative expenses have shriveled, total investment fees have ballooned at a five-year compound rate of 28% a year.

You can be easily confused. It is difficult to learn what your plan is charging you. For example, last year, MONEY reporters and correspondents, acting as regular 401(k) participants, phoned several major employers and plan providers and asked what fees employees like them were paying. Every company eventually answered fully but not before some informed prodding on our part. A few at first mistakenly told reporters that participants paid nothing, thereby overlooking the asset-based investment fees workers pay automatically.

One reason for the confusion is that many 401(k) providers make it tough for employers to understand a plan's true costs. For example, administrative and investment fees may be lumped together, making it impossible to separate the charges. Don't expect much help from the government, either. Thanks to ERISA's minimal disclosure requirements, the only document that your sponsor must send you automatically is a summary annual report, which lists the plan's total gains and losses as well as the administrative expenses. The summary annual report tells you nothing about how much you forked over in investment fees.

Employers can reveal more if they choose, and some do. But more often, companies volunteer little or nothing about costs, even when the information is clearly important to their workers.

LEARN HOW TO FIGHT FOR YOUR RIGHTS

Fees aren't the only things that 401(k) providers don't want to disclose to you. Tight-lipped employers, poorly trained phone reps and lax regulations can make it difficult at best to find out who's handling your 401(k) savings, where your money is invested and how those investments have performed. Says 401(k) creator Ted Benna: "You can be left flying by the seat of your pants."

How much information you can demand depends in large part on whether your employer complies with the Department of Labor's 404(c) regulations. These guidelines spell out what companies must do to protect themselves from employee lawsuits if 401(k) investments perform poorly. One requirement is that companies offer employees enough information to make prudent investing decisions. So start by asking your benefits department: Does our plan comply with 404(c)?

If the answer is no, the most useful document you'll receive when you enroll in the 401(k) plan is the summary plan description. It describes the 401(k) rules, your legal rights and, in many cases, your investment options. Otherwise you are entitled only to an annual benefits statement, a summary annual report and access to your plan's 5500 financial report.

If the answer is yes, you are entitled to the above documents plus a prospectus for any retail mutual funds you buy. A prospectus will tell you the names of the fund managers, their tenure, the fund's investment fees and its 10-year performance. For funds that do not have a prospectus, you'll get information such as objectives, expenses and fees. But once you're in the plan, your company must supply information updates, new prospectuses or a list of assets in each fund only if you request them.

To safeguard your retirement savings, follow these tips:

Scrutinize your 401(k) account statements. Pay special attention to the earnings column, where many mistakes show up. Calculate the quarterly percentage gain or loss reported for each fund on your statement and compare it with the quarterly performance update that normally accompanies your statement. The results should roughly match.

Ask your benefits department to break down fees and expenses. If you are paying anything beyond 1% in investment management fees for a bond fund, 1.25% for a domestic stock fund or 1.5% for an international stock fund, complain in writing to your plan administrator. Since the top brass are usually paying the same percentages as you in their 401(k) accounts, send a copy of your complaint to them too.

If you discover more than inflated fees or honest snafus, call the Department of Labor or hire a professional. Your DOL regional office can pursue allegations of fraud and gross negligence. For a booklet with the phone numbers of the regional offices, call 202-219-8776. If you believe your payout when you retire or change jobs is less than you deserve, you can turn to the private National Center for Retirement Benefits (800-666-1000). The NCRB will review your beef for free but keep as much as 30% of whatever it recovers for you.

CHAPTER 5

WHAT YOU NEED TO KNOW ABOUT CREDIT

Limiting your consumer debt—or repaying it if you can—is among the most important financial moves you can make. Consumer debt (excluding mortgages) has soared 50% to more than $1.2 trillion over the past four years. Of that, more than $520 billion consists of credit-card balances and other revolving credit. In fact, since 1994, consumer debt has grown more than four times as fast as wages. "Unfortunately, the strong economy has seduced some consumers into thinking that high debt is okay," says James Chessen, chief economist of the American Bankers Association in Washington, D.C. But, in fact, there have been calamitous consequences. For example, both in terms of dollar amounts and number of accounts 30 days or more overdue, credit-card delinquencies are near 20-year highs. And bankruptcies have been soaring, with a record 1.26 million people filing for personal bankruptcy in the 12 months through November 1997.

The typical American adult has nine credit cards and average balances totaling nearly $4,000. Principal and interest payments on consumer debt eat up 11¢ of every dollar Americans earn after taxes. Add in home mortgage payments, and debt service consumes a near-record 17% of personal disposable income, up from 15.5% in 1993. Only a little over a third of all cardholders pay off their balances every month. That means that debt payments have an extra-heavy impact on the 64% of cardholders who carry balances. If you're one of them, your best profits in 1998 can come from paying off any credit-card debt (two-thirds of Americans carry such debt). With interest rates ranging from an average of 18% to 30%—and not tax deductible—the effective return on every dollar you spend to pay down your credit-card balances will easily top what you're likely to earn on your investments.

Making the wrong credit moves can be disastrous for your finances. The best advice anyone can give you is to pay off your credit card balance in full each month to avoid paying those steep interest charges. This chapter will also help you avoid other traps.

MAKE SURE LENDERS SIZE YOU UP RIGHT

Credit scoring systems—essentially computer programs that grade your ability to repay debt—have spread beyond credit cards and auto loans. For example, banks and other lenders turned to computer-driven scoring models to help evaluate as many as half of the roughly 10 million mortgage applications they received last year. But that's only the beginning. These computer programs—which can combine information from your credit bureau files with details you provide, such as your income and job history—are tiptoeing into many aspects of your financial life. And that can cause big trouble for you.

You can be denied insurance. On the controversial theory that people who have subpar credit ratings are more likely to file insurance claims, a small but growing number of insurers are relying on a computerized review of your credit history to help determine whether you qualify for homeowners or auto insurance. If you get nixed for an auto policy because of serious credit problems such as unpaid bills, tax liens or a past bankruptcy, you could be forced to deal with an insurer specializing in high-risk policies and pay a 50% or more higher premium.

You can be dunned by collection heavies. Lenders have developed special scoring systems to help them decide whether to give you a bit of slack when you miss a loan payment—or jump on you immediately. For example, Cleveland's KeyCorp divides its auto-loan customers into three risk categories based on their credit scores. If a top scorer is late with a payment, the bank sends a reminder letter. If you rank in the bottom third of borrowers, however, a bank collection officer duns you by phone if your check hasn't arrived five days after the due date.

You can be hit for high deposits. Even some phone and cellular-service companies are interested in your credit rating. The credit reporting firm Equifax, for example, has designed a scoring system that forecasts

Improved accuracy. Banks, department stores and other companies are now legally responsible for the accuracy of the information they provide to credit bureaus. And if you report an error in your file, they must double-check the item you question; in the past they were not required to do so. "This new duty to report accurate information and investigate consumer complaints should mean fewer mistakes in your credit reports," says David Medine, associate director for credit practices at the Federal Trade Commission.

Greater privacy. Your current employer, or a prospective one, is no longer allowed to examine your credit report without your permission.

Less junk mail. You can now tell the big three credit bureaus (Equifax, Experian and TransUnion) that you don't want them to give your name to credit-card issuers or insurance companies looking for new customers. Telephone requests are good for two years; written ones last forever.

A FLAW IN THE LAW

Under the old federal credit law, before Congress expanded it last year, a lender that sent you a solicitation after getting your name from a credit bureau was required to offer you some amount of credit if you responded. Now, however, lenders are under no such obligation. Here's the danger: You could reply to a solicitation assuming you were "preapproved"—and then get turned down. Such a rejection, in turn, could show up on your credit report, making it harder for you to qualify for a loan in the future. So how should you deal with those tempting credit-card come-ons? "Don't repond to the mailing at all," says Gerri Detweiler, author of *The Ultimate Credit Handbook*, "unless the offer looks so great that you would go for it even if you weren't under the impression that you're preapproved." And if you really want to be safe, you can, as we noted above, call the major credit bureaus and have your name taken off the junk-mail lists.

YOU CAN PREVENT ERRORS IN YOUR REPORT

Why are there so many errors in credit reports? For starters, the credit bureaus are sloppy, but some of it's our fault. There is no foolproof way for a credit bureau to collect data on us. The main problem is that variations crop up when we apply for credit or our lenders report information about us to credit bureaus. For example, if you apply for a loan with the name that's on your birth certificate instead of the name you use at work, it's still you, but the computer isn't so sure. If you accidentally misstate your Social Security number or your date of birth, or if the lender makes a typographical error when reporting either one to the credit bureau, the computer will be confused.

But credit bureaus try to figure out whose file the confusing data belong in by using programming instructions called matching logic. They might better be called best guess. When new information comes in, the computer scans all the files to find one with a significant number of details that match those in the new report. So if you're Rog on an incoming credit report but your address, Social Security number, date of birth and credit-card account number all match the ones in the existing file for Roger, the new information goes in the existing file. The more significant the corresponding fact—for example, a matching Social Security number is better than a matching birth date—the greater the likelihood that the computer has located the right file and is inserting correct information. But even matching logic doesn't work with so-called identity theft. When a crook steals your wallet with detailed and accurate identification and then establishes credit in your name, a credit bureau has no way of knowing it's not you.

That's why regulators are approaching the problem of errors from both ends, demanding better collection and faster correction of mistakes by the bureaus. States now have the authority to sue credit bureaus that are excessively sloppy, and consumer disputes with bureaus must be resolved within 30 days.

But there are a few things you can do to help prevent errors. Make sure you always use the same form of your name on all credit applications—Rog or Roger, but not both. And if you've decided to knock a few years off your age, be consistent about your new birth date.

GUARD YOUR PRIVACY OR GO BROKE

As you're receiving your first phone call in the morning, driving past a toll-booth camera en route to work, e-mailing an office colleague, picking up groceries or letting your kids surf the Internet, it's possible that you and your family are being watched, listened to or recorded, while data about your personal finances are being collected—and then sold.

That's right: sold. Companies that get your address and Social Security number and gather information about your assets, buying habits and per-the computer." But you don't need to beat a merchant to the bank to hang on to your money. Credit regulations give you a leisurely 60 days after the charge is posted to dispute it; then the card issuer has another 90 days to investigate the problem. Meanwhile, you don't pay a dime, because card companies maintain a reserve fund to cover charges in dispute. That sure beats forking over $30 to stop a check.

How the Fine Print Can Fool You

"Free minutes!" "Free Trial!" "You're Preapproved!" shout the advertisements. "Not so fast," whispers the fine print.

By now, you may have grown so accustomed to the fine print in advertising, contracts and mail offers that you've stopped reading it—or worrying about it. That's a mistake. When you sign up for a credit card, lease a car, choose an Internet service or enter into almost any financial agreement, you're accepting a host of terms. Many of them are buried in a dense thicket of legalese that can be difficult to read and even harder to understand. But if you don't take the trouble to make sense of them, the conditions, exclusions and exceptions can end up costing you serious money.

If you think you're seeing more fine print than ever these days, you're probably right. Much of it, ironically, is the result of consumer-protection laws that have forced companies to disclose more and more details of their offers. But some consumer advocates believe that extensive disclosure ends up benefiting the company, not you. "Fine print is often used as a defense for the company," says Joseph Goldberg, director of Pennsylvania's bureau of consumer protection. "If you complain, they can say 'We gave notice, so you're stuck.'"

Indeed, you're generally bound by all the terms of a contract (except anything illegal or unconscionable), whether or not you read it and understood it. And you don't have to sign on the dotted line to be obligated. Simply by using a credit card for the first time, for example, you indicate that you accept the agreement. Moreover, you often have little opportunity to modify or eliminate provisions you don't like. True, you may be able to negotiate some aspects of certain contracts—like mortgages or auto leases. But in most cases, including credit-card agreements, your only choice is to accept the agreement as is or take your business elsewhere.

So reading the fine print is essential. Trouble is that tiny type can be awfully tough to see. Many consumer-protection laws require only that information be "clear and conspicuous"—without specifying how big. Thus important provisions may appear in letters 25% smaller than what you're reading now, sometimes in faint shades of gray rather than black. "I believe that's to discourage you from reading it," says Ken McEldowney, executive director of Consumer Action, a San Francisco advocacy group. And key information can be even harder to find on a computer screen. Last year, the Federal Trade Commission forced several online services to improve the way they disclose their terms of service.

To help you decipher the treacherous type and glean the information you need, we spoke with dozens of attorneys, regulators, industry experts and consumer advocates. Below we highlight areas where you should pay especially close attention to the fine print.

Sneaky clauses pump up credit costs.
If you think the advertised interest rate and annual fee accurately sum up the cost of using your credit card, think again. "The credit-card charges that are going up are the ones that can be buried in the fine print," says Will Lund, Maine's director of consumer-credit regulation.

Faced with record delinquencies and shrinking profits, card issuers have been hitting you with numerous new fees and penalties in recent years. A look last year through cardholder agreements and change-of-term notices from some of the 20 largest card issuers turned up the following terms of ensnarement: Citibank, the No. 1 credit-card issuer in the nation, slapped you with a penalty rate of prime plus 12.9% on your outstanding balance—21.4% at one time—if you missed two consecutive payments (vs. a range of 13.9% to 18.9% on accounts that were current at the same); First Union hit you with a $29 late fee if your check arrived late; and the Discover card took to the fine print to explain its two-cycle billing method for calculating interest on your outstanding balance—an unusual calculation that tagged some customers with finance charges even during months they paid their balances in full.

Card issuers are also playing "gotcha!" with their perks. Last April, American Express sent out what it labeled as an easy-to-read guide that spelled out new cardholder terms. One tidbit: If your account is unpaid for even one 30-day billing cycle, you may no longer be eligible for insurance when you use your AmEx card to rent a car or make a major purchase.

Also, take a close look at the next letter you get promising a "preapproved" low-rate credit card. Somewhere in the mailing you may find language noting that after reviewing your application, the card issuer may decide to offer you a higher interest rate, lower credit limit or both.

Self-defense: Since many of the fees and penalties are triggered by late payments, it's more important than ever to stay up to date with your bills. Moreover, once you've established a record of paying on time, you could have a better chance of persuading your card company to waive a late fee if you accidentally miss a due date. Another tip: Before you rely on a credit-card perk, such as rental-car insurance, call the issuer's 800 number and make sure the coverage is still available.

Online services can be hard to log off. Even in cyberspace, you can't escape fine print. And it's harder to read on-screen than on paper. To get the 10 to 15 free hours of time or unlimited access for one month that some services offer, you must first sign up for a subscription by providing a credit-card number. If you fail to cancel your subscription when the free trial period ends, you'll be hit with monthly charges. The fact that it's up to you to cancel—and the instructions for doing so—are buried in the pages of disclaimers that come up on your computer screen when you launch the software.

And once you find them, the procedures can be complicated. For example, at one major service, you cannot end your membership via e-mail; instead, you must do so by phone or in writing at least three business days before your next billing period begins.

Self-defense: When you log on to any online service, read the screens explaining the membership terms and print them out for future reference.

Home mortgages can come with catches. Mortgage documents are loaded with legalese, but today's home buyers need to pay especially close attention to two items: prepayment penalties and private mortgage insurance (PMI).

Prepayment penalties, which disappeared from most mortgages by the early 1980s, are making a comeback. If you're among the one in four home buyers who chooses an adjustable-rate mortgage, a small but growing band of lenders will impose a penalty (generally 3% of the principal, or up to six months' interest) if you refinance your loan in the first three to five years of the mortgage. (A few of these lenders can even hit you with the penalty if you sell your home.)

PMI is another potential trap. When you put down less than 20% to buy a home, your lender requires you to buy PMI, which protects the lender in case you default. The cost is typically half to three-quarters of a percent of the loan amount every year; your payment is tacked onto your monthly mortgage tab. The rude surprise: The terms of a mortgage usually make no mention of how to cancel the PMI after your home equity exceeds 20%.

Self-defense: If you're paying PMI but you think your home equity is at least 20%, ask your lender what you must do to cancel the insurance. For example, you may have to get an appraisal.

Who Has to Pay a Parent's Debts?

"My 82-year-old dad is digging himself deep into debt," a reader recently wrote to MONEY. "He owns a small house in California, collects Social Security and has a modest pension. But he spends a lot more than he takes in. He's maxed out on several credit cards. To get extra cash, he arranged a reverse mortgage on his house, and he's taken out high-interest personal loans. No, Dad's not mentally incompetent. He even seems to agree when I tell him he has to stop this excessive spending. But he doesn't stop. I'm worried that when his bills finally catch up with him, his creditors will expect me to pay. Are adult children legally responsible for their parents' profligate spending?"

MONEY replied that "children are on the hook when we're talking about the national debt. As for personal debts, however, the answer is no. Your dad's creditors cannot demand money from you unless you co-signed any of his loans."

We also advised that the American Association of Retired Persons runs a money-management program for low-income seniors in 22 states, including California (for information, call AARP at 800-424-3410). "If your father's income is too high for the AARP program," we said, "you might want to put him in touch with the Consumer Credit Counseling Service (888-775-0377), which can help him get on top of his debts."

Does Your Rebate Card Still Deliver?

The lure of getting something for nothing is irresistible, which is why so many Americans shop with rebate cards—credit cards that let you earn points toward airline tickets, cash refunds or other goodies every time you charge. Such cards now account for roughly one out of every four credit cards in use in the U.S. But they are becoming victims of their own success. To offset the cost of the incentives, many card companies have begun reducing rewards and raising interest rates and fees on their rebate cards. So you need to take a hard look at whatever card you use to make sure it's still a good deal. "A card that was once well worth its cost may no longer be worth what you're paying to use it," says Sara Campbell, senior vice president at Bank Rate Monitor, a consumer-banking research firm.

Consider these cutbacks: A while ago, GM MasterCard sliced the maximum award that gold-card holders can earn toward the purchase of a new car by 50% to $500 a year or $3,500 over seven years, down from $1,000 annually and a total of $7,000. Sunoco MasterCard cut the cashback rebate on nongas purchases from 2% to 1% (though it upped rebates on gas purchases from 3% to 4%). And major airlines hiked the minimum points cardholders need to earn a free ticket.

Other card companies are making their offerings more expensive to use—or dropping them altogether. Moreover, experts expect the cutbacks to continue. So in light of recent changes—and those yet to come—answer these questions to be sure your rebate card still makes sense:

What is the card costing me? If you carry a balance from month to month, the higher interest rates that rebate cards typically charge almost surely outweigh the benefits you receive. Example: One rebate Visa card recently had a 19.4% interest rate and no fee, and offered a 3% cash rebate on all new purchases if you carried a balance. In contrast, the bank's basic Visa has a 12.25% interest rate and an $18 annual fee. If you ran up a $1,000 balance on the rebate card and made the minimum payment each month, you would have paid $184 in interest after a year and earned a $30 rebate, making your net cost $154. But if you carried the same balance on the standard card, your total cost would have been only $130.

How valuable is the rebate? Free airline miles and other rebates sound great but may not be worth as much as you think. Using one airline card ($50 annual fee; 17.9% annual interest rate), you would need to charge $25,000 within three years to earn a round-trip economy ticket within the continental U.S. A recent 14-day advance-purchase fare for a flight from New York City to Los Angeles is $341. Thus you're earning just 1.4¢ for every dollar you charge. Look at it that way, and you may decide you'd be better off using a cheaper credit card and buying the ticket.

Will I spend enough to collect the rebate? Even the best rebate deal is no deal at all if you never use the benefits. In general, credit-card issuers

figure that only 50% of rebate-card customers ever collect rewards, according to banking industry consultant James Accomando. One reason: The average consumer racks up about $2,000 a year in credit-card charges. But you need to spend $25,000 within three years to earn most airline tickets, for example. If you don't run up big charge bills, rebate cards may not be right for you.

The lesson: Don't let a rebate blind you to the costs of using the card. If you carry a balance, you want a card with the lowest interest rate you can find. If you pay your balance in full each month, you want a card with no annual fee, or one whose rebate is more valuable than the fee. Make sure you've got a decent card, and then any rebate you earn will be icing on the cake.

ARE THE NEW PLATINUM CARDS FOR YOU?

Since 1984, an Amex platinum card has epitomized consumer chic: You are invited to join, pay an annual fee of $300, and receive lavish perks such as free companion plane tickets and access to airport clubs.

So how do the new platinum Visas and MasterCards stack up? Well, they're the same color, but that's about it.

Consider: It's about as easy to get a platinum card as it is a gold card (some 30 million people already have). And the perks are virtually the same. The main difference is that platinum issuers are *required* to offer 24-hour customer service.

Sure, the platinum cards tout credit lines of up to $100,000. But you'd have to earn at least $250,000 just to qualify for that six-figure limit.

So ignore the hype. Here's how to size up platinum:

If you don't carry a balance but pay an annual fee on your current card, a no-fee platinum card will save you money.

If you carry a balance, you can cut your interest cost by transferring the sum onto a platinum card with a low initial rate. After the rate expires, you can continue to save on interest only if your platinum card has a lower regular rate than your current card.

HOW CREDIT CARDS BEAT DEBIT CARDS

Debit cards—those handy pieces of plastic that electronically tap your bank account for the cost of your purchases—are making their way into more and more wallets. But the cards are far from hassle-free. Here's what you need to know to guard against debit debacles—and why it can be smarter to pay with a credit card.

Your ATM (automated teller machine) card may now be a souped-up debit card. Over the past three years, most banks have converted their basic ATM cards to combination ATM/debit cards. These combo cards can be used for purchases as well as for ATM transactions. But the debit feature makes these cards a lot less safe. Here's why: When using an ATM, you must enter a personal identification number (PIN). But when you make a purchase with a debit card, you simply sign the receipt, just as you would with a credit card. That means a debit-card thief may be able to drain your entire checking account simply by faking your signature.

If you are uncomfortable with that risk, consider asking your bank to switch you back to a basic ATM card. Another option may be to lower the spending ceiling on your debit card, thus reducing the amount a thief can get his hands on quickly.

Since January, MasterCard debit-card customers who report the card loss (or money missing in their account) within 24 hours of discovering it will have zero liability for fraudulent debit-card charges. And Visa has eliminated all liability for both its debit cardholders and credit-card customers, as long as you report the fraud within two days of discovery. If you fail to make a timely report, your maximum loss is $50 with both Visa and MasterCard.

But even though your liability is limited, it can take weeks to get your money back. Under federal law, banks can take up to 20 business days to investigate a debit-card fraud claim and return the stolen money. In practice, most banks will give you a provisional credit in one to five business days. While five days is sooner than 20, it can be a long time to wait when bills are due. What's more, you may be stuck with fees for bounced checks. No matter how rapidly a bank acts to make you whole, you may bounce a few checks before the funding comes through. Fortunately, most major banks will waive their own returned-check charges in cases of debit-card misuse. But bank policies vary when it comes to bounced-check fees charged by the firm that deposited the check, such as your electric company.

Bottom line: A credit card still offers key advantages. Even if you swear by the convenience of digital dough or simply prefer to avoid interest charges, don't cut up all your credit cards. The old-fashioned charge-it card still offers benefits that its debit double does not. For one thing, you cannot build a credit history with a debit card, since you aren't borrowing money. And some merchants refuse to accept debit cards because they are not a measure of creditworthiness. What's more, by using a debit card, you may lose the option to withhold payment for faulty or undelivered merchandise. Credit cards still give you the best consumer protection.

TURN DOWN CREDIT LIFE INSURANCE

Most of the estimated 20 million Americans who spend $2 billion or so each year on credit life insurance—which pays off the outstanding balance on your loan if you die—get a lousy deal. Credit life insurance (CLI) often costs more than three times as much as basic term life. For example, annual CLI premiums run $7 for each $1,000 in coverage, vs. less than $2 per $1,000 for a typical term policy for a nonsmoking middle-aged man. As you might guess, CLI is a great deal for the banks that peddle it: Commissions average 40% of premiums, vs. 5% or so for mutual funds and annuities. No surprise, then, that many banks sell CLI aggressively, despite its dubious value to consumers.

Last year, however, new regulations from the Office of the Comptroller of the Currency (OCC)—the chief regulator of the country's 2,800 nationally chartered banks—directed banks to start putting consumers' interests ahead of their own when offering CLI. Specifically, the new OCC regs stipulate that "recommendations to bank customers to buy credit life insurance should be based on the benefits to the customer, not on the revenue from commissions."

A noble sentiment, but unfortunately, the OCC's regulations have little, if any, chance of curtailing credit life pitches. Here's why.

First, the regulations offer no guidelines for how banks should gauge a policy's benefits to borrowers. What's more, the new rules contain no specific provisions for checking up on banks to assure they are even abiding by the new regs. OCC spokesman Dean DeBuck told MONEY that bank examiners will simply consider compliance with the new rules as part of their overall review of bank policies and procedures. Says Mary Griffin, insurance counsel at Consumers Union, a Washington, D.C. consumer advocacy group: "We see nothing in these regulations that will prevent consumers from being duped and pressured to buy expensive insurance they don't need."

State insurance regulators don't offer much protection, either. Only a handful of states, mostly in the Northeast, place reasonable ceilings on what insurers can charge for this coverage. For instance, a credit life policy on a $20,000 five-year car loan would run you $305 in Maine, compared with $1,049 for the same coverage in Mississippi. But for most people, even the strict state limits only make credit life less of a bad deal, not a good one.

Your best protection: Just say no the next time a banker matter-of-factly suggests a credit life policy or even implies you need one to get the loan. (You don't.) "You're almost always better off just making sure that your regular life insurance policy is adequate to cover your debts," says James Hunt, an insurance expert at Washington, D.C.-based Consumer Federation of America. There's a possible exception, however. Because insurers don't take your age or medical condition into account when issuing credit life policies or calculating premiums, the cost of this coverage could be lower than that of regular life policies if you're a smoker over age 40 or have serious health problems.

Finally, if you find that you've unwittingly agreed to a policy in the course of taking out a loan, you're entitled to a refund of the premium provided that you cancel the coverage, typically within 10 to 30 days.

CHAPTER 6

SECRETS OF A RICH RETIREMENT

Looking ahead to retirement, people with household incomes that average $50,000 or more annually—let's call them affluent Americans—appear to be living with unrealistic expectations of how much it will cost and how much they must save to live the way they want when their working days end. According to a recent MONEY poll, they estimate they'll need only 53% of their pre-retirement income to support their retirement lifestyles. Yet, well-off retirees who were polled say they actually require a full 71%. And while the affluent retired people say their single biggest regret is failing to have put more money in tax-deferred retirement savings accounts while they were employed, 60% of them nevertheless say they did invest the maximum the law permits. Only 48% of the affluent nonretirees are doing the same. The bottom line: Unless working Americans begin to plan more realistically, they will not be able to realize their retirement dreams.

Making those dreams come true is not that hard. For example, if you ask Laura and Terrell Danley of Washington, D.C. and St. Petersburg, Fla. how they've attained a financially secure retirement, the former publications editor and former accountant will tell you there's no mystery at all. "People today seem to spend so much time worrying about retirement," says Laura, 63. "Really, it just comes down to doing some intelligent planning." This chapter will help you do exactly that. Starting with six moves you should make to retire with all the money you need, we offer a game plan for your happy, prosperous retirement. It includes strategies for making your money grow, taking advantage of tax breaks and maximizing benefits like Social Security and pensions.

SIX STEPS TO THE LIFESTYLE YOU WANT

The MONEY poll asked retirees key questions about their current finances, plus what they wished they had done differently to prepare for the day they stopped working. Who better to advise readers planning their retirement, we figured, than people who have already gone through the process—and who are willing to share the wisdom they gained from their own mistakes? We distilled our survey's findings into six moves you can't afford to ignore if you want to retire a millionaire. We describe them below, along with steps that accountants, financial planners and investment advisers urge you to take now to capitalize on your elders' wisdom. The figures we cite are for poll respondents with annual household income above $50,000; the average is $78,000.

Figure out how much income you'll need in retirement.

Retirees told us that to support their lifestyles they typically require 71% of their pre-retirement income, which is much more than many of them expected while they were employed. In fact, nearly two in five retirees said they're spending more—an average of 26% more—than they thought they would. "People fool themselves by assuming that when they're retired, they're never going to buy clothes again, or because they fixed the roof a year ago they're never going to have to fix it again," says Paul Yurachek, an accountant and financial planner at American Express Financial Advisors in Bethesda, Md.

To come up with a realistic estimate of your retirement spending, fill out the worksheet on the following page. Don't be too conservative in projecting future costs. Sure, you can expect to get the price break that most insurers offer to retirees on homeowners and auto insurance policies. You can also expect to save on clothing costs, since you will no longer have to buy business attire. But financial planners say that your entertainment outlays will typically double in retirement, because you will have more time to travel and to attend cultural events. You'll likely pay more for utilities and to maintain your residence, because you'll be there more often. And you probably can expect health-care costs to increase as you get older.

Moreover, our poll hammers home the fact that you may have to budget for more people than just you and your spouse. More than a third of retirees with children and grandchildren told us that they are helping to support them financially. And of the 36% of retirees whose parents are living, 23% are giving them monetary assistance. Though such generosity is

HOW MUCH YOU MUST SAVE FOR RETIREMENT

Use this worksheet to figure how much your retirement life will cost—and how much money you must save to pay for it. For the first 10 lines, estimate your annual expenses in today's dollars. We've assumed that you'll live until 92 and earn a modest 8% annually on your investments. We have also assumed that the inflation rate will be 5% a year.

1. Housing (including insurance, utilities, property taxes, furnishings) _____
2. Food (including meals out) _____
3. Transportation _____
4. Taxes _____
5. Clothing, personal care _____
6. Medical expenses (including health insurance) _____
7. Entertainment, recreation, vacations _____
8. Debt payments (including credit cards) _____
9. Savings _____
10. Other (including life and disability insurance) _____
11. TOTAL ANNUAL EXPENDITURES IN RETIREMENT[1] (Add lines 1 through 10.) _____
12. Your expected Social Security and pension income
    (You can obtain estimates from the Social Security Administration
    at 800-772-1213 and from your employee-benefits office.) _____
13. Annual retirement income you will need from savings and investments
    (Subtract line12 from line 11.) _____
14. How much you must save by retirement (Multiply line 13 by factor A below.) _____
15. How much you've already saved (including tax-deferred accounts
    and the total amount you expect your employer to add to them before you retire) _____
16. Inflation-adjusted value of your savings at retirement (Multiply line 15 by factor B.) _____
17. Total retirement capital you still need to accumulate (Subtract line 16 from line 14.) _____
18. HOW MUCH MONEY YOU MUST SAVE EACH YEAR UNTIL RETIREMENT
    (Multiply line 17 by factor C.) _____

Age at Retirement	55	56	57	58	59	60	61	62	63	64	65	66
Factor A	22.2	21.8	21.5	21.1	20.8	20.4	20.0	19.6	19.2	18.8	18.3	17.9

Years to Retirement	3	9	15	20	25	30
Factor B	1.09	1.30	1.56	1.81	2.09	2.43
Factor C	0.324	0.098	0.054	0.037	0.027	0.021

Note: [1] On average, this number constitutes 71% of an affluent retiree's pre-tax, pre-retirement income.
Sources: MONEY poll; Moss Adams in Seattle

laudable, if you can't afford it bear in mind Yurachek's advice: "Your first priority has to be taking care of yourself in retirement."

Start saving for retirement early.
Retirees' second biggest regret is that they didn't begin saving at a younger age. They typically waited until they turned 32 to sock away that first retirement dollar. "It's just silly that I didn't start saving earlier, but I never really felt like I had the money to do so," says Robert Feeney, 80, of Claremont, Calif., a retired engineering professor at California State Polytechnic University–Pomona. "If I had, I would have a lot more money than I do now." An early start is especially crucial for women, whose financial security late in life lags men's at an alarming rate (see the box on page 167).

Let's say you want to have $1 million by the time you're 65. Let's also say your investment money is going to grow by an average 9% a year. If you start at age 22, you'll have to put away $186,190 ($4,330 a year for 43 years) to make that million. If you wait until you're 32 to start, you'll have to shell out $291,854 ($8,844 for 33 years). The reason: compounding. The 10-year head start means you'll already have $63,114 working for you—and compounding—by age 32, rather than having to start from scratch. Wait until you're 40 and your annual investment skyrockets to reach your $1 million goal.

Besides starting young, planners often suggest this approach to boost your stash: Invest your raises and bonuses instead of spending them.

Make full use of tax-advantaged investing.
Financial pros say the only acceptable excuse for not plowing the max into tax-deferred plans is if you need cash to build your emergency fund for daily living. And, says Robert Steffen, a financial planner in Bloomington, Minn., there's never a reason for not investing as much in your retirement account as your company will match, typically half of the first 6% or so of your salary that you contribute. Let's say you put $100 into a 401(k) and your company matches half of it dollar for dollar. Already you're up to $150. If that investment annually earns 10%, you'll turn your initial $100 investment into $165 in one year. Add in tax savings of, say, $35, and you've nearly doubled your money that year. "There's nowhere else you can get a guaranteed return of almost 100%," says financial planner Glen Clemans of the Pearson Financial Group in Lake Oswego, Ore.

Under the new tax law, more people will be eligible for tax-advantaged IRAs. If you or your spouse is covered by a pension plan at work, the income limits for deducting your contribution to a standard IRA will gradually rise over the next decade to $80,000 for couples by 2007 and $50,000 for singles by 2005. If you earn more than that, consider the new so-called Roth IRA. You can open a Roth IRA regardless of whether you have a pension plan at work, but your Adjusted Gross Income can't top $95,000 if you're single or $150,000 if you're married. You won't get a tax deduction for your contribution; instead, once your money has been in the account for five years, you can make tax-free withdrawals, provided you're at least age 59.

Put more money in stocks. Fully 41% of retirees wish they had invested more heavily in stocks. "The stock market seemed risky to me. I never wanted to mess with it," says Rose Brewer, 64, a retired nurse in Bridgeport, Texas. "So my money is in CDs and a savings account. But I missed out on a lot of growth."

Unfortunately, if you're like the people we surveyed, you risk feeling the same remorse when you retire. On average, the nonretired people we questioned have just 53% of their retirement portfolios invested in stocks or equity mutual funds. Investment advisers generally agree that if you won't tap your portfolio for 10 years or more, you ought to keep 60% to 100% of your holdings in stocks. Remember that from 1926 to 1997, stocks returned an annual average of nearly 11%, compared with only 5.6% for long-term corporate bonds. You want your money to stay ahead of both inflation and taxes, so you need as much growth as possible.

Take good care of financial and physical health. Retirees' biggest nonfinancial regret was failing to take better care of themselves during their working years. "You've worked hard to ensure you'll have enough money to live the life you want in retirement," says financial planner Dee Lee of Harvard, Mass. "But if you don't have your health, you won't be able to enjoy any of that life."

To avoid having your retirement blighted physically and financially by illness, take preventive measures now, such as getting plenty of exercise, quitting smoking and following dietary guidelines for a healthy heart. Make sure your health insurance will protect you until you qualify for Medicare at 65 and will then pay for the bulk of any medical needs that the government program won't cover. If your company's insurance coverage will end when you retire, sign up for COBRA before you leave your job. COBRA, named after the federal law known as the Consolidated Omnibus Budget Reconciliation Act, requires your company to continue your health benefits for 18 months. Ask your employee-benefits office for details.

A MONEY poll found that retired men have socked away an average of $105,000 in tax-deferred accounts and other investments, or 24% more than the typical retired woman. In addition, today's nonretired men plan to leave work with average savings of $462,000—nearly 89% more than the $245,000 women expect to save. Yet because American women have a longer life expectancy than men—79 years vs. 73—women need to save a lot more. For example, figures Glen Clemans, a financial planner in Lake Oswego, Ore., a woman who earns $50,000 a year must amass $310,000 by the time she's 60 to retire that year and maintain her standard of living for the expected remaining years of her life, assuming she earns 10% a year on her investments. A man with the same salary would need only $250,000.

To plan for a secure retirement, women must invest more aggressively. Our poll found that even though women live longer in retirement and need the investment returns that only stocks can provide, on average they have a mere 37% of their portfolios in equities before retirement. Nonretired men, on the other hand, keep 51% of their holdings in stocks.

Women also must be smarter about pension vesting. They frequently move in and out of the job market during their child-raising years, which are also typically their peak earning years. "As a result, they accumulate less money in employer-sponsored retirement accounts and have more trouble vesting in a company pension plan than men do," says financial planner Marilyn Capelli of Flint, Mich. So women must pay special attention to vesting dates for pensions and employer-sponsored plans like 401(k)s—and try to time their periods away from work accordingly. (If you're a stay-at-home spouse, take advantage of the new tax law that, starting in 1998, allows people like you to contribute $2,000 a year to an IRA, regardless of whether your husband is covered by a pension plan at work.)

Additionally, women must prepare to live on their own. While 80% of the retired men polled have spouses, only 60% of the retired women do. Spending a portion of your retirement years alone can be financially devastating: A report by the General Accounting Office shows that 80% of widows now living in poverty were not poor before their husbands died. Furthermore, only 28% of divorcing women are entitled to financial support from their exes—and only 34% of those women ever see the money that's owed them, according to the National Center for Women and Retirement Research at Long Island University.

It's critical for women to know their legal rights. If you're widowed and your late husband was covered by a private pension plan, you're generally entitled to survivors benefits unless you waived your rights. You can also collect a Social Security benefit based on your late husband's work record if it's higher than the full benefit you'd receive based on your own earnings. If you're divorced, 62 or older, and were married for at least 10 years, you too can receive benefits on your ex's work record.

In addition, 52% of women and 33% of men will spend at least some time in nursing homes, which typically charge $40,000 a year, according to the United Seniors Health Cooperative in Washington, D.C. And the average stay lasts more than two years. So if your family's medical history indicates that you run a high risk of a long, debilitating illness—and you can't expect your children to care for you—you might consider long-term-care insurance. Unfortunately, the premiums—which are deductible only to the extent they and your other itemized medical expenses exceed 7.5% of your Adjusted Gross Income—can be prohibitively expensive, especially as you get older. For example, a policy that will provide a $100 daily nursing-home benefit and a $50 daily home-health-care benefit could cost a 55-year-old $1,452 a year. Buy the policy at 68, and your annual premium will jump 153% to $3,676.

Don't postpone key retirement decisions. Nearly 25% of retirees said they wished they had spent more time analyzing their pension plans before leaving work. Clearly, a fumbling decision about your pension-plan distribution can be a particularly costly error. Our survey showed that nonretirees generally count on their pensions to provide 26% of their retirement income. Yet 64% of them expect to take their pensions as annuities, even though employers seldom pay more than 6% a year on money left in their care. That's why financial pros usually advise clients to take their pensions as lump sums. You can roll over your payout into an IRA, invest it in stocks and bonds and figure on your money growing tax deferred at an achievable 8% or so annually.

There are other reasons to give yourself a few years of lead time before you quit working. You may find it difficult to drop your current spending and working habits abruptly. Planners therefore recommend that you start trying to live on your expected retirement income at least three years before you leave your job. These also are the years to test your retirement plans. If you think you want to do volunteer work three times a week in retirement, try doing it once a week now, to see if you really like it. If you want to work part time, begin setting up contacts as soon as possible.

CREATE A PERSONAL INVESTMENT PLAN

If you start now you can reach retirement with all the money you need, even if it's in the seven figures. Don't believe it? Just follow the math. Let's say you are 40 with a household income of $84,000, the median for MONEY subscribers, and you want to retire on an inflation-adjusted 80% of your current income. If you put 10% of your salary every year into a 401(k) with a typical 50% in matching funds from your employer and earn 10% on your money (a little below the stock market's average over the past 60 years), you will hit 65 with $1.7 million in your account—even if you are starting from zero today. All right, by the time today's 40-year-olds retire, inflation will have made a million dollars a somewhat less awesome figure than it is today. Even so, it will never be chump change.

You will inevitably face obstacles on the way to accumulating such a sum. If you are just starting out, for example, you may find that your beginner's salary leaves you barely enough to cope with student loans, let alone max out on your 401(k) contribution. If you're married with kids, you will have to find some way to finesse college expenses that loom just one step ahead of your own retirement bills. But the fact is, at every stage of your life, you can control your retirement prospects—by how much you save and when you save it, by how aggressively you invest and by when you plan to retire. Even if you are 50 years old, in the earlier example, without a penny saved, you could still hit retirement with a million in the bank by cranking your savings up to 15% of your salary and staying on the job two years longer than you had planned. And remember that you have help. As we said earlier, the government gives you tax breaks when you save in Individual Retirement Accounts and retirement plans like 401(k)s. There is Social Security too. And chances are, your employer is willing to lend a hand. Some 90% of large and mid-size companies offer 401(k) retirement plans, and 80% of these employers usually match 50% of whatever you save, up to 6% of your salary.

We can help you reach your goal. With help from a panel of six top financial advisers, MONEY devised the following retirement saving strategies for people at two critical crossroads of life.

Strategy for a young single. When she isn't playing alto sax or teaching music to schoolchildren, Laura Griesemer, 26, of Middlebury, Vt. is something of a magician. With an ease that amazes even Griesemer, she can make her $1,450 a month take-home pay disappear. "I don't know where the money goes," she says, a lament that most twentysomethings (and their parents) find all too familiar.

The leaks in her cash flow are about what you'd expect from someone just getting a start on life: a $230 share of the monthly mortgage payment on the two-bedroom condo she and her boyfriend bought last year, $380 in car payments, and $140 for gas and insurance combined. Although she earned an extra $4,200 last year giving private music lessons, that money also vanished into closing costs on the condo and other housing expenses. Not exactly an auspicious start for a millionaire in the making.

Like most people her age, Griesemer finds it hard to sacrifice for a financial goal three or four decades in the future. She socked away only $1,000 of her $24,700 salary last year in Vermont's retirement savings plan for teachers, at a return of about 5%. She'll be vested in nine years. Meanwhile, she also has $2,800 earning the same dismal return in a pension plan from a former teaching job. But at least she understands what is at stake. "I realize that saving early gives you a lot more money in the end than saving late," Laura says. "So I want to put away as much as I possibly can." And she'll have more to salt away later this year when her salary rises to $27,900, thanks to her new master's degree.

Our advice: Save all you can—until it hurts. Take full advantage of tax-sheltered savings plans.

Laura should start saving as much as she can—and so should anyone her age—to get maximum benefits from compounding. The ideal vehicles for the ride to the $1 million mark are those employer-sponsored retirement plans like 401(k)s. Laura qualifies to contribute to a 403(b) plan where she works, a relative of the 401(k) offered to employees of nonprofits. In either plan, every dollar you save effectively counts as a tax deduction in the year you take it. So if you're in the 28% tax bracket, to save a dollar you actually give up only 72¢ in after-tax take-home pay. Our planners urge Laura to save the maximum permitted by her plan, or 20% of her pay.

When it comes to choosing investments, figure on putting at least 75% of your savings into your plan's stock funds, and then do your best to ignore market fluctuations. "A 26-year-old has plenty of time to recover from a market slide or two or three," says Margie Mullen of Mullen Advisory in Los Angeles. If Laura does that, she may be able to mimic the market's long-term average return of just under 11%. In that case, assuming she keeps working for the next 29 years, she could retire a 55-year-old millionaire—and play the sax whenever she wants.

Strategy for marrieds with children. Vickie and Kevin Jones, 44 and 36, of Fremont, Calif. have two of everything: incomes, 401(k) plans, pensions and children. Parents of Jade, 5, and Chauncey, 9 months, they also have two major expenses to face before they can retire: double college bills. Like many baby boomers who have produced 50% more children after age 30 than the previous generation, the Joneses began building their family later in life than their parents did—which means that they will be slogging through college expenses in their mid-50s, just when they should begin their savings sprint toward retirement.

For all parents, trying to squeeze out money to amass a college fund while salting something away for the future empty nest is like asking the same dollar to do two jobs. "It's always the thorniest problem my clients with children have," says Laura Varvel of Briaud Financial Planning in Bryan, Texas. Vickie and Kevin Jones have not made it any less prickly by setting their sights high: When they think about the future, they envision a big-ticket Stanford education for both of their kids and a retirement in which they live as well or better than they do now in pricey northern California.

That won't be easy for the two employees of Bank of America, where Kevin works as an unemployment insurance administrator and Vickie is an administrative assistant. To provide an inflation-adjusted retirement income of $57,600—what the Joneses will need to maintain their standard of living— the couple would need assets of $1.8 million, a long reach from the $61,000 they have today. That cache is divided between two B of A pension plans and two 401(k)s. Kevin puts 5% of his $37,000 pre-tax salary into his 401(k), and the company matches his contributions a generous dollar for dollar. Vickie contributes 3% of her $35,000 and gets a dollar-for-dollar match too.

At the Joneses' current rate of saving, their retirement accounts will total just $906,000 by the time Vickie turns 65. And that's without counting the tuition at Stanford.

Our advice: As your assets grow, diversify. Save for retirement first, then college.

If your retirement plan isn't working, tear up the script and rethink. To make their target, for example, Kevin and Vickie must raise their savings by $2,860 a year (which may mean pushing hard for big salary increases) and earn one percentage point a year more on their investments (which will require slightly more aggressive investing). Fortunately, the couple have no plans to retire early. In fact, with an eight-year age difference, Kevin will be working for quite a while after Vickie retires.

Our panel of planners says that it usually makes sense to review your investments to see whether you can squeeze higher returns out of your portfolio. Judging from the way 401(k) participants overall divide their money, many investors have plenty of room for improvement: The average employee relies far too heavily on safe but low-returning fixed-income funds and keeps too much money in his or her employer's stock.

The Joneses are guilty of both errors. Half of their retirement portfolio is invested in B of A stock and 40% is in fixed-income securities. The rest is in a blue-chip growth fund. "I think it's too risky to tie more than 10% of your portfolio to the health of any one company," says Lisa Osofsky of the financial planning firm M.R. Weiser in Edison, N.J. "That's even more true when it's the stock of your employer, whom you're already relying on for your income and pension." Margie Mullen points out that the Joneses could probably boost their returns from 9% to 10% a year without any increase in risk by moving at least half of their Bank of America stock and half of their fixed-income funds into their 401(k)'s growth funds. To achieve similar returns with even less risk, Mullen advises them to put all but 10% of the B of A stock in the growth funds.

Coming up with any extra cash to save is more difficult. Says Kevin: "With a mortgage and two kids in day care, it's an expensive life." So it's important for the couple to concentrate their saving where they'll get the highest payoff. That's their 401(k) plan, with its handsome dollar-for-dollar match. "Vickie needs to save at least 5% of her income, not 3%," says Osofsky. "By scraping up that extra $700 a year, she'll get another $700 a year from her employer." Even if your 401(k) matches a more conventional 50%, that still amounts to a guaranteed 50% return, instantly. No other investment comes close. Mullen also suggests the couple try to find ways to put still more of their pay—up to 8%—into their 401(k). "Any amount beyond what's permitted by their employer has to come out of after-tax salary, and there's no match," she says. "But the money will still grow tax deferred, making it a better investment option than an alternative that's taxed every year."

As for saving for both college and retirement, the planners say your wisest course—and the Joneses'—is to concentrate first on your own future. By the time your children are college bound, they may be eligible for loans or scholarships that are impossible to foresee today. Mullen points out that you can demand your kids pay some of their own way for college. But there's not much chance that your children will fund your retirement.

MANAGING YOUR MONEY IN RETIREMENT

Conventional wisdom holds that managing your money in youth and in retirement are similar. Of course, conventional wisdom has also held, at various times, that the world was flat, that members of the British royal family do not get divorced and that the Dow could not top 7000. But the main problem with conventional investing wisdom is not that it's wrong but that it fails to consider the real world of retirees. "Asset allocation is about coming up with an ideal blend for an individual," says Tim Schlindwein, an investment counselor in Chicago. "And the way to do that is by matching up the characteristics of an asset with the needs and preferences of the individual."

The conventional stocks/bonds/cash allocation groups are fine if you're 25 and own no investments outside of your 401(k). But what if you're the average American over the age of 55, which means your house makes up 25% of your total assets? Or you receive Social Security and a corporate pension? How do those income streams figure into your portfolio mix? What's the role of stocks in a portfolio that must produce income as well as growth? And what if you plan to leave some money to your heirs?

To manage your money properly in retirement, you need to consider as part of your portfolio some holdings you may never before have regarded as assets and to ignore others you may have always thought were indispensable. And it's important to recognize that your investment horizon extends not just through your life span but into your heirs' as well.

Rethink fixed-income assets.

You should count your Social Security and pension benefits as fixed-income assets. In fact, since corporate pensions were guaranteed up to $33,136 in 1997 by Uncle Sam, you can regard your pension up to that amount as the next best thing to a U.S. Government bond. Moreover, the stability of your pension and Social Security "assets" allows you to tilt the remainder of your portfolio comfortably more toward stocks, even in a high-flying market.

But since there's no market for your claim on Social Security or your company's pension fund, how do you know what value to affix to them? Maria Crawford Scott, editor of the *American Association of Individual Investors Journal*, says it's simple: Their value is roughly equal to what it would cost to buy an annuity promising the same monthly payments for the rest of your life. Add that sum to the market value of your bonds, CDs and stable-value funds to get the true amount you have allotted to fixed-income assets.

Don't factor in your house.

If you're like most retirees, your home is either your largest or your second largest asset. Over the past 20 years, house prices have leaped an average of 249%, and you have long been assured that you can use this store of wealth to ensure a comfortable retirement.

Not so fast. Your home is not part of your investment portfolio unless you plan to sell it. "Your house is there to provide shelter, not to generate income, which makes it a nonworking asset," says Wayne Starr, a financial planner in Kansas City, Mo. The same goes—even more so—for your art collection, jewelry, antiques or other collectibles. Are you really planning to part with that 1963 Stingray or the honest-to-god Stickley dining room chairs in order to invest the proceeds? If not, don't count on them as investable assets.

While you could earn some income from a reverse mortgage on your home, selling the house, moving to smaller quarters and investing the difference is preferable by far. For one thing, that way you get to earn interest on the net proceeds from the sale, rather than owing it, as you would on a reverse mortgage. And because larger homes tend to have higher utility bills, property taxes and maintenance costs than smaller ones, downsizing will free up money so you can make additional investments. Downsizing has one major strike against it, however: Most retirees like to stay put. In fact, every year, just 5% of them choose to relocate.

If you are dead set against selling your place and are short on cash, then a reverse mortgage may be your only choice. But be aware that it will cost you. A reverse mortgage is essentially a cash advance on which you pay interest against the expected future value of your home when you die. You sign over 80% to 90% of your home's value to the lender in return for a stream of monthly payments that last as long as you live. You never have to vacate your house, but the price of that privilege can be absurdly high.

Obviously, a well-executed retirement plan should not force you to take that risk. "A reverse mortgage is an option of last resort," says Peggy Ruhlin, a financial planner in Columbus, Ohio and president of the International Association for Financial Planning. "If you are reduced to it to keep your home, then you really haven't saved enough for retirement."

You can touch your principal. If you needed $100, would it matter whether you took it from your checking account or from your savings account? Of course not. And yet too many retirees persist in defining potential income as only the money that will come exclusively from their fixed-income investments, namely bonds or Social Security. Principal, they reckon, is off limits.

But proceeds from the sale of a stock can pay a month's rent just as easily as the 6.1% payout from your three-year Treasury notes. "When we're talking about income, what we're really talking about is your cash flow," says Ruhlin. "That can mean capital gains, dividends and principal, as well as interest from bonds."

Say, for example, that you retire this year with a $300,000 portfolio and need to take out $20,000 a year to meet living expenses. You could invest your money in 30-year bonds at 6.7%; that would be enough to let you meet expenses without touching principal. By 2017 you'd still have $300,000 in your nest egg, as well as your $20,000 of income—although 3% inflation would have reduced the purchasing power on that sum to just $10,876, not to mention its effects on your principal.

Suppose, instead, that you put the money into a portfolio heavily weighted with stock funds and it returned 9% a year, nearly two percentage points below the average for the S&P 500 since 1926. Because the yield on such a portfolio would likely be less than 2%, you would have to sell securities every year to meet your income needs. Even so, in 20 years, your portfolio would have grown to $697,000, even if you took $20,000 a year from the kitty in living expenses. Alternatively, you could have raised your withdrawals by 3% a year to keep pace with inflation, and your nest egg would still have grown to $416,000 by 2017. And that doesn't account for the fact that you can save on taxes by taking your income out of capital gains rather than interest, which is taxed at your maximum bracket.

Obviously, no stock-oriented portfolio will earn 9% each and every year. But losing years are only paper losses until you have to liquidate your portfolio. "In a year when you're winning, you're tucking away for the down years," Ruhlin says. "So you really have to focus on how it averages out." Your best bet for minimizing losses: Stick with conservative blue-chip stocks that pay dividends, as opposed to riskier, small-size companies.

Invest for both yourself and your heirs. There's another reason to weight your portfolio more toward stocks than the conventional wisdom advises: It's better for your heirs.

Suppose you invest mainly in bonds and bequeath your portfolio to your daughter. For the reasons explained above, you will probably have a smaller legacy than you would have had if you had invested in stocks. Moreover, presuming that your daughter prefers stocks to bonds for her own portfolio, bequeathing her bonds leaves her with two unattractive options: She can hold on to the bonds and pay ordinary income taxes on the interest; or she can sell them, incur unnecessary transaction costs of up to 3.5% or so and reinvest the remainder in stocks.

When you bequeath stocks, on the other hand, you take much greater advantage of a huge tax break. At your death, any capital-gains tax liability on your profits is wiped out. For tax purposes, your heirs' cost in inherited stock becomes the value of the shares as of the day of your death, not as of the day you bought them. So if your daughter sells the stocks right away, she'll owe no capital-gains taxes; if she waits to sell them, she'll owe taxes only on gains incurred since the inheritance. "Appreciated assets are one of the best things you can leave your heirs," says Ellen Fairbanks, a certified financial planner in Pittsburgh.

And be sure you keep those assets separate from the ones you plan on investing for your own retirement. After all, your heirs will have their whole lifetime to ride out the ups and downs of the stock market and they can afford to be more aggressively invested. Which brings us back to where we started: Asset allocation is not a one-size-fits-all strategy. Your heirs won't want to wear the same kind of portfolio you do.

ONLINE HELP FOR YOUR PLANNING

Several sites on the Internet offer advice accessible to even the most numerically challenged retirement investors. But before you fire up your browser, you should be aware of an inherent limitation: Computerized calculators are terrific for crunching numbers but not so great at providing the kinds of judgment and insight a flesh-and-blood financial planner would. For example, FinanCenter (http://www.financenter.com)—a site that includes calculators on everything from planning your retirement to deciding whether to buy or lease a car—automatically assumes a life expectancy of 85 for everyone. But a 65-year-old man who doesn't smoke has a 51% chance of living beyond that age. If your retirement plan is built around living to 85 and you live to, say, 95, your final decade could be a lean one. So boost your life expectancy to 90 or more, as sites typically allow you to do.

With that caveat, here are the top Websites in three key areas.

Figure out retirement living expenses. The FinanCenter site takes a sophisticated approach to this task by splitting expenses into two groups—those that tend to shrink in retirement, such as life insurance and housing, and those that typically grow, such as medical and recreation expenses. The program will then calculate your estimated total monthly expenses in retirement for each of these categories in current and inflation-adjusted dollars. Playing it cautious, the program automatically enters a 4% inflation rate. But you can enter a more reasonable 3% to 3.5%, which better reflects the long-term U.S. average.

FinanCenter's detailed expense planner provides a color pie chart that breaks down your expenses into 11 groups, ranging from housing and loan payments to clothing. The chart instantly reveals which parts of your retirement budget will be sucking up most of your money—and, therefore, which are ripe for trimming.

Calculate how much you must invest. Once you know the expenses you'll face, you can focus on making sure you will have enough income to live comfortably. The retirement area of the Quicken Financial Network (www.qfn.com) can guide you step by step through the various calculations you must make to do this. The QFN program begins by asking how much annual income you will need after you retire. Simply enter the living-cost estimate you put together at the FinanCenter site. QFN then takes a look at how much you will actually have, starting with company pensions and Social Security. If you are not sure what you can expect from Social Security, QFN will help you estimate your benefits. If you are like most people, your pension and Social Security payments won't cover all of your expenses, which means you'll be relying on your investments to cover the shortfall.

This is where QFN really excels. It examines how much you have invested, including company savings plans such as 401(k)s, and then asks how much you plan to continue investing until you retire. Next, rather than simply telling you to estimate how much you will earn on your investments, as some programs do, QFN quizzes you on how much volatility you're willing to stomach. It then assigns a projected return based on your risk tolerance. If you have a moderate appetite for risk, QFN factors in an 8.5% annual return based on a suggested mix of 45% domestic bonds, 35% large-cap stocks, 5% small-cap stocks and 15% international stocks. Changing your risk level immediately changes your return and your investment mix.

Once you have also plugged in the amount you now have invested and what you plan to save, QFN can tell you whether you will accumulate a large enough stash to generate the income you will need. If it appears you will fall short, you can figure out how to achieve your goal by increasing your savings, shooting for higher returns or both.

Choose the most tax-friendly withdrawal plan. If you think figuring out how to save money for retirement is complicated, wait until you have to start spending it. Tax law requires that you begin withdrawing at least a minimum amount from tax-deferred accounts such as 401(k)s and Individual Retirement Accounts starting the April after you reach age 70. (You can hold off taking money from your 401(k) if you are still working.) The minimum you must pull out is based on your life expectancy. The idea is to prevent you from avoiding tax on your money in 401(k)s and IRAs indefinitely. You won't want to take this requirement lightly. If you don't withdraw enough, the IRS hits you with a big penalty.

The site that thoroughly addresses this issue—as well as others, such as deciding whether to take a lump sum from a company pension plan or lifetime income—is Vanguard's retirement planner (www.vanguard.com). For example, the site explains in detail the two different ways of calculating your required minimum distribution. The first is simply to prorate withdrawals based on your life expectancy at the time you start pulling money out; the second is to refigure your life expectancy each year and base the withdrawals on that figure. Though more complicated, the second method results in smaller withdrawals, allowing more of your cash to compound tax deferred.

KEEP TRACK OF BENEFITS YOU'LL NEED

Boost your Social Security payoff. If you've been watching the debate in Washington over how to keep Social Security from going broke in 2029, you may fear that by the time you retire, your benefit will have been cut to a pittance or, worse, you won't get anything. Relax. The politicians can't afford to let America's most popular entitlement program wither or die. After all, 30.3 million people receive Social Security retirement benefits today—the total will swell to 57.5 million by 2025—and most of them vote. So while the pols argue over ways to prevent the program from slipping into the red, you might start thinking about how you can get the most out of Social Security.

That's no joke. The truly good news about Social Security is that throughout your working life you can take steps that will increase your retirement benefit, even if you start receiving checks at the earliest possible date, when you turn 62. We are about to describe benefit-building strategies that could boost your Social Security check. And let us assure you: Your efforts won't be in vain. The likeliest reforms, such as raising the age at which you can receive full retirement benefits—now as old as 67 for some future retirees—won't fundamentally alter the system. Moreover, the changes are likely to be phased in over many years, giving today's workers time to plan for them.

That means you'll have plenty of warning—and enough time—to amend any benefit-fattening strategies you adopt now. Indeed, even in the unlikely event that the system is radically transformed sometime in the 21st century, you would almost certainly collect a benefit based on what you had accumulated up to that point. Thus, come what may, your smartest move is to do whatever you can under the present rules to pump up your benefit.

Before you get started, let's review the basics on how your Social Security retirement benefit is calculated:

1. To qualify for a check, you must earn income in at least 10 years and make a minimum amount that is set by law in each of those years, $2,680 in 1997. The amount rises each year according to the average wage index. For example, someone who worked at the minimum wage for 10 years and retired today at age 62 would be entitled to a monthly benefit of $327.

2. To get the biggest possible payout—$1,609 a month for someone who starts collecting benefits this year at age 70—you must work at least part time for 35 years and earn as much as the maximum amount that is taxed for Social Security purposes in each of those years—$65,400 in 1997. If you work for more than 35 years, the Social Security Administration will replace your lowest-earning years with higher-earning years in the benefits calculation. Only your earnings subject to Social Security taxes are included in the computation; any additional earnings are left out.

3. Every year that your work history falls short of 35 years will be counted as a zero in computing your benefit, and you'll get a smaller Social Security check than you would otherwise.

With those fundamentals in mind, consider taking the following steps to boost your Social Security retirement benefit:

▶ Increase your earnings by moonlighting or starting a part-time business. If your day job doesn't pay you at least as much as the maximum taxed for Social Security, developing a profitable sideline could dramatically increase your benefit. Also, carefully plan absences from the work force. When you're deciding how much time to take off to care for a newborn or an ailing parent, your Social Security benefit is probably not uppermost in your mind—but it's worth considering. That's because, as explained above, years in which you earn nothing can count against you when your benefit is calculated. If you must leave your full-time job, try to work part time to earn money that will count toward your retirement benefit.

▶ If you're divorced, protect your right to a benefit based on your ex-spouse's earnings. You're entitled to Social Security checks calculated according to your ex's work history if you meet the following four tests: 1) One-half of your ex-spouse's age-65 benefit is larger than the benefit you would receive based on your own work history; 2) you were married for at least 10 years; 3) you've been divorced for at least two years; and 4) you are not married to someone else at the time you start to get the benefit. You can begin receiving checks as soon as both you and your ex are at least 62, even if neither of you is retired. (If you remarry after you start to collect, you lose the ex-spousal benefit.)

▶ Know that you can collect benefits for dependent school-age children. When you start receiving Social Security checks, you qualify for an additional amount if you have a child under 18, or under 19 and still in high school full time. The youngster usually must be your biological or adopted child, and you must be able to claim him or her as a dependent on your tax return. The child may also be a grandchild or stepgrandchild who lives with you because his or her parents have died. If you qualify for the extra benefit, be sure to tell Social Security that you have young kids when you apply for your check. You can then collect an additional amount equal to 50% of your benefit if you have one qualifying child and as much as 88% for two or more.

▶ Learn when it pays to delay retirement. Until you turn 70, the longer you postpone filing for benefits after age 65, the bigger your check will be. That's because for each year you delay, your benefit will automatically increase, depending on your year of birth. At age 70, the increases stop.

On the other hand, no matter when you were born, you could start receiving your benefit at 62. If you do, however, your benefit will be permanently reduced. The reduction's size depends on how close you are to your full retirement when you start collecting checks. For most retirees today, it doesn't pay to postpone filing until after age 65, even though your benefit will rise for each year you delay until 70. That's because the increase is usually too small to make up for all of the money you could collect by filing early. But there may be tax consequences that will influence your decision. To learn about them, see "When It Pays to Work after 65" on page 187.

Track down errors in your records. If you were born in 1944 or earlier, Social Security either sent you an estimate of your retirement benefit sometime in the past two years or will mail you one this year. If you were born in 1945 or later, you can get an estimate by filing an application for a Personal Earnings and Benefits Statement. You can get the form at your local Social Security office, by calling 800-772-1213 or by computer at http://www.ssa.gov. The form asks for such data as your name, the age at which you want to retire and your estimate of your average annual income between now and retirement.

About five weeks after returning the form, you'll receive a statement that shows the earnings that the Social Security Administration has on file for each year you worked and a projection of your benefit. When you get your statement, check first for mistakes in your earnings record. If you find one, such as an entry that shows zero earnings for a year in which you made money, report the error to Social Security. To fix the record, the agency will require proof, such as a tax return from that year. If you don't have documentation, give Social Security your employer's name, and the agency will try to correct the error using data from its own records.

As of last year, the Social Security Administration's records showed more than $200 billion earned by American workers that the agency hadn't been able to match with their rightful owners. If some of these earnings belong to you, you could get a smaller monthly Social Security check than you deserve—or miss out on benefits entirely. To get a clue whether this problem affects you, think back to all the jobs you've ever held. Did you always use the same version of your name when you filled out payroll forms? Ever use Bill instead of William or insert your middle initial or middle name? Did you stick with your maiden name, even after you married? Any one of these seemingly innocuous moves raises the odds that you may be in for a boost in the size of your Social Security checks—if you take action when you see an error on your Social Security Personal Earnings and Benefit Estimate Statement. To prevent errors, phone Social Security if you change your name for any reason, including taking your spouse's name after marriage. And don't change your name at work. Make sure that the name that appears on your employment records, such as W-2 forms, is identical to that on your Social Security card. Never use a nickname on those job records, unless it's also on the Social Security card.

Protect against broken promises? Anyone in or near retirement must wonder: Will my employer pull the rug out from under me? From 1995 to 1997 roughly a third of large firms tinkered with their pledges to provide lifetime health benefits, typically off-loading more of the cost onto people like you. According to Foster Higgins, a New York City consulting firm, about 16% of these employers have boosted retirees' health premium contributions and 11% have upped deductibles, co-insurance payments or out-of-pocket maximums. The message is clear: You, the retiree, are going to be more responsible for protecting yourself. Here's how:

First, find out if you are at risk. Your employer has no obligation to provide you with lifetime medical coverage unless the company has unconditionally promised it to you in writing. Ask your benefits administrator for a copy of the summary plan description (SPD), a document that outlines exactly what your benefits include. The SPD can be changed from year to year, so if you're still working, be sure to get the most current one. Retirees should ask for the SPD that was in effect at the time they retired.

As you read it, look for a clear promise along the lines of: "Basic health-care coverage will be provided at the company's expense for your lifetime." Next, check for such disclaimers as: "The company reserves the right to modify, revoke, suspend, terminate or change the program, in whole or in part, at any time." If your SPD has one of these "reservation of rights" clauses—and most plans today do—you're on shaky ground.

If you are still working, count on paying all or part of your health-care costs once you retire. In 1996 only 40% of large employers offered medical coverage to early retirees, according to Foster Higgins, vs. 46% just three years earlier. Fewer still—33% in 1996, down from 40% in 1993—provide health benefits to retirees who are eligible for Medicare.

Whatever your company may have promised, however, it does not have to set aside money to pay for health care, so the pledge can be broken if the business lacks cash. Some do back up their promises by contributing to a voluntary employee beneficiary association, or VEBA. Depending on how the VEBA is set up, the money in it can cover expenses ranging from health benefits to life insurance. Your summary plan description will tell you if your company contributes to a VEBA.

If you are offered a buy-out, negotiate for better health benefits. When you are downsized out of a job, you are often asked to sign a release agreeing not to sue the company for age discrimination. But, says Raymond Fay, a Washington, D.C. lawyer who fights companies that renege on promises to provide lifetime benefits, "you aren't required to sign a release unless you get something extra for doing so." If your company wants you out, that "extra" could be agreeing to extend your health coverage for a few more years or even for life. Be sure to get any such promise in writing.

If your employer reneges on benefits once you have retired, consider bringing a lawsuit. If your SPD is vague or contradictory about how long your benefits are supposed to last, you could sue the company on the basis of misinformation. "Failure to be clear about benefits is a breach of fiduciary responsibility," explains Alan Sandals, a lawyer with Sandals Langer & Taylor in Philadelphia. Early retirees who accepted a buy-out in return for lifetime benefits could also have a strong legal case. But remember, you have no guarantee of winning.

Even worse, these legal wrangles can last for years. To defray expenses, you could enlist other retirees and file a class-action suit. You might also be able to sue for age discrimination. Most employers want to honor their promises, if only so they won't look bad. Sometimes the best leverage you have is to threaten to make them look very bad indeed.

Keep up with Medicare changes. How you'll fare under the new Medicare regulations depends partly on how old you are now. If you are now receiving Medicare, your premiums will rise to $67 a month in five years, rather than the $51.50 projected under the old law. But there are benefits too, including the right to choose from new health plans.

Some new options are of dubious value. Starting in 1999, for instance, up to 390,000 seniors can volunteer to open a medical savings account. Each year, Uncle Sam will provide you with a tax-free cash allowance, based on your age, location and other demographic factors, to cover the premiums for a high-deductible health insurance policy as well as part of the deductible. If you don't have many medical expenses, the money accumulates in your account; once the balance reaches 60% of your deductible, you get to keep the excess cash. That works great—provided you stay healthy. Warns Geri Dallek, director of health policy for Families USA, a Washington, D.C. advocacy group: "If you get sick, you could wind up with four-figure bills and not enough money in your account to cover them."

In an equally dramatic change, for the first time in Medicare's 31-year history you will be able to buy Medicare-style coverage from private insurers. These insurers may pay doctors more generously than Medicare does, meaning doctors might give you more attention than they can afford to under Medicare's parsimonious fee schedule. On the other hand, higher fees to doctors mean that insurers will demand bigger premiums for the coverage and your co-payments will be higher. The new law also allows doctors to accept private payments from Medicare patients at any rate the physicians wish, as long as the patient pays the entire bill himself. But to do this, a physician must agree not to accept any Medicare reimbursements for at least two years. Considering that 93% of doctors who treat the elderly receive

Medicare payments today and that those payments, on average, make up 27% of their income, it seems unlikely that many will give them up.

The smart thing to do now: Read carefully all the informational bulletins and letters you'll be getting on Medicare over the coming months from the Health Care Finance Administration, the agency that runs the program.

If you are in your mid-50s or early 60s, the costs of the new Medicare freedoms will start to weigh heavily just as you become eligible for the program. Starting in 2002, for example, Medicare beneficiaries will be allowed to change plans only once a year, although new enrollees who choose a plan they don't like can replace it during their first year. After the turn of the century, seniors will also face far higher costs than they do today. By 2007, premiums are expected to reach $105 a month. What you should do now is figure out what you like and don't like about your current health insurance plan so you'll know exactly what you want when it's time to enroll in Medicare. Also, keep abreast of what the first wave of seniors who try these plans have to say about them, and learn from their experience. Finally, make sure you've budgeted for the higher premiums and payments you're going to get hit with.

If you are in your early 50s or younger, stay vigilant. Congress scuttled a proposal to raise the Medicare eligibility age from 65 to 67, but the idea will likely come around again. A 17-member commission studying ways to keep Medicare solvent for the baby boomers is scheduled to report to Congress by March 1999. Don't wait for the report. Tell Congress how you feel about various remedies. And sock away extra cash for retirement. No matter what happens to Medicare, it's going to be more expensive by the time you get there.

Pluses and minuses of Medicare HMOs.

Desperate to get a piece of the rapidly growing, increasingly healthy 65-and-over population, health maintenance organizations are selling themselves to the nation's estimated 38 million Medicare recipients these days with the zeal of old-time circus barkers: "Medical benefits far beyond those offered with traditional Medicare! No paperwork! Low co-payments and no deductibles! The highest-quality services and facilities! Doctors who will keep you alive forever!" Well, okay, maybe they don't say you'll live forever. But the rest of the sales pitch has been mighty effective: Medicare beneficiaries are now signing up for HMOs at a rate of one every 30 seconds. As a result, experts say that with both the government and seniors trying to reduce their health-care spending, 25% of Medicare recipients may be in HMOs in five years.

For some of you, joining a Medicare HMO will be a smart move. For others, however, it could be a mistake. MONEY's reporting shows that Medicare HMOs can be a satisfactory option if you're in good health. But if you have a serious or chronic medical condition, HMOs can have significant shortcomings that you need to understand before you sign up.

Studies show that seniors have more trouble getting specialty care in HMOs than with traditional fee-for-service plans and that elderly patients who need home health care or who are chronically ill are likely to get less treatment through Medicare HMOs than from fee-for-service plans. To hold down costs, the HMOs limit your choice of doctors and access to specialists. And, quite critically, Medicare HMO patients lack a timely, efficient appeals process when they don't get the care they think is essential. This can delay urgently needed treatment.

Clearly, however, Medicare HMOs offer several advantages over traditional fee-for-service Medicare. First, members have virtually no paperwork, since the plans handle all insurance forms. Second, HMOs provide more comprehensive coverage, typically offering benefits traditional Medicare doesn't—like prescription drugs, dental services, eyeglasses and preventive care—at little or no charge. And they are inarguably cheaper: To get such extras with fee-for-service Medicare, you'd have to buy a supplemental Medigap insurance policy, which isn't cheap. Last year the average premium cost rose 23% at Prudential, the biggest Medigap seller, and its basic plan can run up to $1,020 a year.

In addition, roughly 60% of HMO members owe no premiums with their plans. Co-payments are minimal in a Medicare HMO too, generally ranging from just $5 to $20 per office visit. And there are no deductibles, even for hospital stays. Indeed, HMOs pick up virtually the whole tab on approved hospital care. Traditional Medicare, by contrast, holds you responsible for up to $760 in hospital charges during a 60-day period.
But critics, like Diane Archer, executive director of the nonprofit Medicare Rights Center in New York City, contend that "HMOs do not compete based on quality of care but on the basis of costs and benefits, which attract healthy patients." Here are three major problems seniors need to be aware of when considering a Medicare HMO, and how to avoid them.

1. Not all HMOs are created equal. Approximately 50% of all Medicare beneficiaries can choose from two or more HMOs in their area. If you're interested in joining a Medicare HMO, check out all the managed-care plans in your area. Start by calling the Medicare hotline of the Health

Care Financing Administration (HCFA) at 800-638-6833. Ask for the names of local plans. In addition, your state or county's local Health Insurance Counseling and Advocacy Program (HICAP) can sometimes provide you with information about individual plans. To get the HICAP number, call Eldercare Locator at 800-677-1116. Once you have a list of the HMOs, phone them and request a benefits summary, cost breakout and lists of both primary and specialty-care doctors.

2. HMOs may offer less care than fee–for–service plans. In 1996 the Journal of the American Medical Association published a study of 2,235 Medicare and Medicaid patients that found that the elderly more frequently experienced a decline in their physical health when enrolled in HMOs than with traditional Medicare. The reason, researchers concluded, was that the HMO patients probably had access to fewer specialists and expensive medical technology than their fee-for-service counterparts. Moreover, in terms of home health care, a 1994 study of 1,632 Medicare patients nationwide conducted by the Center for Health Policy Research in Denver found that HMO patients received less frequent treatment than those with fee-for-service, producing a detrimental impact on their progress. For example, after 12 weeks of home visits, 48% of traditional Medicare patients could feed themselves more easily, compared with just 34% of HMO patients.

So look for a plan that offers doctors, home-health-care agencies, hospitals and skilled-nursing facilities that are easily accessible. Also, while all HMOs are required to cover medically necessary emergency services in hospitals that aren't in the HMO's network, plans vary widely in their definitions of what constitutes an emergency. So be sure to check out the fine print in your plan's benefits summary. And make sure after-hours-care treatment facilities are offered. If you have a chronic condition, you'll want to verify that you'll be able to get referrals and access to the kinds of specialists you'll need.

3. The appeals process is frustrating and inefficient.
Consumer advocates say that one of the most common complaints they get from seniors is that an HMO is denying coverage they believe they deserve. When your Medicare HMO denies you coverage, federal law says it must provide a written explanation of its decision and your right to appeal. If you decide to challenge the HMO's decision, your plan must then rule in your favor within 60 days or forward your claim to HCFA. The government then has 30 days to issue its decision. If it finds in the HMO's favor, you have 60 days to request a hearing from an administrative law judge.

The trouble is, this process almost never unfolds so seamlessly, and it is so time consuming that patients could literally die waiting. For instance, in 1995 the GAO found several HMOs in California and Florida holding on to beneficiary appeals for as long as 200 days before forwarding them. "In Southern California, it was taking two years to get a hearing," says Carol Jimenez, a Long Beach attorney. "By that time, the patient is either in much worse shape or dead."

What should you do? Ask an HMO you're thinking of joining how it handles appeals and the average length of time it takes for a ruling. If you're already in an HMO, make sure that whenever you're denied coverage you get a full, written explanation of your appeals rights and the process.

WHEN IT PAYS TO WORK AFTER AGE 65

First comes the retirement dream: Leave work, head for the golf course, live off your savings and Social Security. Work doesn't really fit in. After all, retirement is supposed to be about not working. But sometimes reality intrudes on the dream. Maybe you have a younger spouse not yet eligible for Medicare and still in need of your company's health insurance. Perhaps you have a child racking up college tuition bills, or maybe you're bored just playing golf. For a multitude of reasons, 3.8 million seniors were in the labor force last year, and according to the Bureau of Labor Statistics, that number will increase 13% to 4.3 million over the next decade.

Does working past 65 make sense for you? As you ponder continuing your career—or starting a new one—beyond the age most people call it quits, consider the following checklist. It sets out both the advantages of working after 65 and the inevitable tradeoffs.

The advantages of staying on the job. You can really shore up your retirement stash. Just a few additional years on the job can have an enormous impact on your financial security. Not only do you gain the additional contributions and growth in your savings plans but you also have fewer years to provide for in the future. For example, let's say a 65-year-old who earns $65,000 a year has $300,000 in her 401(k). Russell Kelley, vice president at the Ayco Co., a financial planning firm, calculates that if she retired today, that sum would provide an inflation-adjusted income of $23,760 over her expected remaining life span of 20 years, assuming she earned 8% on her money. If she worked for just another five years, however, her 401(k) would grow to $481,950, assuming 3% pay raises, a 10% contribution rate and a 3% company match. Add in the fact that her expected life span would be shorter, and her projected income would start at $43,820, an 84% increase.

Working also builds a cushion into your strategy for retirement because, as we pointed out earlier, people frequently don't factor the cost of emergencies into their retirement plans. Continuing to work lets you build up the reserves to cover those unanticipated expenditures—not to mention the occasional luxury.

It may also allow you to hang on to your insurance. You can usually keep your dental, disability and even life insurance. And businesses generally let older workers maintain health coverage for themselves and their spouse.

Finally, you can stay involved. "If you cannot think of anything you would rather be doing than working, there is no reason to stop," says Martin Sicker, the former work-force programs director for the American Association of Retired Persons.

The disadvantages of working. For starters, some perks may disappear. Firms that provide life insurance may decrease your benefit when you turn 65. And some companies will cap your pension after a certain amount of service, typically 35 years.

Be aware, too, that Social Security might cut your benefits. When you work while collecting Social Security, you are subject to an "earnings test" until age 70. If you were one of the people 65 through 69 in the 1997 work force, that meant your Social Security income would have been reduced by $1 for every $3 you earned above $13,500. (Good news: The threshold is slated to rise to $30,000 by the year 2002.) Earning an annual salary of $61,236, therefore, would have wiped out a 65-year-old's maximum 1997 Social Security benefit of $15,912. From 70 on, you can collect full benefits no matter how much you earn.

There's another tradeoff to consider. The higher your wages, the more likely it is that your Social Security benefit will be taxed. About a year or so before you decide whether to work past 65, talk to your tax adviser to figure out the tax consequences. Then call the Social Security Administration to find out how your benefits may be reduced based on the salary you expect to earn. If staying in the work force decimates your Social Security money, you may want to delay benefits until you stop working or hit 70.

Finally, ask your employer which company benefits you can hang on to if you stay on the payroll. If there are few, ask whether you can retire and sign on as an independent contractor or part-time employee. That way, you'll be able to draw your pension without completely leaving your job. (Your employer can't cash you out until you separate from service.) Of course, there's nothing wrong with retiring, collecting your pension and going to work somewhere else. Indeed, that may capture one of the chief benefits of working past 65. At that age, you've earned the right to do what you want.

GET THE MOST OUT OF THE NEW TAX LAW

We can only guess what our public servants had in mind when they dubbed the new tax law the Taxpayer Relief Act, but they surely weren't promising relief from complexity. As usually happens when lawmakers decide to improve the revenue code, taxes came out of Congress even more hellaciously complicated than they went in. But for anyone in or near retirement, it's worth taking the time to untangle those complexities. If you do, you'll find that retirees get a heaping share of the goodies dispensed by the new law. Consider:

A new kind of IRA gives you much more maneuvering room to avoid tax on investment gains.

The maximum rate on long-term capital gains drops from 28% to 20%. While this tax break wasn't aimed specifically at seniors, it might as well have been. "Retirees and those close to retirement hold much of the country's wealth," explains New York City financial planner and C.P.A. Joel Isaacson, "so they benefit most from lower taxes on investments."

For a lengthy overall view of the law, as well as more details on capital gains and IRAs, see chapter 2, "Slash Your Taxes With The New Law." For two provisions with specific significance for soon-to-retire and retired investors, read on.

Estate taxes. A long-overdue increase in the estate-tax exemption—the amount of money you can leave any heir free of estate taxes—could save your heirs as much as $400,000. Previously set at $600,000 per person, the exemption will rise in steps to $1 million by 2006. You can also make larger tax-free gifts starting in 1999, an advantage if your strategy calls for you to shrink your estate below the exemption limit. For the past 15 years, the most you have been able to give each of your intended heirs without triggering the gift tax is $10,000 a year ($20,000 if you give jointly with your spouse). From 1999 on, that figure will increase with inflation, but only in

$1,000 increments. Thus it would take three years of 3.5% inflation before the limit would jump to $11,000.

Home sales. If you have wanted to trade down to a smaller house but felt trapped by the expected tax bill, your capital has been liberated. That's because, for married couples, up to $500,000 in capital gains is now exempt from taxation when you sell your house ($250,000 for singles). "People whose children have left home or who want to retire and relocate can now buy a smaller, less expensive house and add the profit difference to their investment portfolio," says Chicago investment adviser Tim Schlindwein.

You can use this provision as often as every two years. (If you own the house longer, you must have lived there for two of the past five years.) Under the old law, you were limited to just a one-time exclusion of $125,000—and only if you were 55 or older. To defer taxes at a younger age, you had to roll over the proceeds of the sale into a new house of equal or greater value.

In calculating the taxable gains from the sale of your current home, remember that you must also include any tax-deferred gains from sales of previous homes if you have traded up once or more in the past. You can still deduct any money you spent for capital improvements such as new kitchens or bathrooms in any of those houses, so hang on to the records of all such expenditures.

BORROW WHILE THE BORROWING IS EASY

Even if you have a sterling credit history, lenders will be less likely to fork over money once you no longer have a regular paycheck. So if you're thinking of refinancing a mortgage or buying a new car, for example, do so before you retire from work. Also consider opening a home-equity line of credit, in case you'll need it in the future.

DON'T MAKE THESE COMMON ERRORS

Don't leave financial decisions to your spouse. Eoline Patton, 79, who likes to be called Pat, never gave much thought to her retirement. She left the finances to Jack. Pat started working in 1960 as a volunteer at a nonprofit children's nature museum in Charlotte, N.C., eventually taking a full-time job there in 1965. In 1979, her husband Jack quit his job as a chemist with Pennwalt Chemicals because of worsening emphysema. The next year, Pat took a job at Discovery Place, a science museum in Charlotte, and eventually became an administrative assistant, earning $18,000 a year.

For a while, the couple were able to manage on her salary plus the $920 they received monthly from Jack's Social Security payments and his $500-a-month company pension. By 1987, however, Jack's breathing became so bad that he didn't have the strength to drive, and he fell into a depression. Selflessly, Pat quit her job to spend time with him. "I wanted to make his last years happy ones," she says.

After Jack died in 1990, though, Pat stopped getting his pension because her husband had not signed up for the joint-and-survivor option that would have paid lifetime benefits for both spouses. So at age 71, Pat realized that she would receive only the $984 a month from her own Social Security earnings. She wasn't sure she could live on that. "Women should pay more attention to their finances than I did," she says.

Indeed, the biggest mistake that women make in managing their money is not doing it until it's too late. The motivation for action typically is a divorce or the death of a husband. These two common events can have devastating financial, as well as emotional, effects. As we noted earlier, a report by the General Accounting Office shows that about 80% of widows living in poverty were not poor before their husbands died. "A crisis is no time to be figuring out what your assets are and how you should be investing them," says Ann Benson, who has been conducting women's investment seminars for Merrill Lynch for more than 12 years. "Women are starting to take a more preventive approach, but the change is not happening fast enough." In preparing for retirement, you and your spouse should jointly meet with your financial planner or accountant for a so-called needs analysis, which forecasts your likely future expenses year by year and shows whether they will exceed your projected income from sources such as work, your pensions and investments. Since women live longer than men, it is especially crucial for them to participate in the planning.

Don't move too fast when choosing a new place to live.
Four years ago, Juanita Rippetoe, now 69, and her husband Bill, then an owner of a car-leasing business, retired to a dream house they had built in the suburbs of Fort Worth. Four months after they moved in, Bill died of a massive heart attack. After that, Nita says, "I hated the house. It brought me nothing but sadness."

Her sister-in-law and other relatives urged Nita to move to Houston to be near them, so she agreed. Her family directed the search for a new place, picking out a $147,000 three-bedroom house in a new gated community in Katy, about 10 miles outside of Houston. "It's an elegant house," Rippetoe says, but it was "a big mistake." Only a few others have sold, so Rippetoe doesn't have many neighbors, and most of them are young families who don't share her interests. She doesn't see her relatives much either, because they work full time. She feels marooned. "Every time I go to an aerobics class or play bridge, I have to drive about 30 miles," Nita says. She would like to move to Houston or even back to Fort Worth, where she has friends. But with new homes moving at a glacial pace in her subdivision, she would probably have to take a big loss to unload her house.

So, before relocating to a retirement paradise, rent an apartment or a house in the area to see if you like living there. Widows should be particularly cautious about uprooting soon after a husband's death. In their grief, they often rely on a child or another relative to make difficult decisions like selling the house or moving to a new city. Then they wind up in places that don't suit them—for instance, a community that has a shortage of eligible men of a certain age.

CONS THAT TARGET RETIREES

Could a con artist scam you? No way. You know you are too savvy to fall for an investment pitch claiming you can earn an easy 25% to 50% a year, guaranteed. Only the terminally gullible would swallow a line like that, right?

"Don't kid yourself," warns Neal Sullivan, executive director of the North American Securities Administrators Association. "With blue-chip stocks returning 25% or more a year recently, the lofty returns touted by flimflam artists don't sound so far-fetched." Besides, many con artists are masters at making their sham investments seem like real ones. Says Massachusetts attorney general Scott Harshbarger: "We're seeing some very sophisticated scams these days."

And make no mistake about it: The favorite targets of professional swindlers and unscrupulous investment advisers are retirees. More than half of the people on con artists' hit lists confiscated in 1995 by state and federal law-enforcement agencies were age 50 or older. The main reason charlatans prey on retirees is that older investors are the ones most likely to have big bucks. And they also make inviting targets because they tend to be more courteous and trusting than younger generations. The longer you stay on the line, of course, the more likely you are to fall for a con man's patter.

Here are examples of the six come-ons that experts say scamsters are most likely to inflict on retirees today. If you hear these spiels—or any variations on them—don't invest a cent.

The safety pitch. "I'll guarantee you a high return with almost no risk to your principal. This investment is as safe as a bank CD."

Safety is a big selling point with retirees, who are usually more cautious than younger investors. So to give a scheme a convincing ring, con artists often invent a name for a bogus investment that sounds as safe as a certificate of deposit. For example, the Securities and Exchange Commission says that over the past few years scamsters have sold millions of dollars of so-called prime bank notes. Con men still peddle these fake notes—citing potential returns of as much as 150% a year—by claiming they are backed by institutions like the World Bank, the Washington, D.C.-based organization that provides loans to developing countries. Of course, no such notes exist. The crooks peddling these notes simply issue sham securities and then run off with their victims' money.

The cyberspace scam. "As one cyberinvestor to another, I'd like to pass along this incredible stock tip I heard about on the Internet."

If you visit investment chat rooms, you're a likely target for a cyberspace scam known as "the pump and dump." Here's how it works: Typically a con artist will send you an unsolicited e-mail or approach you in a discussion forum with a piece of seemingly friendly advice touting the stock of a tiny company with outstanding growth prospects. What's really going on, explains Susan Grant, director of the National Fraud Information Center in Washington, D.C., is that the promoter and his cronies already own tons of the stock and are simply trying to drive its price up by reeling in other investors. After the share price soars, says Grant, "the people behind the scheme sell and reap their profit, and innocent investors get crushed when the stock price plummets."

Investors who fall prey to "pump and dump" and other scams on the Net stand little chance of recouping their money. "It's difficult for regulators to figure out who is actually posting these messages," says Grant. "The technology seems to have outpaced the regulators."

High-tech hokum. "Our new high-tech product promises unmatchable returns with little risk—if you buy now."

"High-tech has been big news, and investment fraud follows the headlines," says Dean Graybill, an associate director in the Federal Trade Commission's Bureau of Consumer Protection. That's why con artists often spin schemes involving high-tech products.

Lately, to capitalize on the mobile communications boom, telemarketers have been hawking airwave licenses issued by the Federal Communications Commission, claiming investors can earn returns of up to 100% by selling or leasing the license to a large communications company. In reality, there is no market for the licenses, since anyone who wants one can go straight to the FCC—and get it for thousands of dollars less than what these promoters charge. In one such scheme, an Atlanta-based company in 1994 sold 15 mobile radio system licenses for a total of $115,000—some for more than 200 times their actual cost—to 14 seniors ages 63 to 87 in Montana. State auditor Mark O'Keefe shut down the operation and charged the company with, among other things, falsely representing the license's value.

The scare solicitation. "Stop worrying that you will outlive your assets and become a burden to your children. Just transfer your nest egg into a secure Internal Revenue Service-approved investment for Individual Retirement Accounts."

This scheme begins when unscrupulous investment firms run television infomercials and radio advertisements designed to fan seniors' fears of spiraling health-care costs and possible cuts in Medicare. The ads then offer a solution: a supposedly IRS-approved investment for your IRA. Hapless listeners who respond by calling a toll-free number receive a package of documents that pledge returns of as much as 800% within a few years and include instructions on how to transfer their IRA stash directly into the new investment, which can be anything from a risky real estate pool to an ostrich farm.

The IRS, of course, doesn't sanction or endorse specific investments. So claiming that the agency has approved these products is a ruse. Even worse, though, these investments are almost never overseen by a qualified pension administrator, as is the case when you set up an IRA with a mutual fund, bank or brokerage. Thus any gains on your investment would not qualify for the tax deferral of an IRA. If you send money, therefore, you could end up not just with a lousy investment but a major tax headache as well. "If someone claims to have the magic elixir for your retirement nest egg," says Vermont deputy securities commissioner Richard Cortese, "you've got to question the investment."

The friendship fraud. "I've helped your friends and relatives improve their financial situation. Let me help you too."

This is the type of pitch used in what securities regulators call affinity fraud, so named because a charlatan gets his hooks into one member of a church, a family or an ethnic group—or even a set of friends or neighbors—and then gradually begins to attract others.

One such operator allegedly convinced at least 15 residents of a small Southern town to plow $3 million in what he described as commodity accounts invested in silver. To add an air of authenticity to the scheme, he had rigged up an elaborate home office with a computer bank and faxes going back and forth, supposedly from a commodities trading floor. But after one suspicious investor got in touch with the Commodity Futures Trading Commission, the commission filed a complaint against the salesman for selling unregistered securities and froze his assets. He then fled. Investigators are unsure how much of their money investors are likely to recover. Most of the people who were taken were either friends or at least a friend of a friend. Just because an adviser handles your best friend's finances doesn't mean that he or she is on the up and up.

The savior smoothie. "I understand you've been a victim of investment fraud. I'd like to help you recoup your losses."

This is, hands down, the cruelest pitch. If you've ever lost money in a scam, your name is probably circulating on a "sucker" or "mooch" list. Con artists often pay as much as $200 apiece for names off such lists and then call the victims, offering new investments that can supposedly wipe out past losses. Many people bite, says the FTC's Graybill, "because they're desperate to get their money back."

After more than $25,000 of their money disappeared in a bogus oil-and-gas investment, a Los Angeles couple received a call from a man who claimed to have been duped in the same scheme. He was very cordial and said he could help them get their money back if they invested several thousand dollars in his new company.

After they invested, he paid them $500 or $600 in supposed dividends from his oil-well venture, and the couple eventually put in $102,000. But they ultimately discovered that there was no oil-well company. The man was convicted of defrauding the couple and selling unregistered securities. But they were able to recover only $10,500 of the $102,000 they invested.

So be alert. Swindlers are constantly spinning out new schemes. Be wary of any tempting financial pitches—not just the ones we've mentioned. Before you put money in any investment, here are three steps you should take:

▶ **Check up on the salesperson.** Start by making sure that the broker or adviser who approaches you is registered with the appropriate regulatory agencies and that he or she doesn't have a disciplinary record for abusing customers. You can investigate a brokerage firm or a securities sales representative by calling the National Association of Securities Dealers (800-289-9999). To check out an investment adviser or a financial planner, call the SEC (202-942-8090) as well as your state securities commission. (You can get the number for your state office by calling the NASD number listed above.) If someone is pushing commodities, get in touch with the Disciplinary Information Access Line (DIAL), operated by the National Futures Association (800-676-4632). If you have questions about an insurance agent or the investments he's hawking, call your state insurance department. You can look up the number at the National Association of Insurance Commissioners' Website (www.naic.org) or call directory assistance in your state capital.

▶ **Demand documentation.** Always get information in writing. If you're considering a stock, bond, mutual fund or commodities investment, you should get a prospectus. For an insurance product, demand a copy of the policy. Since insurance policies seem almost designed to confuse everyone but actuaries, you may want to consider spending $40 to have an expert at the Consumer Federation of America (202-387-6121) analyze it—and let you know if it lives up to the sales rep's promises.

▶ **Never invest under pressure.** If you're unsure about an investment, run it by a trusted adviser such as your accountant or lawyer. If you suspect a scam, call the National Fraud Information Center (800-876-7060), a watchdog group that offers tips on spotting fraud and tells you which regulators and law-enforcement authorities to report it to. Finally, never hand over your money because you're afraid that by delaying you'll miss out on a great deal. If the investment is legitimate, it isn't going to disappear tomorrow.

▶ CHAPTER 7

THE BEST REAL ESTATE MOVES TODAY

Housing prices are cooling down, but there's hot news for some sellers. Specifically, the new tax law will make trading down a smart strategy for many homeowners in a year when home values are likely to outpace inflation. And if you live out West, you can profit from the nation's highest booming real estate market.

Overall, homeowners across the nation will see prices grow at a slower pace this year. The median home price will rise just 3.2%, versus 4% in 1997 and 5.3% in 1996, according to the forecasters at Regional Financial Associates in West Chester, Pa. But the prices in 25 of the 50 largest U.S. metropolitan areas are projected to beat the 3.2% rise, with San Jose, Seattle, Salt Lake City, San Diego and Orange County, Calif. all expected to see hikes of 5% or more. Generally, in most areas of the country, buyers can be selective and take their time making bids. And they will continue to see mortgage-rate bargains: The 30-year fixed rate will probably not go very far above or below its '97 average of 7.7%, according to Keith Gumbinger, vice president of research at HSH Associates, a mortgage research firm in Butler, N.J.—the second lowest reading for any six-month period in 25 years.

THE OUTLOOK FOR HOUSE PRICES

Even though housing-price increases will slow this year, homeowners in most places will enjoy their third straight year of inflation-whipping returns, as long as the rise in the cost of living remains below 3%, as MONEY predicts. Of course, precisely how much your house will appreciate—and ultimately sell for—depends on your local economy and even your particular neighborhood. For a glimpse of the future in your area, consult the table "The Hottest Housing Markets" on the following page. It lists the projected median home prices and appreciation rates for the nation's 50 largest metropolitan areas.

San Jose, with an anticipated 5.7% gain, occupies the No. 1 spot for 1998, mainly because of the demand fueled by job growth in the Bay Area's booming high-tech industries. Seattle is next, with a 5.6% gain forecast, followed by Salt Lake City, where prices are expected to rise 5.4%. In contrast, slowing local job markets and adequate housing stock have landed New Orleans, Indianapolis and Orlando at the bottom of the heap for 1998. Where you live will help determine your strategy for buying or selling a house this year. Consider the following advice.

Sellers must price carefully. Unless your home is in a sizzling market where bidding wars have flared lately, the generally temperate market in '98 will likely force you to ask a reasonable price for your home—if you hope to sell it within 90 days. To see what similar properties in the area have sold for over the past six months, ask a local real estate agent or check out the National Association of Realtors' Website at www.realtor.com. In a strong market, takers are likely to respond even if you're as much as 5% above comparable recent sales; in weaker markets, they may look for a price as much as 5% below.

Buyers should be aggressive. In most cases, your best move in '98 is to snare a 30-year fixed rate mortgage, rather than an adjustable-rate mortgage (ARM). That's because fixed loans are generally considered a better deal whenever the spread between fixed and adjustable rates narrows to two percentage points or less. In 1998, mortgage mavens expect the spread to hover near two percentage points, with the fixed rate at about 7.7% and the one-year ARM near 5.7%. "For most home buyers, locking in a fixed loan at less than 8% is worth the peace of mind, even if the spread between fixed loans and ARMs were to widen a bit," says Gumbinger of HSH.

A five-year ARM—which is likely to average 7.3% in '98—may make sense, however, if you plan to move within five years and thus want to lock in the lowest rate possible during that time. Similarly, an ARM can be a good choice if you need to stretch to afford the home you want. At the projected average rate of 7.7% on a 30-year fixed-rate mortgage in '98, for example, your monthly payment on a $250,000 loan would be $1,782. With a five-year ARM at 7.3%, you could take out a loan for $260,000 for the same monthly outlay.

When you are ready to make a bid, be prepared. Many sellers, especially in hot areas, expect buyers to have preapproved mortgages—commitments

THE HOTTEST HOUSING MARKETS

Home prices in 25 of the 50 largest U.S. metro areas are expected to beat the projected 3.2% rise in the median-priced home next year—and 14 of the hottest markets are out West. No. 1 San Jose, also the priciest, will surge 5.7%, while cellar dweller New Orleans will limp along at 1.1%.

RANK	METROPOLITAN AREA	PROJECTED GAIN IN '98	'98 MEDIAN PRICE[1]	RANK	METROPOLITAN AREA	PROJECTED GAIN IN '98	'98 MEDIAN PRICE[1]
1.	San Jose	5.7%	$318,800	26.	St. Louis	3.2	99,700
2.	Seattle	5.6	182,600	27.	Detroit	3.2	121,100
3.	Salt Lake City	5.4	134,300	28.	Kansas City	2.9	107,900
4.	Orange County, Calif.	5.0	238,400	29.	Tampa/St. Petersburg	2.9	86,700
5.	San Diego	5.0	192,700	30.	Miami	2.8	121,500
6.	Las Vegas	4.9	128,300	31.	Columbus, Ohio	2.8	119,400
7.	Phoenix	4.9	119,400	32.	Philadelphia	2.8	128,100
8.	Dallas	4.4	114,700	33.	Cincinnati	2.7	111,800
9.	Boston	4.3	199,100	34.	Buffalo/Niagara Falls	2.6	84,800
10.	San Francisco	4.3	296,100	35.	Nashville	2.6	116,100
11.	Los Angeles	4.2	181,000	36.	Fort Lauderdale	2.6	125,200
12.	Washington, D.C.	4.1	176,000	37.	Greensboro/		
13.	Newark	4.1	200,600		Winston-Salem, N.C.	2.5	119,400
14.	Oakland	4.0	282,500	38.	New York City	2.5	181,800
15.	San Antonio	3.9	90,100	39.	Minneapolis/St. Paul	2.5	119,000
16.	Sacramento	3.8	120,700	40.	Pittsburgh	2.3	88,500
17.	Houston	3.8	93,700	41.	Long Island, N.Y.	2.2	166,000
18.	Atlanta	3.8	110,900	42.	Milwaukee	2.2	125,900
19.	Fort Worth/Arlington	3.8	88,800	43.	Hartford	2.1	138,800
20.	Portland, Ore.	3.8	156,700	44.	Cleveland	2.1	118,100
21.	Denver	3.4	144,400	45.	Norfolk/Virginia Beach	2.0	108,100
22.	New Haven	3.4	139,100	46.	Baltimore	1.8	119,500
23.	Riverside, Calif.	3.4	117,800	47.	Orlando	1.8	95,300
24.	Chicago	3.3	164,800	48.	Indianapolis	1.4	103,600
25.	Charlotte, N.C.	3.3	126,200	49.	Bergen/Passaic[2], N.J.	1.4	208,800
	U.S. MEDIAN	3.2	126,600	50.	New Orleans	1.1	90,400

Notes: [1]Projected [2]Counties. **Source:** Regional Financial Associates

from lenders proving they'll be able to borrow a specific amount. Says San Jose real estate agent Monica Farnsworth: "You won't get the house you want by dreaming about it. You have to let your money talk."

Indeed, in desirable neighborhoods all around the country, eager buyers are finding that they must compete to snare prize properties. We canvassed real estate experts nationwide for tips to help you land your dream house without breaking your budget. They agree that a preapproved mortgage is essential. They also offered up the following advice to help you in your search.

First, make sure your area is really hot, not just hyped. Don't just take the word of your real estate agent. Ask at least three other local agents how long homes in your price range stay on the market, as well as the average difference between the asking price and selling price. Says Joseph Cummins, author of the book *Not One Dollar More! How to Save $3,000 to $30,000 Buying Your Next Home*: "If homes sell in less than a month for within 5% of the asking price, that's a strong market."

It's important, too, to set your limits. You should ask the real estate agents about the selling prices of similar houses in the neighborhood. Try to avoid paying more than 3% or so above what comparable properties are fetching. Remember: If your lender determines your home is worth less than the amount you bid, you may not get enough mortgage money.

Experts also say you should make your first bid count. When there's a lot of interest in a house, you may have only one shot at nailing the deal. "If your initial offer is too low," warns Denver real estate agent Ann Atkinson, "the seller is likely to accept someone else's bid." So offer as much (or nearly as much) as you are willing to pay the first time around. If the bidding goes beyond your target price, consider moving on to another house. But if you remain a truly determined buyer, there are ways to stretch your budget and still qualify for a mortgage (most lenders require that your monthly payments equal no more than 28% of your monthly pre-tax income). One option is to increase your down payment. Another option, as mentioned earlier, is to raise your carrying power with an adjustable-rate mortgage rather than a fixed-rate loan.

Finally, you must know which important compromises you absolutely must not make. For example, when you sign a contract to buy a home, the deal is usually contingent on your receiving mortgage approval. In an overheated market, though, a seller may ask you to waive that so-called financing contingency. The danger: If you can't complete the purchase, you could lose your deposit (usually 10% of the price). So unless you are absolutely certain that you will get your loan, don't agree to such a request. Otherwise you risk winning the bidding battle but losing the war.

Cash in on new tax breaks. An important provision in the 1997 tax law now lets sellers take tax-free profits—up to $500,000 for couples and $250,000 for singles—when they unload their principal home.

The main beneficiaries of the new law will be couples who have larger houses than they need but have been loath to sell because of the potential tax hit, such as Iris and Sebastian Nola of Upland, Calif., a tony community near San Bernardino. When the Nolas sold their three-bedroom home in 1996 for $410,000, the only way to avoid a $72,961 tax bill on their $260,575 gain was to buy a house of equal or greater value than the selling price of their previous home. So they purchased a four-bedroom house for $484,000, although "it's much too big for us," says Iris, 49. Thanks to the new law, Iris, who teaches interior design, and Sebastian, 54, an energy company executive, will now be able to fulfill their dream of trading down to a smaller place in Hawaii when they retire, without owing any tax.

Some sellers—such as people with vacation homes—will have unique ways to take advantage of the new tax law. Here's why: The law lets you take tax-free profits on the sale of your primary home as often as every two years. So you can sell your current residence, reap the tax-free gains, move into your vacation home for at least two years, and garner tax-free gains again when you sell that home. "We wouldn't be surprised to see quite a few retirees with vacation places in Myrtle Beach using this strategy," says James Pearman, a financial planner and C.P.A. in Roanoke, Va.

Like couples who want to scale down, couples who want to split up could also see their tax burdens ease because of the new law. Previously, when a home owned by a divorced couple was sold, the spouse who had moved out was often hit with taxes on his or her share of the gain because the home was no longer considered his or her primary residence. Under the new law, if your ex lives in the home under the terms of your divorce decree, you will qualify for the tax-free exclusion on your share of the gain—even if the sale takes place years after the divorce.

WHY OWNING A HOUSE IS A GOOD DEAL

Sure, the median house price nationwide is expected to appreciate no more than 3.2% this year, no great hike compared to the returns you can get on other investments like stocks and bonds. But owning a home offers a host of advantages you'd be hard-pressed to find in any other single investment. Among them: leverage, tax breaks and, at times, inflation protection. For a typical homeowner, those pluses can translate, even with today's piddling rates of appreciation, into an after-tax return as high as 15% and make a home a smart move. "Home ownership has clear financial advantages over renting," says Baltimore financial planner J. Michael Martin. "At the very least, you'll own a sizable asset by the time you retire."

One caution: While a home may be an underappreciated asset right now, it doesn't necessarily follow that every dollar you dump into it will pay off big. To make the most of your largest investment, you need to understand what it can do for you and what it can't.

Figure the real return on home ownership. Okay, so double-digit gains in home values petered out about the same time as the Bee Gees. But a rising price tag is just one component of a house's return, says Peter G. Miller, author of the book *The Mortgage Hunter.* "A home remains a good investment for most American families because you buy it with a small amount down, put aside money gradually and build substantial equity, which is likely to be tax-free." Because of these angles, a home can enrich its owner as much as a taxable stock mutual fund returning 20%.

How did we get that figure? For one thing, even if you don't own your residence, you must pay monthly housing costs. The only issue is whether those payments enrich a landlord or build equity for you. On a $100,000 mortgage with 20 years to go, for instance, $150 or so of the monthly $735 reduces the loan principal and increases your ownership stake. (The rest is interest.) That's like making $150 monthly payments into a mutual fund.

So what, you say, if your investment figures to grow only 3% a year, if that? That question overlooks the fact that your equity stake in the house typically amounts to a fraction of its actual value for most of the time you own it. As a result, when the property appreciates, your equity expands much faster. For instance, if you put 20% cash down on a $100,000 home that rises in value by $3,000, or 3%, the return on your $20,000 investment is 15%.

And that's in today's low-inflation economy. If the rate of inflation were to pick up, your home would probably appreciate more rapidly. A fixed-rate mortgage offers a second type of inflation protection. In a time of rising prices, your payments would stay the same, even as all your neighbors' rents were escalating.

Another notable plus to home ownership is taxes. If you itemize deductions on your tax return, not only can you deduct mortgage interest but you can also write off local real estate taxes on your federal return. As a result, you may end up paying less to own a home after taxes than you would to rent a comparable one.

Better yet, when you sell, you can permanently avoid paying taxes on any profits.

A mortgage is not a millstone. One of the alleged drawbacks of home ownership is that it saddles you with a debt that takes as long as 30 years to pay off. That's why mortgage prepayment plans seem so enticing: If you have a $100,000, 30-year fixed-rate mortgage at an 8% interest rate, volunteering an additional $50 a month would cut your total interest expenses by nearly $40,000 and let you burn the mortgage six years early.

Gratifying as that may be, however, it's usually not the most profitable use of your money. Says Clarence Rose, a finance professor at Radford University in Radford, Va.: "In general, the lower your mortgage interest rate and the higher your marginal income tax rate, the lower the likelihood that prepaying your mortgage will be worthwhile."

Why? The "return" you get from prepaying a loan is equivalent to the interest charges you avoid. But because your mortgage interest is deductible, your after-tax interest charges are typically low. If the choice is between prepaying or investing in a tax-deferred retirement plan, the case for letting your mortgage live out its natural life is even stronger. You may feel getting a sure return on a loan prepayment is preferable to the uncertainty of the stock market. Even so, you probably have other higher-rate, nondeductible loans you should attack first. Notes Portland, Ore. financial planner Glen Clemans: "It amazes me that people put $50 extra toward their mortgage every month when they're carrying an 18% credit-card balance."

GET HELP FROM AN ALL STAR TEAM

It's crucial for home buyers to dump outdated notions about real estate and master the new realities of today's housing market. Our single biggest tip for you: Why go it alone? "The housing market has gotten increasingly competitive and complicated over the past decade," explains author Peter G. Miller. "To get a winning edge, you must have a team of sharp, professional advisers."

We will help you assemble just such a roster of All Stars to get the best return on your housing dollars.

Buying at the lowest price. Before you begin seriously shopping for a house, the first pro you should seek out is a relatively new breed of agent known as a buyer broker. Unlike traditional real estate agents—who actually represent the home seller's interests—buyer brokers work to negotiate the best deal for the home buyer. Typically, you don't have to pay a buyer broker. Rather, he or she usually splits the 5% to 7% sales commission with the seller's broker, although the buyer broker may ask you for a retainer of $200 or so, which gets deducted from the final fee.

A knowledgeable buyer broker can lead you to the right neighborhood and house for your needs, plus help you decide how much of your financial resources to devote to a potential home given local appreciation prospects. More often than not, ace buyer brokers today will advise you to buy only as much house as you need to live comfortably, rather than following the old rule of stretching for as much house as you can afford.

The biggest advantage to hiring a buyer broker, however, is that he or she can help you negotiate the best possible price and loan terms. "House hunters who enlist a buyer broker can wind up paying at least 5% less than shoppers who rely on traditional agents," says real estate expert Joseph Eamon Cummins. Such savings are especially valuable today given the limited prospects for price appreciation.

Thomas Forrester, 48, an executive at a waste-management company, and his wife Eva, 47, found out just how profitable hiring a buyer broker can be when they began looking for a house in Orinda, Calif., near Oakland. Frustrated after house hunting in vain for three months, the Forresters decided to hire their own advocate, Soheila Smith, a broker whose practice is split between sellers and buyers. Says Tom Forrester: "I worked with a number of agents until I found the one to help us get what we wanted." Within two weeks, Smith steered the family to a 1,400-square-foot, three-bedroom with a panoramic view listing for $279,900. Smith then helped the Forresters drive down the price to $268,000. Next, she persuaded the sellers to fork over $12,000 for repairs and kick in another $3,000 toward closing costs. All told, Smith saved the Forresters $26,000, more than 9% off the list price in one of the country's hottest housing markets.

For names of buyer brokers in your area, call the National Association of Real Estate Buyer Brokers (415-591-5446). To assure that the broker is working solely for your benefit, try to hire an exclusive buyer broker—that is, someone who represents buyers only. There are only about 2,000 or so such purists nationwide, however, so like the Forresters, you may have to hire an agent who also takes seller listings.

Be sure to have your pro sign a buyer broker agreement that legally obligates her to put your interests above all others, including sellers represented by brokers in her agency. Before choosing, interview at least three candidates. Pick the one who can refer you to at least three recent clients and who displays the keenest understanding of home values in your area—past and future.

Financing and refinancing wisely. Whether you're lining up financing for the house, condo or co-op you plan to buy or trying to refinance a home loan you already have, you'll face a daunting challenge sorting through the panoply of mortgage options offered by lenders today. For help, you'll probably want to hire a mortgage broker, as about half of 1996's 7.5 million mortgage borrowers did. The best of these pros can steer you to banks or mortgage companies offering the lowest loan rates. Often a top mortgage broker can save you a quarter of a percentage point on your rate. Equally important, these brokers can help you select the most appropriate mortgage. In exchange, the broker typically charges 1% to 2.5% of the mortgage amount, although the lender usually picks up the tab. For names of mortgage brokers in your area, call or e-mail the National Association of Mortgage Brokers (703-610-9009; cdf@.namb.com) or ask your real estate attorney for a referral.

A recent class-action suit accused some mortgage brokers of pocketing cash kickbacks for steering clients to lenders offering high-rate loans. So make sure the rate on the loan your broker suggests is within a quarter of a point or so of the average mortgage rates listed in your newspaper. Also, call your state banking department to see if your state is one of the 43 that license mortgage brokers. If it is, check that your broker's record lists no violations.

Perhaps the greatest service a mortgage broker can offer is matching you with the type of loan that best suits your housing profile. For example, if you lack cash, a resourceful mortgage broker can direct you to a lender offering low-down-payment loans. Despite the enduring myth that you need to put down 20% of the purchase price of a house, the reality is that half of all buyers two years ago made down payments of 10% or less. Such mortgages usually carry the same rate as conventional loans, but if your down payment is less than 20%, lenders typically require that you buy a mortgage insurance policy, guaranteeing your loan will be repaid if you default.

Borrowers may also want to enlist government officials to join their housing squad. Reason: Federal, state and local government agencies oversee a variety of programs designed to help cash-short, lower- and middle-income people buy homes. For example, the Federal Housing Authority runs a program—with an appropriately bureaucratic-sounding name, the FHA 203 (b) plan—that helps buyers qualify for mortgages with as little as 3% down. The amount you can borrow, however, is limited to between $81,548 and $160,950, depending on housing costs in your area. In October 1996, Freddie Mac, a government-sponsored private corporation that buys mortgages from lenders, launched a similar plan—Affordable Gold 97—that also provides 3%-down loans and lets you get some of the cash from relatives. While FHA and Freddie Mac insure the mortgages in these programs, the loans are actually made by local banks and mortgage companies. To get the names of affiliated lenders near you, call the FHA at 800-225-5342 or visit Freddie Mac's Website at www.freddiemac.com.

Remember also to check your state and local government housing offices for mortgage deals. They not only make low-down-payment loans but often offer grants to help cover closing costs, and teach classes explaining financing alternatives to would-be home buyers. In December 1995, for example, David Mareira, 31, manager of a Boston furniture delivery business, attended a home-buying class offered by the city of Boston. Not only did his class instructor, Doreen Treacy, explain all the financing options offered by city and state agencies, she became a key member of his housing finance team. Treacy helped Mareira secure a 5%-down loan from the Massachusetts Housing Finance Agency (MHFA) and grab a $750 grant from the city of Boston for closing costs. Last September, Mareira bought a two-family house for $160,000 in Boston's revitalized Dorchester neighborhood, becoming the first person in his family to own a home. Says Mareira: "The city offered a step-by-step plan, and Doreen helped me follow it."

If you already have a mortgage, you might want to consider trading in the loan for one with a lower rate—as long as you expect to stay in the house long enough for the lower monthly payments to compensate for the closing costs, usually 2% to 3% of the loan amount. Don't bother refinancing if you think you'll stay in the house less than five years, unless the rate on your new loan is at least one percentage point lower than that of your existing mortgage. That's because it'll take you three to five years to recoup closing fees. But if you're certain you won't sell your home for five years or longer, investigate replacing your loan even if you'll cut your interest rate by as little as half a percentage point.

Selling at the highest price. To get top dollar when you sell in today's housing market, you need to recruit a real estate agent with plenty of experience selling your kind of home in your specific area. Why? Because demand and resulting appreciation rates for different types and prices of houses can vary dramatically even within the same city.

For example, prices for starter homes in Cleveland (median price: $60,000) shot up 14.4% between 1995 and 1997, according to Cambridge, Mass. housing research firm Case Shiller Weiss, in part because of aggressive government lending programs designed to increase home ownership among lower-income residents. During that same period, however, prices for Cleveland trade-up houses (median price: $152,000) rose a mere 1.2%, reflecting slack demand for luxury homes. Says Case Shiller Weiss president Allan Weiss: "It's a mistake to assume that the economics of your city automatically drive home prices in your neighborhood." To get top dollar when you sell, therefore, look for an agent who specializes in selling homes in your neighborhood and monitors prices there daily.

When they wanted to unload their house in Denver's historic Congress Park district, attorneys Matt Dalton, 44, and wife Gigi, 43, signed up real estate broker Sonja Leonard Leonard largely because she had scads of experience selling there. "Sonja had been selling homes in our area for 17 years and knew more about our neighborhood than any other broker," explains Gigi. Based on her knowledge of the local market, the broker advised the couple to list their house for $315,000, or about 4% higher than the average asking price in the neighborhood for comparable homes. The Daltons received (and eventually accepted) an offer for $312,000 in just 10 days, much quicker than the 45 to 60 days the average home spent on the market at the time.

To find such a sales champ, interview at least three candidates at different real estate brokerages. In his book *How to Sell Your Home Fast, for the Highest Price, in Any Market*, author Terry Eilers lists more than two dozen questions to ask prospective agents. The most essential one: What listing price do you recommend for my house and why? (A broker should have a ready list of prices that homes like yours have recently sold for, as well as a strategy for selling your house within 90 days.)

Choose a broker who shows some creative marketing skills as well. Leonard Leonard's repertory includes, for example, an Internet site, customized color brochures for each client's house and attention-getting events such as hosting English "high teas" in houses that she is selling. "A broker has to be prepared to pull out all the stops, especially for a house that may be a tough sell," she says.

Online mortgage lending is projected to surge this year. Technology experts estimate that loan volume on the Internet will increase nearly threefold, from $265 million in 1997 to $750 million. True, that's just a tiny fraction of the total $725 billion U.S. mortgage market. But it represents a huge opportunity for home buyers. The companies that operate mortgage Websites are hoping to steer you to their advertisers—generally, lenders, moving companies and real estate agents. But to get your attention, they're adorning their Web pages with vital consumer tools, such as up-to-the-minute mortgage rate data. In addition, many provide electronic worksheets to let you calculate how much you will likely be able to borrow and what your monthly payments would be on a multitude of mortgage options.

To help you navigate the world of cybermortgages, we asked experts in mortgage banking and Internet financial services to divulge their favorite sites. We then vetted their picks for accuracy and ease of use. Our overall impression: Mortgage shopping online can save you considerable time and effort in sorting through dozens of loan options and hundreds of potential lenders. But to make sure you're getting the best deal, compare any seemingly attractive online mortgage with terms offered by lenders in your area.

Here's how to get the most out of an online money hunt, organized according to the steps involved in landing a mortgage.

▶ **Getting started.** At **interest.com** and **mortgage-net.com**, you'll find topnotch instructions, worksheets and calculators for making basic financial projections, such as the payments you'll face on, say, a 30-year fixed loan vs. a five-year adjustable. You'll also get answers to questions you probably haven't even thought of: interest.com, for instance, offers advice on securing hard-to-find mortgages such as loans on vacant land or remote properties; mortgage-net.com lists the top 10 home-buying mistakes.

▶ **Finding the best interest rate.** Once you've decided on the type of mortgage you want, a computer search can help you find the lender with the best interest rate. For the most comprehensive and timely data available online, visit **hsh.com**, sponsored by HSH Associates, the country's largest publisher of mortgage rate information. Once a week, HSH updates the rates offered by 2,500 lenders. Just click on the area where you plan to buy to find the rates and phone numbers of lenders who make loans there. If you don't have the time to rummage through a vast database, try **GetSmart.com**, which has links to 20 lenders nationwide, or **QuickenMortgage.com**, which has six bank affiliates. These sites give you a broad sense of the range of available mortgage options.

▶ **Applying for a mortgage.** Roughly 80% of the 2,000 lenders with Websites will pre-qualify you for a loan based on information you provide them over the Internet. But bear in mind that "pre-qualification" simply means the lender will do some quick calculations to estimate the size of the loan you're likely to qualify for. Don't confuse pre-qualification with "preapproval," which typically constitutes a commitment from a lender to make you a loan.

Finally, don't forget to ask each prospective broker for a list of former clients. They'll know best whether the pro you're considering has the potential to be a Most Valuable Player on your team.

PULL PROFITS FROM RENTAL PROPERTY

Rental property provides nice diversification to an investment portfolio, and you'll get some tax breaks too. Moreover, economists such as Robert Sheehan, with the nonprofit National Apartment Association in Washington, D.C., see rental-property values as a fairly decent inflation hedge, rising by around 4% annually, on average, during the next decade. In addition, you'll get monthly rent checks from your tenants (about $1,500 for the average duplex).

Of course, investing in real estate comes with its share of headaches and heartaches. When the pipes freeze, you could get a cranky call in the middle of the night. The wrong tenants could turn your apartment into a war zone. And you might not be able to find a buyer when you decide to sell. You'll raise the odds of success by following these tips:

Buy below market value. One of the best ways to secure rental property on the cheap is to purchase bank foreclosures or properties held by the Internal Revenue Service and bankrupt builders. Usually such property is sold at auction. Under federal law, notices of where and when such auctions will take place must appear in local newspaper ads.

Limit your search for rental properties to within an hour's drive from your home. That way you can easily inspect any property being auctioned off before making a bid. If you find an attractive building, visit similar ones in the area to help calculate how much rental income you can expect to rake in. (Then subtract roughly 50% of that figure for expenses like repairs, taxes and insurance.) If you decide to make an offer, "turn in a written bid that's at least 20% under the current market value, since that's what these places typically sell for," says John Reed, editor of the newsletter *Real Estate Investor's Monthly*. You can calculate the market value by getting the sales prices of similar rental properties in the neighborhood from a local real estate agent.

If your bid wins, you'll probably immediately need to come up with cash covering the entire purchase price.

Check out all prospective tenants. A good way to weed out tenants who may have trouble paying their rent is by subscribing to a service that sells credit report data to landlords. These firms, found under "Credit Reporting" in the Yellow Pages, generally charge a one-time application fee of about $50 and an additional $10 or so for each credit report you want.

Hire a savvy manager. Your best bet is to find a trustworthy, handy local homeowner to manage the property. Employ this person to show the apartments, keep an eye on them and handle minor repairs. Typical cost: $15 an hour, or about $55 a month per unit. "If you hire someone who owns a home in the area, he'll have a vested interest in finding good tenants, since he wants to keep property values up," says Reed.

GOOD TIME TO BUY A VACATION HOME

The American dream once meant owning the house where you lived. These days, for 10% of American households, it also means owning a place where you can escape from it all. And why not? What's more alluring than the thought of dipping your toes in a crystal lake a few feet from your second front door? Or strolling on the beach below your rural sunporch? Or relaxing before your fireplace after a day on the slopes?

Now is a great time to make that dream a reality. Because price appreciation has barely kept ahead of inflation in most areas during the past three years, vacation homes are still very affordable. Moreover, some of the most important costs of ownership have actually dropped in recent years. Most mortgage lenders have stopped charging higher interest rates for second homes than for first ones. And some big insurers are lowering policy premiums on second homes, which in the past have cost as much as 25% more to insure than comparable primary residences. No wonder that a 1995 survey by the American Resort Development Association, a real estate trade group, found that about a third of Americans not only want to buy a second home in the next 10 years but also believe they have at least a fifty-fifty chance of doing so. That's more than double the percentage found in a similar survey five years earlier.

The time to start making your move is now, before baby boomers inflate the prices of vacation homes the way they did those of primary homes in the 1970s and 1980s. Most of today's buyers are either boomers or Americans in their mid-50s to early 60s who plan to live in second homes at least part of the year in retirement, according to John Tuccillo, chief economist for the National Association of Realtors. As baby boomers begin to swell the ranks of those pre-retirement buyers, forecasters say, second-home price increases will accelerate. Indeed, in the ski resort town of Snowmass, Colo., for example, prices have already gone up an average of 19% from 1996 to 1997.

In most vacation havens, however, second homes remain affordable: as low as $100,000 or so in some areas. Prices are quite variable, of course; you'll pay up to twice as much for a house on the water, say, than for one a couple of blocks away. Conversely, condos often cost 15% to 20% less than houses in the same area. And homes in resort areas on the coasts tend to cost up to twice as much as those in the middle of the country.

If you buy now, you can also take advantage of favorable developments in the costs of owning a second home. Until the early 1990s, mortgage lenders—fearful that mortgages on second homes posed a higher default risk—charged interest rates that were a quarter to three-quarters of a per-centage point higher for second homes than for primary residences. That could add as much as $80 to the monthly payment for a $160,000, 30-year, 7.75% fixed-rate mortgage. No more. A survey conducted for MONEY by financial researcher HSH Associates shows that more than 90% of lenders in the 11 states with the most vacation homes charge the same rate for first-home mortgages as for second-home loans.

The insurance picture looks brighter too. Traditionally, a second home costs up to twice as much to insure as a first home. That's because second homes are empty much of the time, leaving them more vulnerable to bur-glaries, fire and other risks. But in the past couple of years, big Warren, N.J.-based insurer Chubb has been slashing its second-home premiums in 13 states that contain lots of vacation homes. (Chubb plans to do the same in the rest of the country in the next year or so.) Chubb's rationale: Most peo-ple have fewer and less valuable belongings in their second homes than in their primary residences. So the insurer's plan offers lower than usual cover-age levels on those items in return for an annual premium bill that might run $700 a year, vs. $1,000 for a primary residence. Other insurers are expected to follow Chubb's lead.

Of course, you can cut your carrying costs on a second home even more by collecting income from renting it out for part of the year, as approximately a third of second-home owners do. If you expect to rent, decide before you buy how often you plan to do so. That's because if you rent out your new vacation property almost all the time, both mortgage and insurance costs will be higher than they'd be otherwise.

If you and your family stay at your vacation home fewer than 14 days or 10% of the number of days it's rented, it will be considered a rental property, not a second residence. Mortgage rates for rentals are as much as three-fourths of a percentage point higher than for regular second homes, and insurance bills are higher too. Tax breaks partly offset those costs, however: You get to deduct not only interest charges but also repair and other maintenance costs. And, of course, you collect all that rental income.

If you'll rent out your home for fewer than 50 weeks a year but more than two, you can deduct some of the repair and maintenance costs (consult your tax adviser for details). You can deduct real estate taxes and mortgage interest so long as your mortgages on your first and second homes do not total more than $1 million.

Here are more key tips to make you a savvier second-home buyer.

▶ **Be ready to part with cash up front.** While mortgage rates for second homes have come down recently, strict down payment requirements have not. The HSH survey shows that 38% of lenders still require a higher down payment for a second home than for a first one—often 20%. And government programs that can cut down payment requirements on first homes to 5% or less don't apply to second homes.

▶ **Stay close to a city.** Favor properties within a three-hour drive of a major metropolitan area. A home that's close enough to make a practical weekend getaway will reduce the wear on your car and your psyche. It will also increase your chances of renting the property and eventually reselling it profitably. Among the communities that meet the reasonable-drive test are Rehoboth Beach, Del., which is less than three hours from both Philadelphia and Washington, D.C., and ski resort Steamboat Springs, Colo., about three hours from Denver.

▶ **Look for water or snow.** Activities like skiing, hiking, boating and fishing will not only keep you entertained, but will also draw renters or buyers. Nearby restaurants, movie theaters and other entertainment for adults and kids are pluses too.

▶ **Choose a year-round area.** If vacationers throng to your area all year long, rental and resale prospects rise. For example, Big Bear Lake, Calif., in the mountains about 100 miles east of Los Angeles, features skiing in the winter and fishing and boating in the summer. As a result, the value of properties sold there dropped only 3% to 5% in the past three years in the lingering aftermath of the early-'90s California recession. By contrast, the value of desert getaways in Palm Springs, which is popular from November through May, fell a whopping 10% to 20%.

▶ **Consider a condo.** While 62% of prospective buyers prefer a house to a condominium, according to the American Resort Development survey, a condo's advantages can be compelling. For one thing, a condo can cost 30% less than a comparable single-family house. For example, a two-bedroom house in Old Orchard Beach, Maine with a direct ocean view typically runs $200,000. But two-bedroom condos with views of the harbor are available for just $140,000.

Hassle is low too. You can leave yard work and maintenance of everything outside your apartment to the condo association. Such services aren't free, of course. In addition to your mortgage payments, you'll owe monthly condo fees that range from as little as $50 to as much as $500 in luxury units. But owners of single vacation houses also have to pay for maintenance services, such as cutting grass, raking leaves and simply checking the house periodically to make sure all is well.

▶ **Don't compromise on living space.** Tastes vary widely, of course. But consider holding out for a home with an open design that allows people in the kitchen to converse with those in the family room—one feature that both renters and home shoppers crave. Also look for a home that has at least two bedrooms; it will be much easier to rent than a smaller dwelling. Finally, buy a home with ample storage space to stow your personal possessions out of renters' way.

▶ **Budget for furniture.** If you plan to rent, "your furniture needs to be appealing but bulletproof," counsels Claire Walter, co-author with Ruth Rejnis of the book *Buying Your Vacation Home for Fun and Profit.* "People won't be satisfied with a place that looks like a 1956 motel." If you're in a rush, look for ready-made furniture packages, offered by many furniture stores in resort areas. For instance, the Mountain Comfort Furnishings store in Vail, Colo. will provide new furniture for an entire two-bedroom condo for as little as $6,900.

▶ **Plan for insurance costs.** Know insurance prices before you buy. Your second-home insurance cost may double if you choose a remote location more than five miles away from the fire department, for example. If you buy property in a low-lying coastal area, you may be required to carry special federal flood insurance that can add $500 to $1,500 to your annual insurance bill.

▶ **Be willing to give up prime time.** Consider renting out your place during part of the high season if you're after maximum rental income. If you own a typical two-bedroom condo near the ski slopes in Telluride, Colo., for instance, you might make as much as $3,000 by renting it in February, compared with $900 in July.

▶ **Check out the area before you buy.** If you like an area, rent for a season or two, then buy. Spending one or two weekends in a mountain or beach town when the weather is perfect doesn't give you a real feel for the region. Renting will let you see if you really like the area, even when there is no sun or little snow.

▶ **Pick a place you love.** Even if you plan to rent out your second home much of the time, your overriding concern should be whether it will make you and your family happy. A weak economy or other problems could prevent you from collecting all the rental income you expect. But if you own a place you love, nothing can deprive you or your family of the pleasures of a great getaway.

AVOID HEADACHES WHEN YOU REMODEL

Our national anthem should be the Star Spackled Banner. Last year, Americans were expected to spend a record $119 billion on home improvements, and the National Association of Home Builders (NAHB) believes the growth in remodeling outlays will exceed inflation by 2.5 percentage points annually in the next several years, reaching a colossal $180 billion by 2005. And that doesn't include the psychiatrists' bills for the stress that invariably accompanies renovations.

What's behind this drywall revolution? For one thing, as the baby boomers slouch toward middle age, Americans are staying in their homes longer than they used to. The median number of years Americans remain in one home is now 13, compared with 10 a decade ago. Just as important, today's demanding dwellers want their nests feathered just so. According to the NAHB, nearly $2 out of every $3 now spent on home renovation projects is targeted not for unglamorous repairwork but for optional upgrades.

Just seven years ago, the dollar split was close to fifty-fifty. What's also notable today is that many of those upgrades—a jazzy kitchen, a family room, a major addition—are eye-poppingly opulent.

What hasn't changed, though, are the headaches of home remodeling. That's where we can help you. After consulting more than a dozen contractors, consumer advocates and other experts, we've distilled the most crucial advice on how to create the home of your dreams without losing your mind—or too much of your money.

Typical of today's renovators are Larry and Patty Glenn. When their four-bedroom home in Voorhees, N.J. began to feel cramped two years ago, they faced a decision: Spend to move (and uproot their kids from their neighborhood and school) or spend to stay (and get the house they wanted, where they wanted it). They stayed, shelling out $180,000 (completely financed with an 8.25% loan Larry took from his medical testing business) to add 1,500 square feet of extra living space to their 2,300-square-foot house. The additions include a new playroom, sunroom, deck and a double-size kitchen. "We are ecstatic," says Larry. "We can't believe how well it turned out."

As with most such projects, however, the Glenns faced nightmarish moments. Among them was a six-month delay as the New Jersey Department of Environmental Protection pondered the impact the project would have on the small lake in the family's backyard. Then there was the battle of the beams: A newly installed wood-laminate beam had to be ripped out after the Glenns' architect concluded that it wasn't strong enough to support the new addition. After a month of disputing and delay, the Glenns—eager to keep the job rolling—forked over $5,800 to remove the beam and replace it with a sturdier steel support. And then there were the unanticipated extras the Glenns discovered they wanted. As the noisy, invasive, five-month job progressed, they decided to re-side the existing home to match the addition ($4,000) and to insulate the garage and a loft ($2,500). In the end, the Glenns found they had overspent their original budget by $40,000.

Discouraged? Don't be. The numbers show that renovating is often a better move than moving. Sure, you're unlikely to recoup 100% of your remodeling costs when you eventually sell your home. But the cost of paying a broker to sell, plus the actual moving tab, can easily total 10% of the value of your old home. There's also the fact that a new home's price and therefore carrying costs will probably be more expensive. Add it all up, and improving what you've already got can look pretty good.

That's what Martha and Walter White of Houston concluded. They happily spent $200,000 last year to nearly double the size of their 2,500-square-foot brick ranch house, remaking it into the spacious two-level abode they'd always dreamed of for themselves and their three kids. "We loved the area and wanted to stay," says Martha. "But buying a bigger house nearby would have cost $400,000, and we would still have had to remodel to get exactly what we wanted."

The Whites make a good point. Even if you do decide to move, you may feel compelled to remodel once you get there. That's partly because three of four homes bought last year weren't new. The average American house is 28 years old—and is a lot smaller than today's models. Houses built in the 1950s, for example, averaged 1,500 square feet; today the typical new house is close to 2,000 square feet. "Older homes don't have a family room, the kitchen tends to be small and closed in, and the bathrooms are smaller than what people want today," says Gopal Ahluwalia, research director of the NAHB's economic department.

Whether your remodeling desires are modest or massive, here is a blueprint for getting the house you want:

Hammer out the best loan deal.

To pay for remodeling projects above $15,000 or so, chances are good that you will need a loan. (Be careful not to hit financial overload; monthly debt payments for all your loans should total no more than 40% of your gross monthly income.) If you anticipate needing years instead of months to pay for your project, your best bet is a home-equity loan (also known as a second mortgage), since the interest rate you'll pay is fixed. If your project is relatively inexpensive—say, $15,000 or so—consider instead a home-equity line of credit; rates are variable, but you can tap the line whenever you need it.

Nail down a smart spending plan.

As we mentioned earlier, homeowners rarely recoup 100% of their remodeling costs at resale. You'll fare far worse if you turn your otherwise unprepossessing place into the ritziest ranch on the block. "If you live in a $150,000 house in a neighborhood of $150,000 homes, spending $25,000 for a new kitchen and $20,000 for a bath may improve your lifestyle, but your home still won't sell much above what's typical in your neighborhood," says Bill Bucher, a partner in a Harrisburg, Pa. home-building and remodeling firm.

The smart move is to create new space that pleases you, without going overboard. "Intricate and expensive details, such as decorative moldings and intricate tile patterns, do not necessarily increase resale value," advises Palo Alto architect Michelle Belden. "They may create curb appeal for buyers, but appraisers don't care about them." Tip: To make your house easier to sell when the time comes, try to make sure that the value of your home (including the cost of improvements) does not exceed that of the priciest place on the block.

Expect cost overruns. Whatever you decide is the most you can afford, construct a spending plan that equals only 80% of that amount; reserve the other 20% for overruns, which are inevitable. Trust us, stuff happens. Mistakes occur, unforeseen problems arise—finding asbestos behind old walls is a common nightmare in pre-1970 homes—or you may decide mid-project that you simply must upgrade that Formica laminate countertop to fancier imported granite.

Get your design done right. If your project is an easy one, such as a simple bathroom remodel or a conversion of unused basement space into an office, you can save money by bypassing an architect. Many contractors can draw up basic plans, then have a structural engineer convert those plans into a final blueprint. That approach can cost as little as half what an architect might charge, which typically runs from 8% to 15% of the project's cost.

If your job involves knocking out walls, though, you'll need an architect to render an aesthetically pleasing design that is visually and structurally sound. To find a good one, get at least three referrals from friends or from your local chapter of the American Institute of Architects (800-242-9930). Make sure you hook up with an architect who normally works within your price range; the architect who designed the $100,000 kitchen you saw on a local home tour is probably not the right person for your $20,000 project.

Before approaching a pro, consider using a home renovation computer program to help you block out ideas. "The more you steep yourself in the problems of design, the more prepared you'll be," says Steve Thomas, host of the PBS television series *This Old House*. A computer-generated design can also help the designer you choose get a quick idea of what you're after.

Find a contractor who's on the level. Once you have your project's design, you need to hire a contractor to execute it. "In some states, anyone with a pickup truck can call himself a contractor," says Kermit Baker, director of the Remodeling Futures Project at Harvard's Joint Center for

Housing Studies. "But there's also a core of dedicated professionals who are longtime players in the business." The challenge is to find the dedicated pros, not the fly-by-nights. And that requires some serious gumshoe work.

Start by asking friends, colleagues and the folks at the local building-supply company for references, or call the National Association of the Remodeling Industry (NARI; 800-440-6274) for member contractors in your area. Your architect can direct you to favorite contractors, but you will still need to check out their suggestions by visiting a few projects. "Contractors can give you their mother-in-law's phone number, so it's crucial that you ask to see actual projects that they have completed," says Jordan Clark, president of the United Homeowners Association. Ask contractors to show you a state license, then call the agency that issued the certificate to confirm that it is up to date and that no complaints are on file. Also, call your state's consumer-protection agency and the local Better Business Bureau to see whether other remodelers have run into problems with the contractor. Ask each contractor to have his insurance company send you a copy of his liability and workers' comp policy so you can verify he has coverage too.

Get bids from at least three contractors. Tell them to break out specific costs in their bids. Such breakdowns help you compare bids more accurately and discern where there may be some negotiating room. According to Harvard's Baker, materials typically account for 40% to 45% of a project's cost; the rest covers labor, overhead and the usual 10% profit.

Then sit down with each contractor and ask how he plans to manage the project. If he will be hiring subcontractors such as electricians and plumbers, you need to check their references as well. Find out how many projects the contractor will be managing simultaneously; if you're not content with the contractor's commitment to your renovation, move on to the next bid. Don't jump at the lowest one: It can signal a cash-strapped contractor desperate for business. (You can check a contractor's financial status by asking his suppliers if he pays bills on time.)

Draw up a detailed contract. Once you pick your contractor, your job is only half done. "You get what you ask for," says Steve Gonzalez, a Fort Lauderdale home builder. "Put everything in writing to cut down on arguments once the project gets rolling." Consider using the solid six-page contract from the American Homeowners Association (888-470-2242).

In addition to spelling out when the contractor will start work and when you both estimate he'll finish, the contract should specify the exact materials to be used. If you want solid oak cabinets instead of laminated particleboard, for example, you'd better say so. The contract should also require your contractor to obtain lien releases from every subcontractor and supplier. That way, if the contractor doesn't pay the subs, you can't be sued for the dough.

Most important, the contract should lay out the payment schedule. Never make a down payment of more than 10%. "The more you pay up front, the less leverage you'll have," says Joseph Goldberg, president of the National Association of Consumer Agency Administrators. Schedule four or so additional payments to coincide with the completion of specific stages of the project. Save the final 20% of the bill until after the project is finished and final inspections have been passed.

BUILD YOUR DREAM HOUSE

After trekking through dozens of dwellings old and new, maybe you simply can't find a house you want to call home. Solution: Build your dream by commissioning a custom home. You'll get exactly the digs you want—assuming you can pay the tab. The National Association of Home Builders estimates that custom-designed homes cost about 25% more than development.

Unfortunately, the same as with remodeling, dream-house plans can disintegrate into nightmares of cost overruns and endless bickering among the owner, architect and builder. To assure that your project proceeds smoothly, follow this advice in four crucial areas:

Find the right lot to build on. This is key, since land alone can eat up 25% to 50% of the price of a custom-built home. Be sure to figure into your budget the cost of turning the land into a buildable lot. For example, ask a local builder or your town's building department about access to water and sewer facilities. If you build near a city, you can probably tap into municipal lines. In remote locations, however, you may have to drill a well (typical cost: about $4,000) and install a septic system ($3,000 to $6,000).

Choose a creative architect. Adding an architect to your dream-house team will boost its price by about 10%. That's usually money well spent, since a well-designed abode can fetch a higher resale value. Focus on finding a respected local architect who can provide you with the names and phone numbers of satisfied clients. The American Institute of Architects can refer you to three or four pros in your area. After you and the architect agree on an overall design, get the working drawings and specifications you'll need to solicit bids from the person who will actually build the house—the general contractor.

Hire a reliable contractor. Essentially, follow the same advice we just gave you for finding a contractor to remodel your home. For starters, get price estimates from three or more contractors who have at least five years of building experience, and don't automatically pick the one with the lowest bid, since he may resort to shoddy materials or construction short-cuts to ensure his profit.

Line up advance financing. Your goal is to get a bank or mortgage company to grant you a construction loan that automatically converts to a mortgage when the home is completed. In most cases, lenders limit this loan to 80% of the house's estimated value. While the house is being built, you usually pay only the interest on this loan. After the lender inspects the finished home and you get a certificate of occupancy from the local building inspector, you get your mortgage, which pays off the construction loan. Then you can move into your dream digs—and start making monthly mortgage payments like legions of other homeowners.

TURN DOWN THIS HOME-EQUITY LOAN

You probably think the most you can borrow with a home-equity loan is the difference between your house's market value and the balance on your mortgage. Well, you can toss that outmoded notion into the closet along with your old bell-bottoms. Today, lenders are aggressively hawking a new breed of loan—known as a high loan-to-value (HLTV), or negative-equity mortgage—that lets you borrow as much as 25% more than your home is worth. Say you could sell your home for $100,000 and you're carrying an $80,000 mortgage. Under the old rules, you could borrow $20,000 tops, if that. Now, however, lenders might offer you as much as $45,000, boosting the total debt on your $100,000 house to $125,000.

Although lenders initially pitched these loans in states where home values had declined, such as California, negative-equity loans have caught on nationwide. Moody's Investors Service analyst Jonathan Lieberman predicts HLTV borrowings will soon hit $8 billion, up from $3.5 billion in 1996 and just $200 million in 1995. It's easy to see why homeowners—especially those tapped out on credit cards—are snapping them up. After all, paying off credit-card balances with an HLTV loan can reduce your annual interest rate from 17% or more to as low as 12%. Another plus: The interest on HLTV loans is typically tax deductible (though you may not be able to deduct interest on the loan amount that exceeds the value of your house); you can't deduct credit-card interest.

Problem is, these loans endanger your financial health. First off, they're costly. Unless you have a sterling credit rating, for example, chances are you will pay interest of 15% to 16%, not the 12% to 13% touted in ads. You'll also likely face an outrageous six to 10 points in closing costs. Since each point equals 1% of the loan amount, closing fees could add as much as a $3,300 charge for the average $33,000 HLTV loan. Many lenders also penalize you for paying off your debt within the first three years. Such prepayment penalties can total nearly $1,700 on the typical $33,000, 13% loan. Add that sum to closing costs, and borrowers who pay off their loans early can face effective interest rates of almost 22%.

Furthermore, with housing experts projecting only modest rises in home prices, overloading your house with debt could turn your home into a prison. If you needed to sell your house soon after taking out a no-equity loan, you might not be able to cover your mortgages. Take the $100,000 home with the $80,000 first mortgage and the $45,000 HLTV loan. Even if real estate values climbed a generous 4% annually for four years, the house would fetch around $117,000. Subtract $7,000 for the standard 6% real estate agent's commission, and you'd net $110,000—meaning you'd have to dig into your pockets for another $13,000 to repay your mortgages.

▶ INDEX

go online to boost profits,
116–18
growth, 95–6
in retirement, 172–76
portfolios for life's stages,
88–94
retirement saving, 168–72
selling short, 98–100
to minimize taxes, 58–63
value, 96–7

J
Junk bonds, 35

L
Liability insurance, 115
Life insurance, 79, 115
Loans
home-equity, 221
shopping for, 146
student, 50, 64

M
Medical benefits, 182
Medicare
HMOs, 184–87
coverage by, 183–84
reforms of, 183–84
Mortgages
adjustable rate, 199
brokers of, 206
online loans, 209
outlook for interest rates,
199
prepayment, 204
reverse mortgages, 174
Municipal bonds, 92
Mutual funds
balanced, 89
bond, 85, 91–4
fees charged by, 36, 111
focused, 37
foreign, 39, 89–90
global, 39
growth, 40–1, 90

money-market, 103
prospectuses, 111–12
taxes on, 58–63
value, 38, 40, 90, 93

P
Pensions, 167–68
Privacy
and personal finances,
149–51

R
Real estate
and taxes, 46–8, 202–4
brokers, 208
building a home, 220
buyer brokers, 205–6
housing market outlook,
198–200
remodeling, 215–220
rental property, 210
reverse mortgages, 174
vacation homes, 211–15
Real estate investment trust
(REIT), 41–2, 85
Retail deposit notes, 112
Retirement
amount of money
required, 162–65
con artists, 192–96
new tax rules on, 54–7,
165
income in, 163, 173–74
online advice, 176–78
planning for, 88–94, 162–
72, 178–84
reverse mortgages in, 174
spending, 164, 174
tax-deferred plans, 52–8,
100–2, 128–42, 165, 177
working after, 187–89

S
Social security
and divorce, 180

benefits, 178–80
taxes on, 188
Software
investing online, 116–18,
176–78
tax returns, 60
Stock scams, 103, 105–7, 193
Stocks
All Star brokers' picks,
14–23
blue chip, 26–31
foreign, 31–5, 85
growth, 40–1
market forecast, 12
small company, 24–6

T
Tax preparers
how to choose, 69–70
Taxes
audit attractors, 70–2
best software for 1040, 60
business owners, 79
capital gains, 45–6
changes for 1997, 44–52,
189
credits for tuition, 48–50,
64
estate, 76–9, 189
new retirement rules, 52–8
on investments, 45–6, 58–
63
on sale of home, 202
Social Security, 188
Treasury bonds, 35, 94
Trusts, 75–7
living trusts vs. wills, 76

W
Wills, 72–5
living trusts, 76
Women
retirement planning, 167
Working after retirement,
187–89